FEAR!

At all ages and all stages of life, fear presents a problem for almost everyone. When your fears are appropriate to the circumstances, you can control them. But sometimes fear takes over. Terrified of what might happen, you avoid certain actions, challenges, relationships. You may change your goals from promotion or pleasure or closeness to a single and negative goal: to limit the fear reaction.

The inability to handle fear can narrow and confine your life, even cripple you as a human being. To deal with your fears effectively you must realize:

- You are not alone
- It is never too late to change
- By following certain specific techniques, you can start to cure yourself right now . . .

SOME PEOPLE SPEND THEIR LIVES
RUNNING SCARED.
DON'T BE ONE OF THEM!

STOP RUNNING SCARED!

FEAR CONTROL TRAINING
HOW TO CONQUER YOUR
FEARS, PHOBIAS, AND ANXIETIES

by
Herbert Fensterheim, Ph.D.

Clinical Associate Professor of Psychology in Psychiatry, Cornell University Medical College, and Head, Behavior Therapy Treatment and Study, Payne Whitney Clinic, The New York Hospital

and Jean Baer

To Anita Diamant Berke
agent and friend

Published by
DELL PUBLISHING CO., INC.
1 Dag Hammarskjold Plaza
New York, New York 10017

Dell ® TM 681510, Dell Publishing Co., Inc.

ISBN: 0-440-37734-X

Reprinted by arrangement with
Rawson Associates Publishers, Inc.

Printed in the United States of America
September 1978

10 9 8 7 6

"Little Miss Muffet
Sat on a tuffet,
Eating some curds and whey,
Along came a spider,
And sat down beside her,
And frightened Miss Muffet away."

Diagnosis: Spider phobia (arachnophobia)
The nursery rhyme shows:

- Appearance of fear trigger
- Typical surge of automatic fear reaction
- Miss Muffet's fear-maintaining escape behavior

CONTENTS

AUTHORS' NOTE

The techniques and concepts of Fear Control Training stem from Behavior Therapy. So many people have contributed to and influenced our thinking that it is impossible to thank them all, but we would like to express special appreciation to three leaders in the Behavior Therapy field: Andrew Salter, the New York psychologist who is generally regarded as the father of modern Behavior Therapy; Dr. Arnold A. Lazarus, professor of psychology at Rutgers University; and Dr. Joseph Wolpe of Temple University School of Medicine.

We are also indebted to Dr. Helen S. Kaplan, clinical associate professor of psychology at Cornell University Medical College and head of the Sex Therapy and Education Program at the Payne Whitney Clinic, not just for her creative thinking in the area of sexual behavior but for many years of friendship.

We would also like to say a word of thanks to Drs. Isaac M. Marks of Bethlehem Royal and Maudsley Hospitals, London, and Leslie Solyom of McGill University, Montreal, for their insights and research in the area of phobias and obsessions . . . to Dr. Martin E. P. Seligman of the University of Pennsylvania for his work in the area of learned helplessness . . . and to Drs. Gerald C. Davison and Marvin R. Goldfried of the State University of New York at Stony Brook for

their concept of the importance of self-command behaviors in the control of fears and anxieties.

Drs. Gerald Kroetsch and Gerald Pulvermacher of
Fear Relief Centres of Canada were particularly helpful in providing material for our "Overcoming Your
Fear of Flying" chapter, as were Captain "Slim" Cummings and Jay Beau-Seigneur of Pan American World
Airways. And a special acknowledgment to David Mc-
Laughlin of McKinsey & Company, New York, for his
assistance in the preparation of the "Conquering Fear
on the Job" chapter.

Our very heartfelt thanks go to Eleanor Rawson of
Rawson Associates for her really loving interest and
concern about every word in this manuscript.
                                    *Herbert Fensterheim, Ph.D., and
                                    Jean Baer*

ABOUT THE COLLABORATION
THAT PRODUCED THIS BOOK

Stop Running Scared! marks the second collaborative effort for Dr. Herbert Fensterheim and Jean Baer, who in private life are husband and wife. Their first was *Don't Say Yes When You Want to Say No,* which received an award from the American Psychological Association for "a noteworthy contribution to the public's understanding of psychology."

Dr. Herbert Fensterheim received his M.A. in psychology from Columbia University and his Ph.D. from New York University. He spent twenty years as an analytically oriented therapist before becoming one of the first clinicians involved with Behavior Therapy. Currently in private practice in Manhattan, he is clinical associate professor of psychology in psychiatry, Cornell University Medical College, and head, Behavior Therapy Treatment and Study, Payne Whitney Clinic, The New York Hospital. He has taught psychology at undergraduate, graduate and postdoctoral levels at leading universities and medical colleges. In addition he has written almost a hundred professional papers, co-edited two professional books on Behavior Therapy, and is the author of *Help Without Psychoanalysis.* A recognized leader in Behavior Therapy, Dr. Fensterheim has given many talks to and workshops for the professional community at meetings of such groups as the American Psychological Association and the American Group Psychotherapy Association, thus enabling other therapists to learn behavioral techniques and teach them to patients.

Jean Baer has written extensively on contemporary problems. In addition to co-authoring *Don't Say Yes When You Want to Say No* with Dr. Fensterheim, her previous books include *Follow Me!, The Single Girl Goes to Town, The Second Wife,* and *How to Be an Assertive (Not Aggressive) Woman in Life, in Love, and on the Job.* She is a frequent contributor to *The Christian Science Monitor* and the major women's magazines. She has worked for the Mutual Broadcasting Company and the U.S. Information Agency and spent many years as senior editor and special projects director of *Seventeen* magazine.

The substance and most details of the case histories presented in these pages are authentic. But the material has been greatly condensed to save the reader's time, and names and incidents have been disguised with great care to protect the privacy of patients.

I WAS A
PHOBIC KNOW-NOT

by Jean Baer

Some people's lives are ruled by fear and they know it.

Some people's lives are ruled by fear and they don't know it.

Until recently I belonged in the latter category.

I've always thought of myself as rather intrepid. After all, at a very young age I took off for Greece when no tourists traveled to Greece. I've logged thousands of miles flying to remote corners of the world like Samarkand. I can manage a job and a home. I can address an audience of hundreds without a quiver. In fact, I love standing center-stage and hearing the applause at the end. If I can't perform a tear-jerker death scene or dance *Giselle* and have admirers pelt me with red roses, lecturing will do.

I never realized that I spent most of my waking hours living with fear.

I knew I had certain eccentricities (like my fear of such mechanical gadgets as blenders and electric can openers). I just dismissed them. I pretended other fears were rather "cute" (like my inability to make left turns or virtually drive a car at all). For years I dined out on the story of how I would take a ten-mile detour to see my stepmother in Mount Vernon in order to avoid the left turn at the Triborough Bridge. I'm sure that one reason I married my husband, Dr. Herbert Fensterheim, who is clinical associate professor at Cornell University Medical College, is that not once did he say—as every other man in my life always had—"How come a girl as smart as you can't do something as easy as driving a car?" I never told him, or anyone else, that every time I got behind the wheel I died ten thousand deaths imagining all the drivers behind me out "to hit me"!

I had a certain intellectual recognition of other fears. For instance, rejection. I wanted other people to like me. So I was completely other-directed. Everything I did in life was based on getting the whole world to approve of me. Seven years of analytically oriented therapy did help me to see that I turned everyone—co-workers, bosses, friends, attractive men— into mother figures. "My own mother didn't care about me no matter what I did, but maybe I can win him/her even if I couldn't win my mother," I thought. So I always strove to please. If I didn't do what others wanted (or what I thought they wanted), the only alternative was rejection.

Sometimes I set up the rejection. I was single for so long because over and over I picked difficult, demanding, hostile men who *would* reject me. I had the luck to meet Herb, who is a kind, generous man. After we got married, he told me, "You were so terrified of making any major life decision that I could see asking you to marry me was out. You would automatically say no. So I just kept announcing, 'We are getting married.' I took the decision out of your hands."

I was completely unaware of the extent and irrationality of my fears and how the phobic irrationality governed almost everything I said and did. It's crucial to the situation to know you have a problem. How can you change unless you know what to change? I didn't know. For example:

•*At work:* For years I had a job as senior editor and special projects director at *Seventeen* magazine. Despite that fancy title, in reality I handled public relations. Every January *Seventeen* had an issue highlighting accomplishments of outstanding teens around the nation. I would get out hundreds of releases to hometown papers about these girls, even if there was just a one-line mention in the magazine. Even though I had a staff to do the dirty work, I came in at 7:00 A.M. to staple and stuff. None of the other editors cared about my accomplishment and all the resultant clippings. The boss said, "Wastebasket stuff." I had to do it. If I left a stone unturned—in this case, one release not written—*someone might criticize me.* Now I know this is a neurotic *fear of making mistakes.*

•*In my day-to-day existence:* My mother died lengthily and painfully of cancer. Following that, there wasn't a day in my life that I didn't have a whole series of anxious thoughts beginning with, "I'll find a lump today . . . I won't have the operation. I won't sign that clause permitting the doctor to operate . . . I won't be able to kill myself with pills . . . Herb will have to give them to me." No suspicious sign ever appeared but in the days before visiting the doctor for my twice-yearly checkup, I was ready for the loony bin. I viewed my behavior not only as rational but as a preventive device: "If I think this way, it won't happen."

•*Social life:* I constantly created scenarios in which people rejected me. To me, my reasoning had complete validity. I just overlooked the fact that I based it on a false premise. For example, over lunch I presented my fifth book to a friend whom I had quoted in it. That was the last I ever heard from her. "Well, she's finished as a friend," I told Herb. "She didn't like what I said." For months I agonized over her desertion. One day Frances called up full of apologies. "John has taken a new job at Colorado State; we're moving next month," she said. She hadn't rejected me. She had been too busy to think about me. This happened over and over but I never seemed to learn.

•*In my marriage:* Much as I love my husband, I lived in fear of him: that he would not think I was a "good wife" because I sometimes put deadlines before duties . . . that he would criticize me if every meal were not gourmet-style . . . that I was not the "good stepmother" to his children.

Most of all I feared his ex-wife. I have never met her but I hate her because I work so hard and she gets lifetime alimony. After Herb and I wrote *Don't Say Yes When You Want to Say No,* Doris brought a court action against my husband that involved a subpoena of all his financial records on that book—a book which I had initiated and sold and which we had written together. I nearly died. Was That Woman going to get my hard-earned money? She didn't. However, the fear of "What next?" mounted until I lived with it day and night. The daily arrival of the mailman was the trigger. I got so jumpy that Herb had to give me permission to open any letter from her to him because I couldn't wait until he got home to see what might be in it. Meanwhile my thoughts got worse: "Would I have to go to court again?" . . . "Will I have to stop writing with my husband because there might be other subpoenas, other court hearings?" I was a soul in torment.

One day the mail came, containing an official-looking document with a return address something like "Second Judicial Court of New York." I opened it. The heading read "Petition of Bankruptcy." At the bottom line was the name of some unknown man whom I immediately judged to be Doris's new lawyer.

That was at 9:00 A.M. For six hours I lay writhing on the bed, crying my heart out: My thoughts whirled around like a day's wash in a Bendix, "She'll take what little he has. . . . Why does this have to happen to me?" By the time Herb came home at 3 P.M. from the hospital, I was in a state of collapse, my eyes sunk in a sea of circles.

He took one look at me. "What happened?"

"Doris," I croaked. "She's bankrupt. You'll have to pay all her bills. We'll never come out from under this." I relapsed into a fit of hysterics, screaming, "The letter. Look at the letter."

Herb looked. Then he regarded me with an expression I had never seen in his eyes before: the way you'd look at an out-of-control child, compassionate, caring yes, but "Oh, the futility of this."

"Did you see the name on the letter?" he asked.

"Sure . . . that must be her new lawyer," I said.

"Jean," he said tenderly. "The letter has nothing to do with Doris. It's a notice that a patient of mine has gone into bankruptcy. He can't pay me the sixty dollars he owes me."

In my neurotic fear of Doris, I had seen something *that was not* there at all and gotten myself in such a state that I couldn't work for a week.

Soon after, I started Fear Control Training with my husband, who had been so successful in giving my Assertiveness Training.

Frankly, Fear Control Training is hard. It's much harder than Assertiveness Training, through which I had overcome many problems in standing up for my rights, saying no, and asking favors of others. There I knew what was wrong. Here I had to search for it. In AT I learned to improve my relationships with others. In FCT I had to learn to improve my relations with *myself*.

The main thing I learned was that what I thought of as fears were really phobias. Until then, I thought phobias were confined to things like fear of heights, spiders, animals. In FCT I learned that any fear so strong that it keeps you from doing what you want to do is really phobic. Thus phobias can include the "things" phobias like fear of mice, thunderstorms and planes but they also include a wide range of other emotions not commonly thought of as phobic: intense, irrational fears of responsibility, not being in control, going to social events, doing things alone and, of course, rejection (my *bête noire*).

You can be a phobic know-not. You don't even realize you possess these strong fears.

You can be a phobic know-it-all. You take the approach, "Phobic people are crazy. I'm not nuts . . . I don't go crazy when I have a dream [oneirophobia] or see a lake [limnophobia]."

You can be a phobic snowball. You let the phobia take over and spread to many other life areas.

You can be a phobic cop-out. You don't cope with it at all.

Fear Control Training helped me in so many ways.

In every area of life I have learned that I can control my awful self–put-down thoughts. Recently, while on deadline for this book, I had one of those days where my fears got completely out of control. The anxiety whirlpool began. At dinner I said to Herb, *"The Ladies' Home Journal* will reject my article. . . . My editor won't like this book. Oh, they'll publish it but the reviewers will say it's terrible. I'll never get a contract from anyone again. I'm through. I'm finished." Then I caught myself. I would *not* let this irrational fear of failure take over. I used an FCT technique. I made myself relax, then for sixty seconds I breathed deeply through my mouth. Each time I breathed out, I pictured a pleasant scene (the usual ones people choose, like beautiful beaches, don't work for me; I visualized buying an antique highboy on Route 7 in Connecticut). I stopped the thoughts. Soon I was able to say, "I was acting like a child. Let's have a drink."

I analyzed my Pandora's Box of fears. One strong one is any situation where I'm not in control, thus the fear of mechanical gadgets. I realized that while I constantly said to my husband, "You do nothing in the house," I didn't let him do anything. I had to be in control of my domain. I set about organizing a program where I would relinquish control. He took on certain chores. I let him. I knew I had succeeded when one night I came home very late from an assignment. Dinner was ready. He had made it. I enjoyed every mouthful. Two hours later I said, "I can't believe it . . . I don't feel guilty."

I determined to conquer the driving phobia. This was difficult. It involved my husband's teaching me a technique called Systematic Desensitization in which you *imagine* feared situations. I scoffed at this. "How can imagining you're turning left at an intersection help you to do it?" But it did help. I can now turn left.

I recognized my core fear of making mistakes. This came from childhood. Everytime I did anything wrong (like putting the fork on the wrong side of the table setting), I got chastised, sometimes spanked. As an adult, I coped with the fear by being a perfectionist. Like Avis, I tried harder. I don't have to do this any more. I can say, "Enough." I'm still very conscientious, but I hope not as compulsive.

As I grew in self-understanding I saw the extent of the phobic reaction in friends. Mary's fears of being turned down at a job interview are so strong that she won't even look for a job, even though she hates "being just a housewife." Joan's fear of closeness in personal relationships is so strong that she makes every romance go wrong, then cries, "I've picked another bad one." Because of Alice's fear of being ignored, she has created a series of mythical eye diseases to gain sympathy even though a series of ophthalmologists said, "There's nothing wrong." Understanding their problems has made me more sympathetic to them and stronger myself.

I have learned what a phobia is, that many people I like, honor and respect have them, and that you can do something about them.

Here are some basics of Fear Control Training.

•Most phobic fears (not all) are learned. Even if you've had them for years, you can unlearn them.

•When you unlearn them, you do not develop substitute fears. You become a better-adjusted human being.

•Phobic fear is a habit. Like other bad habits, it can be changed. You can change it.

•With will and knowledge you can clear up these fears in a matter of months, not years.

•You may not lose all the fear. But you can cope with the feeling.

Recently, after paying our income taxes, my husband and I decided to buy a country house. Because we had good friends in New Jersey, we looked there and found a beautiful old stone house in which I could indulge my antiques addiction. We bid on it and got it. We signed the binder. At about 3:00 A.M. I woke up shivering and ran for my map. Disregarding poor Herb asleep, I started poring over it with a magnifying glass. He woke up and asked, "What are you doing?"

"The house . . . we better get out of it," I said.

"Are you worrying about the high mortgage?" he asked.

"No, the Lincoln Tunnel," I said. "I'm trying to find another way back. Listen, Herb, as long as I live I will not be able to manage driving that New Jersey entrance to the tunnel where the seven lanes come together. We can't buy the house."

We didn't. We bought another one in Connecticut. I get there coping with three left turns and two major thruways. I think that's pretty good for a woman who, until recently, would rather throw herself into the East River than get behind the wheel of a car. Someday I will be able to manage the Lincoln Tunnel!

As a result of Fear Control Training, I learned how to face (not completely master) my lifelong fear of cars, other people not liking me, not being perfect and a whole host of social anxieties. The experience had a Rip van Winkle quality. I've come out of a deep sleep.

You too can get rid of those feelings "I'm scared . . . I'm scared that I won't make it . . . I'm scared that I will . . . I'm scared that I will make it and no one will care." You don't have to go through life wondering if you're going to panic in the subway, experience torture at the very idea of a plane trip, or die by degrees at the thought of ending a relationship, even though it tries you to the depths of your soul.

You were not born a fearful, anxious person. You learned to be one. As I did, you can unlearn this.

In this book we will tell you how.

YOU CAN FIGHT
YOUR FEAR AND WIN

Some people spend their lives running scared.

Are you one of those people?

Rita is. A twenty-five-year-old copywriter, she spends evening after evening, weekend after weekend by herself. Whenever she receives a social invitation, she quivers with anxiety at the thought of going to the event. Now a very personable co-worker has invited her out. She yearns to accept but wonders, "Will his friends like me?" . . . "Will I bore him?"

Roger is. While going through medical school, he developed a fear of failure. Although he got his M.D., when it came time to take his medical boards, he was so frightened of them that he rationalized, "I need another year's study." For ten years Roger has refrained from taking his exam. Avoiding medicine completely, he has worked as an insurance salesman. He misses medicine terribly.

Jane is. Terrorized at the possibility of a panic attack, she avoids tunnels, bridges, movies, theaters, hairdressers ("What if I get a panic attack under the dryer?"), supermarkets ("The check-out line is the worst"). At first she could leave her home for short periods. Now she can't go out of the house at all.

At all ages and all stages of life, fear presents a problem to almost everyone. "We are largely the playthings of our fears," wrote British author Horace Walpole many years ago. "In one, fear of the dark; to another, of physical pain; to a third, of public ridicule; to a fourth, of poverty; to a fifth, of loneliness— for all of us our particular creature waits in ambush."

When your fears are appropriate to the life circumstances where they occur, you are in command of the fear. However, sometimes your fears are hidden; you are afraid but do not know why. At other times, the fear takes over. Looking at life through your fear-tinted glasses and terrified of what might happen, you don't take on certain challenges, actions, relationships. Often you change your goals from increased closeness, professional advancement, pleasure, being the kind of person you want to be to a single and negative goal: to limit your fear reaction.

Your problems come from the way you handle your fear. Your inability to deal with it can narrow and confine your life, even cripple you as a human being. To deal with it, you must realize:

•*You are not alone.* Millions of others suffer from the same or different fears. They too possess the doubts and dreads that shame and embarrass you. They share that deep humiliation, "something is really wrong with me."

•*It is never too late to change.* The oldest patient I have treated was a seventy-nine-year-old man with a fear of traveling outside New York by any means. We removed that fear; he was then able to fly to Washington, D.C., to see his grandchildren. I also treated a seventy-five-year-old lawyer with a fear of impotency. His first marriage had been filled with sexual difficulties. His wife died. His next marriage lasted for forty years with occasional sexual problems. This wife also died. Dave wanted to remarry but feared the sexual aspects. With the aid of a lovely woman, we reduced that fear so that he functioned better than he ever had before.

In another case, at sixteen, Louise, a brilliant student with a 150 IQ, developed a school phobia. She had such a fear of tests and being asked questions in class that one day she left school in the middle of an algebra exam and never went back. She eventually took a job as a file clerk. She never tried for promotion ("I might have to take a typing test"). Working with me, at twenty-seven, she overcame this school fear, took her high school equivalency exam, acquired both a B.A. and M.A., and got a job as a personnel director.

Even if you have had the fear since childhood, you can change. The length of time you've had the fear makes no difference.

•*If you follow the advice given in this book, you can definitely cure yourself*. There are four important steps.

F   *Find* out what your fears are. Some fears are obvious. You know you're afraid of planes, elevators, tunnels, success, failure. Others, like the fear of rejection, may be disguised. You're dimly aware of it, but don't realize the effect on your life.

E   *Educate* yourself: as to how you learned the fears, how they work, the bodily reactions they produce, how they influence your life, what you do to maintain these fears. Do you see great dangers when the dangers are actually very small? Do you imagine danger when none exists? Do you suffer that "I'm afraid" feeling to a paralyzing degree where others would experience a far lower level of anxiety? Do you keep away from that imagined danger? You do not take that flight, give that speech, ride to the fiftieth floor, attend that social event.

A   *Act.* Follow the training program we are going to give you. Do the things you need to do in order to learn not to be afraid.

R   *Rally.* Call upon your energies and inner strength. Apply what you learn in the program to your life. Change your life pattern so that you can live with the fear—or free yourself completely from it.

You can do this through the new technique of Fear Control Training.

THE NATURE OF FEAR

Scan a psychology dictionary and you will see many categories defining disturbed emotions.

Fear (from the Old English *faer,* meaning sudden calamity or danger) denotes a state of alarm or dread. When you experience fear under certain conditions, it can immobilize you. It usually prepares you for the three Fs: flight, fight or freeze.

Normal fear can serve as a useful emotion. If you are confronted with the threat of fire or accident, fear can spur you to take life-saving measures. Faced with psychological rather than physical danger, you also take protective measures. For example, when you see a co-worker wants your job, you see what is going on and take necessary action. The feeling of fear can also sharpen your perception, mobilize your energies, quicken your reflexes, clarify your thoughts so that you perform better *with* the feeling of fear than you would without it. For example, when you give a speech, that inner feeling of tension can make your mind keener, your manner livelier.

Irrational fear: With this, when minimal or no danger exists, you act as if great peril were involved. For example, you fear dogs, see a small dachshund a block away and behave as if he has actually attacked you. Or your spouse looks at you in an annoyed way and you get the gut reaction, "He is going to leave me."

Anxiety: This upsetting emotional state is marked by a continuous fear, a feeling of threat. Often you can't put into words what actually threatens you; you just feel terribly nervous.

Phobia (from the Greek word *phobos,* meaning *flight,* and from the deity of the same name who could provoke fear and panic in one's enemies) means a persistent fear of an object or idea that ordinarily does not justify fear. You know this is ridiculous but cannot overcome it.

Panic (deriving from the Greek rural deity Pan) denotes a sudden surge of acute terror.

For the purpose of this book we consider irrational fear, anxiety, phobia, panic interchangeable.

A Capsule History of Fear

For the length of human history people have suffered from fears. Literature and history are full of examples. In the fourth century B.C. the Greek physician Hippocrates wrote about Damocles, who "could not go near a precipice or over a bridge or beside even the shallowest ditch; yet he could walk in the ditch itself." In *The Merchant of Venice* Shakespeare described "some that are mad if they behold a cat," while in 1650, Descartes alluded to "the strange aversions of some who cannot endure the smell of roses, the sight of the cat or the like."

Such fears have not been confined to the average individual. Rank, fame and talent do not serve as guards. Tully and Demosthenes had stage fright. Augustus Caesar could not sit in the dark. Queen Elizabeth I feared roses. Feydeau, the French dramatist, practically never went out during the day because of a morbid fear of daylight. Samuel Johnson had an intense fear of death.

Yet, until the middle of the nineteenth century such problems were not considered a matter of clinical concern, and it was not until the early twentieth century that Freud advanced his theory that an individual develops a phobia as a defense.

The Freudian Theory of Phobias

Freud believed that phobias were a shield, serving as a protection against other, more disturbing unconscious fears. These fears stem from an unresolved Oedipus complex. Should these fears threaten to become conscious, you develop a phobia to protect yourself from what really worries you. Thus you can reassure yourself, "It is not my parent who frightens me but elevators . . . dogs . . . heights." To help keep the fear within bounds, you usually become phobic to an object you can avoid.

There is Freud's famous case study (1909) of "Little" Hans, a five-year-old boy who refused to go out into the street for fear a horse might bite him. Freud felt that behind the fear was Hans' unconscious fear that his father would punish him (by castration) because of Hans' strong sexual drive for his mother. By displacing his fear and anxiety from daddy to horse, Hans could avoid the object of his phobia and love his father instead of fearing him.

In psychoanalytic treatment, you use free association and dream interpretation to work through the underlying Oedipus complex. As you resolve your conflicts, the phobia itself disappears because you no longer need it. This is a long, complex mode of treatment, and real doubt exists about how well it works in the area of the unreal fears.

The Behavioral Approach

While Freud and his followers believed that all people are basically helpless until they gain knowledge of

the conflicts and fantasies that reside in the unconscious and the childhood fears that generated them, behavioral psychologists have always considered fears as
learned reactions. Instead of asking, "What in your
unconscious has produced your fear?" they asked two
core questions:

How do you learn to be fearful?

What keeps you from unlearning the fear?

Two classical demonstrations, proving that emotional reactions can be learned and unlearned, took
place in the 1920s.

•In 1920 John B. Watson, founder of the psychological school of behaviorism, and his collaborator,
Rosalie Rayner, taught an unreasonable fear to Albert,
an eleven-month-old boy (a truly distasteful demon-
stration which today would be considered unethical).
First, they established that Albert was *not* frightened
of a white rat (in fact he reached for it) and that he
was frightened of a sudden loud noise. Then, when
they showed him the white rat, they also made the
sudden loud noise. After they did this several times,
Albert showed fear at the sight of the rat even when
there was no loud noise. Furthermore this fear then
spread to a whole group of objects—a rabbit, fur
coat, dog and even a mask of Santa Claus with a long
white beard—that previously had not frightened him.
Albert had learned to be phobic to furry objects.

•Four years after the experiment with Albert,
psychologist Mary Cover Jones showed that conditioning can be used to remove fears. Peter, a child of
almost three, feared rabbits. While looking at the rabbit (in a cage), and at a distance (to keep the fear
low), Peter was given candy. Here the feared rabbit
was paired with the pleasure of the candy. Within six
weeks Peter was gleefully playing with the rabbit.

Having conducted these experiments, the researchers now faced the difficult problem. If fears can be
unlearned, why do unreasonable fears linger on in
life situations? What keeps them going? To answer

these questions, in the late 1930s Dr. O. Hobart Mowrer of the University of Illinois proposed a two-stage theory.

First stage: Just as did little Albert, you learn the fear. Once frightened, you usually want to get rid of the fear.

Second stage: You quickly learn you can reduce the fear most easily by two techniques: (1) *Avoidance* of the feared situation. If subways terrorize you, you always take a bus. (2) *Escape* from the feared situation if you do manage to get yourself in it. You take the subway, get panicky, then make your getaway at the next stop. Each time you utilize one of these methods, your fear decreases. However, you also strengthen your avoidance-escape pattern.

This has a major consequence: You keep from getting into the feared situation. You prevent yourself from learning that your fear reaction is inappropriate or excessive. In this way your fear endures and dominates.

FEAR CONTROL TRAINING

Fear Control Training has a basic premise: What you have learned, you can unlearn. During the past several decades researchers and clinicians have developed a number of highly effective retraining techniques to help people change these inappropriate learned fears. These new methods are still unknown to many professionals as well as to the general public.

Fear Control Training is a branch of Behavior Therapy. In Behavior Therapy you take your problem as it exists *in the present,* identify the specific behaviors you must change to resolve your difficulties. You take these behaviors one at a time and teach yourself to act differently. You replace the behavior you don't like in yourself with one you do like.

Behavior Therapy teaches that if you have learned

a set of fears in certain conditions (whether impersonal like riding in elevators, or interpersonal like fear of closeness), you can change your behavior so that you respond without fear. You can free yourself of unwanted behaviors, like thinking obsessively "I will fail," and replace them with desired habits. Behavior Therapy says you can free yourself of tension, supplanting this state with one of calmness.

To change your habit of fear, you must think of fear as a behavior. Behaviors can be changed.

Fear Control Training has two main goals:

•*To enable you to be less frightened in the fear situation itself;*

•*To get you to carry out certain actions that will weaken your fear rather than strengthen it.*

Learning to Be Less Frightened

Feeling frightened in a nonfrightening situation comes about through a process psychologists call learning by association. Little Albert learned to associate fear with the white rat. Little Peter learned to associate no fear with a rabbit. To break your fear pattern you must learn to associate no fear with what you now regard as a dangerous situation. To set up your retraining program you must know:

There is a fear trigger. Certain things set off your fear reaction. Although some situations or objects are more common triggers than others, you can learn to become disturbed by literally anything. You can feel fear because of elevators, thunderstorms or even the sight of pigeons on the sidewalk. Other people may frighten you because they look angry, bored or say something tender. You can learn to respond to your own thoughts ("I'm sure the plane will crash") or to your own internal sensations (like dizziness).

Your reaction to the thing you fear is as automatic as if you were a robot. No thought, will or desire is involved. This Robot Reaction has two parts: (1)

Subjective feelings. Usually you experience these as fear or anxiety but they can also take the form of anger, depression, withdrawal or other disturbed emotions. Whatever the form, it is unpleasant. (2) *Physiological reactions.* Here you may experience knots in your stomach, difficulty in breathing, heart pounding, weakness, dizziness among others. You may have such outward manifestations as sweating or blushing. Again, each has an unpleasant quality.

To break up this pattern, you go into the fearful situation a step at a time so that your fear doesn't get too strong. At each step, you practice associating no anxiety with that situation. Through this graduated approach, eventually you will be able to conquer the most frightening situation. In this book we will show you how to apply this principle to many kinds of fear. Here is the story of how one woman conquered a fear of cats.

CASE

A fear of cats dominated Wendy's whole life. This had been true since childhood. Even now, as a thirty-five-year-old homemaker and mother of three, before she would go shopping she would send a friend to scout local stores, checking out the possible presence of a cat. She wouldn't visit friends who possessed cats. This not only limited her social life but proved harmful to her husband's career. Because of Wendy's cat fear, he was often unable to socialize with business contacts. His work took him to France, where cats are often household pets. Wendy refused to accompany him. He started taking vacations alone. Before their marriage her husband knew of Wendy's cat phobia and thought it "cute." Ten years later he felt impatient and annoyed.

It wasn't fear of cats that brought Wendy to me. Her marriage was about to break up.

My treatment was aimed at changing her fear association to cats. It had three parts.

•In my office I had Wendy imagine scenes in which cats jumped on her, scratched her, rubbed against her. At first she experienced tremendous anxiety doing this, but I taught her the technique of relaxation to counter her fear association.

•I actually brought a cat into my office and placed it at the far corner of the room. Session by session I brought the cat closer. Gradually Wendy lost her fear. Eventually she touched the box containing the cat. Then, for a brief split second, she touched the cat. Finally she picked up the cat and walked around the room, proudly stroking it.

•She carried out a series of assignments, each aimed at changing her association to cats.

She had to walk into the local butcher shop where a cat usually slept in the window. Then she had to walk out. Gradually she stayed for longer periods of time.

She started going to other stores with cats on the premises.

She visited friends with cats. Realizing her fears, they cooperated. One neighbor even kept her cat on a leash at the far end of the room.

She set little tasks for herself. One friend's cat had kittens. Knowing the kitten had no claws or teeth, Wendy was able to pick it up and hold it.

After some time Wendy acquired a cat of her own. She rationalized that "It was for the children" (who had started to learn the cat fear from her) and that "I need it for completion of my therapy." Actually Wendy had started to develop a fondness for cats.

Carrying Out Actions That Weaken Your Fears

Here you deal with a different kind of learning—what you learn through reward, rather than association. When you avoid or escape from a situation, the reduction of fear serves as your reward. Reward can work in an even more subtle way to maintain your fears. You become frightened by your feeling of fear and the physical symptoms it brings on. This secondary fear causes you to pay a lot of attention to the prospect of becoming frightened and the fear itself. In this instance, the attention functions as a reward and so you train yourself to be frightened.

Your avoidance, escape and fear of being frightened all stem from your great feeling of helplessness. In this area the FCT methods revolve around decreasing your feeling of helplessness through giving you control over your fear-maintaining behaviors. You learn to stop your agonizing anticipatory anxiety, keep yourself in the fear situation, find out that what you're frightened of in the fear situation rarely occurs. In this way you stop being frightened of your fear.

CASE

At twenty-three, newly married John R. was riding in a bus on his way home from the office when he got his first panic attack. He thought his legs would collapse under him and that he'd faint. He got off the bus, managed to get home and his wife phoned their doctor. After checking him out, the internist assured John nothing physical was wrong with him. But from then on, John felt terrified of a recurrence. The panic attack did recur in a subway (he got off at the next stop and rushed home) and in an elevator. Thereafter he was afraid of traveling in any vehicle and arranged his life to cope with this fear. He walked to his third-floor office. He lived within twenty blocks of his work, good restaurants, theaters. But he felt imprisoned. So did his wife. She divorced him.

When John came to me, he was thirty-three. Much to his humiliation, he had recently had a panic attack in a business conference and had to rush out of the room. He told me, "I've got alimony and child support. I've got to keep my job."

Together we worked out the number of situations

which, because of his fear of panic attacks, he kept avoiding and arranged them in order of the difficulty he would have getting into each situation. He ranked elevators as the easiest, saying, "I think I can make myself get into an elevator but nothing will get me into a subway or bus."

For John the elevator in his apartment building would be the easiest starting point; he was used to it and it was so near his front door. The principle: to get him into that elevator for an extended period of time. From this he would learn two things: (1) that if he had the panic reaction, it wouldn't destroy him; (2) if he stayed long enough, the panic reaction would subside. His first assignment: to go up and down in his apartment-house elevator forty-five minutes a day from top to bottom. In the course of just a few days John saw he was capable of riding elevators.

The next step: his fear of subways. We decided he should take a half-hour ride downtown in a nonrush period, using locals (more stops—hence more chance of escape in case he couldn't manage it), get out at his planned destination, cross over to the uptown side, and ride the half hour back to his original starting point. For three weeks John kept finding excuses not to do this. This was *conditioned avoidance*. Finally, I told John that I had some time on Friday morning and that if he had not ridden the subway by then to come to my office and I would go with him, put him on the subway and ride in the next car. If he did the assignment before Friday, he should leave a message with my answering service and skip the session. Late Thursday evening my service called with a message that had been left at 10:00 P.M.: "John wants you to know that he rode the subway."

This proved the turning point. Thereafter John was able to stop his avoidance behavior (for example, he stopped avoiding business meetings that took place on high floors of his office building). With pride he watched his anxiety and panic diminish. We considered his treatment over when he flew to Nassau for a vacation.

Special Fear Control Training Program Points

1. *You must understand your nervous system.* In your nervous system you have a built-in capacity to experience a wide range of feelings and emotions. This capacity is biological and inborn. You have your central nervous system made up of the brain and the spinal cord. Through this you control your voluntary movements; you can direct your arms, legs, head, trunk. This system also contains the thinking and problem-solving centers. You also have an autonomic nervous system which controls your involuntary muscles and also such things as your digestive system, circulation and heart, breathing, endocrine glands. This is the part of your nervous system most directly involved with feelings and emotions. When you experience a fear reaction and your heart races or you get a knot in your stomach, this results from the action of the autonomic nervous system. You don't "will" this reaction; it is mindless and not under your control.

The point: The autonomic nervous system can be trained to respond with fear to inappropriate objects and situations or to thoughts of these inappropriate objects and situations. These responses are immediate, automatic and bypass the thinking centers of the brain. The very word *autonomic* indicates its freedom from the central nervous system and the fact that no thought, will, volition, motivation or conscious activity on your part is involved.

Just as you have trained your autonomic nervous system to respond to *imagined threat,* you can retrain it not to respond. Once you achieve retraining through FCT and learn not to fear specific things—the job, social events, elevators, planes—you will no longer have all these frightening symptoms.

2. *Understand how you learned your fears.*

Direct learning: You can learn inappropriate reactions in a number of ways. You may have had a really bad experience (you actually were in a plane crash) or a series of less disturbing experiences in the same situation (you keep hearing about plane crashes). You may have seen someone else frightened in a situation and you use that person as a model for your own reaction. Or someone—parent, teacher, friend, coworker—may actually have told you to be frightened (during your teen years mother warned, "You should know that at any party there will be always someone who will criticize you and this will ruin your evening." So you become frightened of criticism or of parties or of both).

Generalization: Your emotional reaction does not stay confined to the one situation where you learned it. It spreads to other situations.

You are not afraid of just that one cat. This may spread to other kinds of animals. In one woman I treated it had spread to what she called "catlike people."

You learn to be frightened of parental authority. This may spread to all authorities: teachers, policemen, supervisors. It may spread to anyone to whom you attribute authority: store clerks, waiters, building superintendents. It may even spread to complete strangers who happen to possess an air of confidence.

CASE

In college Patty F. was both a good student and a campus queen. During finals week of her junior year, she gave a talk to a student group and, because she felt tense from overwork and exam pressure, her voice quavered and her hands trembled. A friend commented, "I've never seen you so nervous."

All summer the incident preyed on Patty's mind. "Will I get that nervous at other events?" . . . "Will other people see my trembling hands and realize how anxious I am?" she asked herself. During her senior year the fear increased. After graduation Patty married her campus beau and got a teaching job, but the fear expanded to a series of situations.

She stopped playing bridge (the trembling hands), wouldn't invite friends for dinner (too difficult to serve coffee). She soon stopped going to other people's houses (they'd notice her anxiety). In the classroom, she was afraid to hold a book (students would see her trembling hands). Patty quit her job and soon had a social life confined exclusively to her husband and one other couple. The presence of a single, simple fear, "People will see my hands tremble and think I'm nervous," had spread to almost every life area. It was determining and ruining her life.

Note: Not all fears are learned. Some evidence exists that certain fears are built into the nervous system. At birth human infants already have an innate startle reaction to noise. Some fears like fear of strange objects, animals, and strangers start early in infancy and decrease by the age of three or four. Other fears—like fear of the dark—usually start at age two. Generally, such childhood fears disappear by themselves unless you learn something that keeps you being frightened of them. A frightening experience in the dark may keep that fear active.

Some panic attacks also seem to occur without previous learning. Suddenly, sometimes for no apparent reason, you find yourself in the grip of a terrible panic. You learn to associate these attacks with different situations, and it is this learning that keeps them going.

3. *Think through how your specific actions keep your fear alive and influence your life-style.* Do any of the following fear types represent your behavior pattern?

SEVEN FEAR TYPES

The dodger: You keep clear of the fear situation. For example, one legal secretary with an intense fear of elevators gave up her profession to work in a first-floor boutique, then moved to a small town so she could live in a one-level ranch house.

The runaway: You get into the fear situation but leave it as quickly as possible without giving the fear a chance to subside. For instance, you fear crowds, force yourself to enter a mobbed department store, take one look at the jammed main-floor aisle and bolt.

The doomsayer: Anytime you think about an impending fear situation, you concentrate on the worst possible consequence and then fix on that. You may take a low-probability event ("The plane will surely crash") and make it seem imminent, or you may focus on a higher-probability event ("People won't be interested in me at the party") and exaggerate the consequence ("This will surely ruin my whole life").

The manipulator: You continually enlist the aid of others to keep the fear situation from arising ("Please lock your cat in the bathroom when I visit") or to help you through it. Some people find this kind of control of others very satisfying. For example, even though she had never had the slightest sign of a heart attack, one woman was phobic about getting one. Interpreting any bodily change as the signal for an impending attack, she used this as a device to have friends and family fetch and carry for her. Her enjoyment of the situation reinforced the fear. If she gave it up, she would lose the attention.

The distorter: In the fear situation you lose control of your thoughts. You may use rationalization ("Of course, animals carry germs") to make your fear reaction seem reasonable. Or you may be a *cud-chewer*. Instead of just foreseeing disaster like the doomsayer, you constantly mull about it, exploring each detail and seeking the implications and consequences of it for you as a person, for its effect on others.

The non-coper: You allow yourself to get into the fear situation, but, once there, you concentrate so much on your feelings of fright that you can't cope adequately. For example, you are so concerned about being called on to speak at a meeting that when your turn comes you (a) haven't thought through what you want to say or (b) do something completely inappropriate—turn red and can't say a word or start and have to sit down in the middle of a sentence.

The silent sufferer: You hide your fear. Instead of frankly confessing, "I'm afraid of heights," you say, "I'm not in the mood to go to that particular restaurant today. Let's go to the quiet one around the corner." Silent sufferers often develop another fear—they think they're going crazy.

4. *Realize the relationship between the intensity of your fear and your sense of self-command.* If you have a low-intensity fear but even less self-command in the fear situation, the fear will persist. If you have a high-intensity fear but possess an even higher sense of self-command, the fear will not persist. The most severe fear victims are those with a high-intensity fear and very little self-command.

In Fear Control Training your object is to *decrease the intensity of your fear and increase your sense of self-command.* Every method presented in this book aims at achieving one or both of these. The Freudian techniques of "insight" and "getting at the roots" possess importance only when they affect achieving these goals.

Sometimes a single fear that has nothing to do with people can influence an important personal relationship.

CASE

As a fifteen-year-old Sally had been left alone by her parents. She was sure she could manage, but at 2:00 A.M. she panicked, called her aunt and took refuge with her. The fear lasted. Now twenty-seven and married, Sally was afraid to stay home alone at night, feeling sure she'd be robbed or raped. When her husband, a salesman, would go out of town for several weeks, Sally stayed with friends. This was inconvenient. Her husband had to give up several business trips. His work suffered. He was both sympathetic and angry.

Through Fear Control Training I taught Sally the principle that she had to go through her fear and taught her methods of relaxation to counter it. We arranged for the husband to be away but get home at 4:00 A.M. She would have to spend most of the night without him. If during this time she got in a state of terror, she was to call my answering service and the service would call me. Sally did not call. She performed this assignment successfully twice. Then the husband stayed away until 5:00 A.M., then 6:00 A.M. At this point Sally could stay alone with minimal anxiety. Conquering this simple fear had a tremendous impact on her marriage and sense of self-respect.

Sometimes a single fear may have influenced your whole life-style, without your realizing the effect.

CASE

Thirty-eight-year-old Dick R. came to me with the problem "I lack confidence." Scion of an affluent family, Dick described his mother as a "selfish woman" who created a tense, formal household atmosphere, and his father as a "meek man" who paid little attention to him. Dick had been raised by nurses, sent off to boarding school ("At mail call I was the one who got no letters"). The background had set up the fear that "No one cares" . . . "I'll never be loved" . . . "I'll go through life unloved and unloving."

He did. The fear propelled him into two marriages where he felt lucky to get any scraps of affection. With each wife, he interpreted any anger or criticism as "She doesn't love me." This created so much tension that by mutual consent, both marriages ended in divorce. Fearful of repeating his marital failure pattern, Dick had withdrawn more and more from the world. He had stopped going out.

FIRST STEP: To make Dick see the impact this fear had had on his life. I had Dick recall certain incidents where he had distorted things to maintain his fear: the time his uncle had failed to answer a letter and Dick had interpreted this as "He doesn't care about me" . . . the time his first wife had lunched with an old boy friend and Dick had felt "She knows I'd disapprove. It meant she didn't care." He also saw that he had used promiscuity to set up situations where he avoided testing whether a woman "really cared."

SECOND STEP: Dick had to remember various past incidents and imagine them taking place now: the time his mother gave him permission to have a business cocktail party at her Fifth Avenue apartment and then reneged a few days before the event . . . the time wife number one had accused "You're no fun to live with." Over and over Dick imagined the situations, gradually learning to react with a mellow sadness rather than sharp anxiety.

At about this point Dick started to go out again.

THIRD STEP: We discussed problem situations that might come up and showed him how his incorrect thinking led him to wrong conclusions. For example, if a date expressed annoyance over something he said, it didn't mean no one would ever love him. Suddenly Dick saw that (a) he had a group of concerned friends; he had blocked this out; (b) his ex-wives had loved him; as a matter of fact his first wife kept asking him to remarry her.

Dick started to live with a woman. However, because his fear of not being loved had been reduced, he felt no sense of urgency to rush into a rapid marriage and was able to give the relationship a chance to develop.

Before switching to Behavior Therapy, I spent twenty years as a practicing traditional psychotherapist. Therefore, I can understand that many people frequently find it difficult to adjust to the empirical approach of Behavior Therapy and its Fear Control Training program. They ask pertinent questions that deserve pertinent answers.

Q. Do I have to know how my fears began before I can change them?

A. No. Many people know how their fears began and that doesn't help them one bit. The important things for you to know are the specific things that set off the fear and the things you do to maintain it.

Q. Are fears inherited?

A. Some fears—like fear of the dark or of snakes— seem to be inherited or built into our nervous system. However, even these are influenced by life experience. Most fears are learned.

Q. What kinds of people are most apt to become phobic?

A. Anyone can develop a phobia and most people do develop phobias of one kind or another at some time in their lives. I have seen phobias in people who were frankly psychotic as well as in people who, by any criteria except for the presence of a phobia, must be considered psychologically normal. The main difference is that the more normal a person is, the easier it is for him/her to get rid of the phobia.

Q. What kinds of people are the most likely to remain phobic?

A. There are four general types who are most apt to cling to their phobias: (1) the introvert who pays a lot of attention to his internal experiences and, in this way, nurtures his fear feelings; (2) the obsessive person whose thoughts get out of control. He dwells on his phobias, thus increasing his anxiety and doing nothing to change them; (3) the passive, unassertive person who is resigned to his phobias and has the attitude "This is the way it has to be . . . there's nothing I can do about it"; (4) the tense person who feels nervous about many things and exaggerates any anxiety reaction.

Q. Do cultural factors influence phobias?

A. Yes. Broad cultural influences affect the popularity of certain phobias. In the sixteenth century fears were prevalent about demons, witches and sorcery. In the eighteenth century people feared venereal disease. In this century we find tremendous fears of cancer, heart disease, atomic destruction or outer space. As new objects and concepts evolve, some people are bound to develop fears of these new situations and express them in new ways.

Q. If you take the symptom away (the phobic response), won't I get another and worse one in its place?

A. In Freudian thinking, if the protective phobia is removed while it is still needed as a defense against unconscious conflicts, the person will develop another symptom to serve the same purpose. However, in reality this does not happen. Recent careful studies show that when you remove a phobia, the development of substitute symptoms is either nonexistent or very rare

—so rare that we can exclude it from consideration. You do not have to worry that if you eliminate your phobia, something bad will happen to you. Just go ahead and get rid of it.

Q. What is the difference between Fear Control Training and Assertiveness Training?

A. Fear Control Training and Assertiveness Training share a common goal: to teach you to have an active attitude toward life—in other words, to do something about your problem. However, in Assertiveness Training we concentrate on your inability to stand up for yourself (passive behavior) or coming on too strong (aggressive behavior). Usually we put the emphasis on the social skills needed to relate to the people around you. In Fear Control Training we deal with your learned fear reactions in many areas. We try to help you unlearn these fears (whether they apply to objects, people, personal or impersonal situations) so that you can change your behavior to react without fear. Both AT and FCT are techniques used by behavior therapists and concentrate on changing your present behavior, not on investigating the trauma of your unconscious.

Through Fear Control Training you can learn to face the fear, cope with it, conquer it and live without it so that you can become the human being you want to be.

In 1933, President Franklin D. Roosevelt made his first inaugural address to the nation, saying, "The only thing we have to fear is fear itself—nameless, unreasoning, unjustified terror which paralyzes needed efforts to convert retreat into advance." In this book we cover the personal lifetime crises that "nameless, unreasoning, unjustified terror" provokes. Our aim: to help you convert personal "retreat" into psychological and practical "advance."

CHAPTER 2

WHAT ARE
YOU AFRAID OF?

What things set off your irrational fears?

Are you especially afraid of objects or do your fears occur more in interpersonal situations?

Are all your fears at the same level or do some produce just a little anxiety and some actual terror?

How can you get started on Fear Control Training and perhaps turn your life around?

To change a fear, you must know what it is and exactly what triggers it. Only when you possess this knowledge can you commence constructive action.

In Fear Control Training you don't have to work through every discomfort in your life. Few people feel at ease at the thought of bats, blood, boating in stormy waters, public embarrassment, becoming mentally ill. In FCT, only the fears and anxieties that prevent you from functioning at work or home possess importance. A surgeon who fears blood had better do something about it. So should the construction worker who fears heights.

Other fears have a more subtle effect. The woman who cannot tolerate the touch of any man, including her husband, will not have a successful marriage. A mother will not rear mentally healthy children if her discipline of them depends on her impulsive reactions during temper outbursts, rather than the children's needs. Many fears are of the subtle and incapacitating variety.

THE LEVELS OF FEAR

In trying to overcome fear, you cannot think of it in terms of either/or. You must not reason "Is it a reasonable or unreasonable fear?" Instead, you must think how much a certain fear disrupts your life, the extent to which it keeps you from achieving your goals and from being the kind of person you want to be.

•My wife Jean is extremely sensitive to flying insects. All she has to do is see one and she runs for insect spray, uses enormous amounts of it and becomes fidgety. Sometimes she sees flying insects where there are none. This is a *minifear*. Its greatest effect is on me. Because she gets so nervous from the bugs, she creates enormous tension. On the other hand, her very awareness of bugs serves as a protective device. Her carefulness keeps her from accumulating large amounts of insect bites.

•She has a continuing fear of rejection. For example, after Jean left *Seventeen,* she didn't hear from a certain co-worker, to whom she had been close, for three months. Jean agonized over the rejection: "She has dropped me. All those lunches all those years meant nothing to her. She never was my friend." Then, by accident, Jean discovered that the woman had been hospitalized and in traction for months with a slipped disc and hadn't wanted to burden Jean with her troubles. This is a *midifear*. It kept Jean from contacting the woman, acting like the kind of friend she really wanted to be, and also made her feel bad about her own behavior.

•For seventeen of her twenty-one years on *Seventeen,* Jean worked for a highly talented but exacting editor. This editor demanded extraordinary dedication and hard work from her staff. As long as she got that, she rarely fired anyone. Jean gave her a ten-hour day, achieving a national reputation as a publicity director in the process, but spent half the night worrying, "She is going to fire me." This was a real *maxifear*. While it sharpened Jean's work in a limited area, it also served as a major career detriment. She spent all the time that should have gone to thinking about "What would be the next best professional step for me?" in brooding over "What will I do if she fires me?"

Jean has always insisted that her reactions were perfectly normal: "Bugs bite me more than anyone else" . . . "Ellen could have let me know she was sick. It was her back that was hurt—not her voice" . . . "Mrs. Brown was difficult. There was the danger of getting fired." She fails to realize that it was the intensity of the reaction that caused the disruptive effect on her life.

THE FIVE BASIC KINDS OF FEAR

Placing fears in categories has just one purpose: to help you take action about them. Although all fears share things in common, enough differences emerge to make classifications meaningful. Here are the most important ones:

1. *Fear of things and places.* These are the most easily recognizable, exemplify what most people mean when they talk about phobias, and, in the main, constitute those that have been given Greek names. In your reaction to things and places you can run the phobic gamut. I have known people fearful of tomatoes, mirrors and snow.

Some basic "things and places" phobias

acrophobia	heights
ailurophobia	cats
aictiophobia	sharp, pointed instruments
anthophobia	flowers
aquaphobia	water

astraphobia	lightning
aviaphobia	flying
bacteriophobia	bacteria
brontophobia	thunder
cancerphobia	cancer
cynophobia	dogs
claustrophobia	closed spaces
equinophobia	horses
herpetophobia	lizards, reptiles, creeping or crawling things
melissophobia	bees
mysophobia	dirt, germs, contamination
nycotophobia	darkness or night
ophidiophobia	snakes
pathophobia	illness
sitophobia	eating
taphophobia	being buried alive
zoophobia	animals

2. *Interpersonal and social fears.* These are the most difficult to recognize and may include such fears as that of rejection, anger, tenderness, failure, success. Two factors make it hard for you to spot and deal with this kind of fear.

•Often you persist in an elaborate pattern of avoiding or escaping from the feared situation. If you never take on a challenging task, you may never recognize that you fear failure. If you never get close to a member of the opposite sex, you may never understand your intense fear of closeness and/or getting hurt.

•You may recognize the fear and attempt to make it seem reasonable, seeing only the element of truth and not your exaggerated response. With most people, if things go wrong in a close relationship, they feel upset, unhappy and hurt but not destroyed. Life goes on. However, the person who is phobic to being hurt builds up the danger, does feel destroyed if it happens and takes fewer and fewer risks.

In dealing with interpersonal and social fears, you must first identify the basic fear or situation that triggers your intense fear. This is harder than planning an FCT program for someone who fears elevators.

3. *Fear of internal fears.* In this, your feelings of anxiety, panic or body changes form the phobic aspect rather than the place or situation in which the feelings occur. It is the dizziness, heart palpitations, knot in the stomach or feeling of blushing that frightens you. Because you can't avoid your own feelings, you try to have nothing to do with the situations in which you experience them. However, since they may occur anywhere and sometimes even come "out of the blue," you tend to avoid more and more places. When you have this fear of internal fears to an extreme degree, it is called agoraphobia (from the Greek word *agora,* meaning marketplace or place of assembly).

4. *Fear of thoughts.* Instead of being fearful of your feelings, you fear your thoughts. They may take the form of a thought that intrudes suddenly ("I will get in a car accident"), bringing with it a surge of anxiety or obsessive rumination where you constantly repeat the same thought ("I said something foolish at the party"), thus gradually building up your fear and anxiety. As with the fear of internal fears, because these thoughts are internal, you cannot avoid them—the way you can elevators and tunnels. It is even more difficult to escape from them than from your feelings. Sometimes you can get away from them only by performing a compulsive act over and over (repetitive handwashing) or carrying out security routines like endlessly checking over and over to see that you locked the door.

5. *The derivative fears.* Sometimes the fears themselves are secondary to other problems. People who live under stress are apt to develop fears. One man, under a lot of job pressure, suddenly became afraid to go into restaurants. Because he was so generally tense, his resistance became low and he became fear prone.

People who have not learned the necessary social skills may develop fears simply because they don't know how to do what they have to do. For example, Howard married at twenty, became a widower at forty-five. He didn't know how to cope with the social life of a middle-aged single man. Instead of learning how, he concentrated on avoiding social activities because they made him feel insecure. Thus Howard, who, during his marriage, had had a normal social life, turned into a recluse with a fear of meeting new people. This stemmed from lack of skills.

PINPOINTING YOUR FEARS

UPTIGHT INVENTORY—I

Aim: To recognize the situation that sets off your fear reaction.

STEP ONE: Buy a large-sized notebook. This will be your Fear Control Thinking workbook and you can use it for this exercise and others throughout the book. Don't make the mistake of thinking it too mechanical or simplistic to take the questionnaires and jot down thoughts about your answers. In FCT those who achieve the most important psychological gains usually turn out to be the ones who keep good notes. Keeping a record will also help you to monitor your changes in fear patterns.

STEP TWO: In your FCT workbook make up a chart with seven columns. The left heading should read "Uptight Checklist" and the next six should be your disturbed reactions: *none, very little, a little, much, very much, terror*. Remember, your reaction can be fear, anxiety or any other disturbed unpleasant feeling. Your heading should look like this:

Uptight Checklist
none   very little   a little   much   very much   terror

STEP THREE: Copy the following list into your FCT workbook under the left-hand heading "Uptight Checklist." The list includes the most common fears. Leave space at the end for your own unique disturbed reactions. These can be very important.

1. lightning
2. darkness
3. dirt
4. weapons
5. sudden noises
6. sirens
7. fire
8. loud noises
9. deep water
10. thunderstorms
11. worms
12. cemeteries
13. dogs
14. one person bullying another
15. feeling angry
16. drugs
17. hurting others
18. homosexual thoughts
19. being with people of the opposite sex
20. entering a room where people are already seated
21. being ignored
22. masturbation
23. blood
24. failure
25. making mistakes
26. success
27. being trapped
28. high places
29. doctors
30. elevators
31. injections
32. crowded places
33. dead people
34. illness
35. becoming insane
36. new things
37. airplanes
38. being a leader
39. arguing with parents
40. tunnels
41. traveling alone
42. strange foods
43. strangers
44. driving a car
45. life after death
46. being punished by God
47. thoughts of starting a fire
48. giving orders
49. death of a loved one

50. sexual inadequacy
51. love
52. closeness
53. commitment
54. marriage
55. children
56. pregnancy
57. harmless spiders
58. harmless snakes
59. crawling insects
60. flying insects
61. rats
62. mice
63. cats
64. losing control
65. other people getting angry with you
66. fainting
67. dizziness
68. suffocating
69. missing a heartbeat
70. falling
71. large open places
72. crossing streets
73. blushing
74. pleasure
75. cancer
76. dentists
77. sick people
78. surgical operations
79. church
80. being independent
81. accidents
82. spending money
83. losing a job
84. thoughts of suicide
85. thoughts of having a defective child
86. making decisions
87. being watched working
88. being criticized
89. moving to a new home
90. speaking in public
91. bridges
92. taking responsibility
93. giving off an offensive odor
94. leaving home
95. tests
96. being dressed unsuitably
97. tough-looking people
98. ugly people
99. people with deformities
100. being teased
101. others

STEP FOUR: Using the *none* to *terror* scale, indicate under the six headings from left to right the extent to which each of the items sets off any kind of uptight feeling in you. Put your answer next to each item, and, in giving it, show what you feel *at this moment*, not how you reacted at some time in the past or think you should react.

Pay particular attention to the last item: "others."

These are fears that have not been listed that are important to you. *Note:* Merely because they are not listed does not mean they are uncommon. Odds are that you share them with many other people. Here are some patients have listed:

Not having locked the doors	Ocean waves
Feeling helpless	Full moon
Being fired	Insufficient retirement income
Choking to death	Forgetting an important detail at work
Not being excellent at everything	

One woman who listed "violent movies on TV" added, "I made myself sit through one, and for days after I was enraged, terrified and depressed. I am not sure whether I am afraid I will get hurt and feel humiliated, or that I will hurt the other person and feel shame and guilt."

STEP FIVE: After you have completed this book and have applied some of the Fear Control Training methods to your fears, go back and take the quiz again. In the process you may realize you have fears you never knew you had.

CASE

Mary and Fred A. came to see me because of marital difficulties. In the initial session Fred did most of the talking. He complained that Mary failed to take responsibility in the home, never left him alone, always pushed him to "do things." Calling her "lazy and over-dependent," Fred said, "She constantly asks me, 'What should I wear?' She's twenty-eight years old. She should know what to wear." For Fred, Mary's dependency was the core of the difficulty. For her part, Mary felt

Fred expected too much of her and didn't realize how hard so many things were for her to do. She said, "It's easier for other people to get a lot done. I can't."

Among the forms I gave them to fill out was the Uptight Inventory—I. As a result of filling it out conscientiously and honestly, Mary came in the next week with the realization that her whole problem stemmed from the fear of making mistakes. She told Fred and me, "I suddenly knew that all my life I had been terrified of doing something wrong. It didn't matter so much what other people would think . . . I would know if I did wrong and I'd be upset." Because she avoided any occasion where she had to "do things" and chance a mistake, Mary had become a dependent person.

I had Mary *deliberately* make all kinds of mistakes. At first these consisted of errors only she would know about—like deliberately not dusting a piece of cherished antique furniture or "forgetting" to buy needed staples in the grocery store. Later she deliberately made mistakes other people might notice—overcooking a certain dish or wearing a combination of clothes that wasn't *Vogue*-perfect. As Mary performed these actions and saw the world didn't come to an end, she became less frightened of making mistakes, acquired the ability to take on more responsibility and began to act like the grown-up woman she was. The marriage improved. Both Fred and Mary liked Mary more.

UPTIGHT INVENTORY—II

Aim: To recognize the specific cues that trigger your fear and to choose the starting point for your Fear Control Training program.

STEP ONE: Take your *very much* to *terror* fears. List each one on a separate sheet of paper in your Fear Control Training workbook.

STEP TWO: About each *very much—terror* fear, answer the following questions:

Example: claustrophobia

1. What is it you're really afraid of?	Is it that you'll suffocate . . . be trapped and unable to get out of the room . . . become nervous . . . panic and start to scream, thus disgracing yourself . . . faint?
2. What are the things that stimulate smaller and larger amounts of fear?	Does whether the door is open or closed have a big, small or no effect? Does the number of people in the room matter? The size of the room? Whether there's a lock on the door or not? If there are people in the room, does it matter how well you know them (some people become more uptight if there are others in the room; others are most upset if they're alone)? *Get the pattern of your fear reaction.*
3. What is the worst that can happen in the situation?	You'll panic, scream, run out of the room and everyone will think you're peculiar . . . you'll collapse from lack of air and have to be taken to the nearest hospital with permanent brain damage . . . you'll die!

STEP THREE: Answer the question: What do your *very much—terror* fears do to you? Do they make you avoid situations? In deciding this, note the difference between *active avoidance* and *passive avoidance*. In passive avoidance, you do *not* do things (for instance, with claustrophobia, you think, "If I go to that meeting, the room will be small and I'll become frightened, so I won't go"). In active avoidance, you feel you have to do something to avoid the feared situation (for example, you think, "If I don't go around making sure the doors are unlocked, I'm going to feel trapped," so you get out of bed at 3:00 A.M. and make sure all the doors are unlocked).

STEP FOUR: Do a cost analysis. Ask yourself: "What price am I paying for this fear?" Try these questions:

What have I lost in my career because of my fears?

What have I lost in social situations because of my fears?

What have I lost in personal situations because of my fears?

What have I lost in terms of my feelings about myself because of my fears?

In answering, (a) list specific situations and (b) label the price tags: minifear, midifear, maxifear.

STEP FIVE: Using your answers to all these questions, arrange your different fears into groups. Put those together that go together. For example, here is a list of *very much–terror* fears of one female patient (item numbers are from Uptight Inventory—I).

2. darkness	66. fainting
7. fire	78. surgical operations
27. being trapped	79. church
28. high places	81. accidents
30. elevators	91. bridges
31. injections	99. people with deformities
32. crowded places	
37. airplanes	101. escalators
56. pregnancy	

In grouping them, she examined her answers to the questions in Uptight Inventory—II. She noted that in an airplane she was most comfortable in the middle section of a 747; that when she was near a window, she would get the same dizzy feeling she got on a bridge. From this she realized that her main fear of airplanes was the fear of heights. Going by her actual answers rather than what the fears seemed to be upon superficial examination, she made the following groupings:

Fear of heights

37. airplanes
91. bridges
101. escalators

Fear of being trapped

27. being trapped
30. elevators
32. crowded places
79. church

Fear of physical deformity

7. fire
31. injections
56. pregnancy
66. fainting
78. surgical operations
81. accidents
99. people with deformities

Unrelated fears

2. darkness

STEP SIX: Choose the starting point for your Fear Control Training program. You want to start where you have the greatest chance of success in an area that really matters to you. The principle: *to begin with the least frightening of your most meaningful fears.*

•Go over your fear groupings and see which one has the greatest impact on your life at this moment. In the case cited above, the fear of deformity probably had the most *overall* effect on the patient's life. However, her fear of being trapped was having the greatest *immediate* effect; it was keeping her from job hunting. So we started with her fear of being trapped.

•Within this "immediate" impact area, rank your different specific fears from least to most, according to how much fear is involved. Now go back to Uptight Inventory—I and see if there are any lesser fears that would fall into the same category. Add them to your list in the proper place. The lowest-ranking fear in this category is your starting point. As you conquer these lesser fears, you will also weaken the greater fears in that area and so make them more manageable.

TWO FEAR DISGUISES

Many times your fears lead to two behavioral patterns that may have severe effects on your life-style: *hypervigilance* and *counterphobic repetition.* Each is subtle and often difficult to identify as part of a fear reaction. You know only that you feel things or do things without reason. Both behaviors assume particular importance in the area of social fears.

Hypervigilance: With this condition, you are so frightened, have such a need to avoid the feared situation, that you (1) are constantly alert to the smallest sign that what you fear may take place; (2) react to false signals; you behave as if the fear stimulus is there *when it really is not.*

EXAMPLE ONE: John is terrified lest someone become angry with him. When it does happen, he loses control and blindly lashes out in a verbal counterattack. Sensitive to even the slightest cue that may signal anger, he often sees anger where none exists. Nevertheless his counterattack is automatic.

•At work a colleague under deadline pressure makes a rather brusque request of him. John answers with a sarcastic crack.

•At home his wife is upset by something that doesn't concern him at all. He responds by yelling and berating her.

John is unaware of his fear and the fact that he responds to false signals. He knows only, "I can't get along with anyone."

EXAMPLE TWO: Roger is severely phobic to criticism and hypervigilant in this area. To avoid criticism, he constantly performs "nice guy" favors for others (before they ask) and never makes requests for himself. When others do criticize him, he smiles, mumbles "I'm sorry" and remains upset for days. Often he leaves letters from friends unopened, fearing they contain criticism. If he sees two friends chatting at a party, he thinks, "They're criticizing me." He also continually questions people about the content of their conversations: "Were you talking about me?" This questioning became so constant and inappropriate that his co-workers began to tease him about being "paranoid." When Roger came to consult me, his first statement was, "I have a persecution complex."

In checking to see if you practice hypervigilant behavior, realize that:

•While hypervigilance often seems to resemble the *ideas of reference* (the fear that actions and words of other people refer to you when they don't) found in paranoids, it is not a paranoid condition. Generally paranoid ideas stem from the schizophrenic process, which is primarily biochemical and can be treated with medicine. The hypervigilant process stems from learning. Because of your fear, you have learned to be oversensitive. Unlearn it, and your delusions disappear.

•The important thing is awareness of your hypervigilant behavior.

Counterphobic repetition: Even though you do your very best to avoid certain things, the very things you fear may come about. You cannot have absolute control over this nor can you control your disturbed reaction when it does happen. The one thing you can control is failure. You can act in ways that are fairly certain to bring on anger, criticism, rejection or whatever it is that frightens you. It is the only thing you can control, and the need to be in command of something is so great that you are willing to pay the destructive price involved. So you keep placing yourself in the phobic situations over and over, failing each time, and each time strengthening the pattern.

Of course, you lack awareness of what you are doing. Probably you don't even know that a phobia forms the core of your pattern. You realize only that you have a compulsive tendency to repeat certain types of situations over and over, always with the same disastrous results. Identifying the phobic core is the necessary first step to breaking the pattern.

EXAMPLE ONE: Sally W., a twenty-nine-year-old social worker, came to consult me because of her problems with men. Over and over, she kept getting involved with men who turned out to be hypercritical of her and who would constantly berate her, occasionally with violent temper outbursts, sometimes with physical beatings. All of these relationships quickly became impossible and Sally had to get out of them.

Sally herself realized several things about the problem: (1) this was the way her father had always treated her; (2) that somehow she sought men who would act this way to her; (3) that when she went out with nice, gentle men, she did not feel comfortable; (4) that she repeated the same pattern over and over. What Sally did not realize was that she was phobic to being criticized by men. Her experience with her father had taught her that there was little she could do to keep that situation from happening. *The one thing she could control was to bring it on by deliberately selecting men who would act in just that way.* In this way, even though the consequences were so unhappy, she felt she gained some degree of mastery.

EXAMPLE TWO: Dan S. had a fear of being trapped. In high school and college he had a mild claustrophobia. This eventually disappeared but it generalized into a social claustrophobia: the fear of being trapped in a relationship. Dan would get formally engaged, but, as the wedding date approached, without realizing the similarity to the previous claustrophobic reaction, he'd start feeling he couldn't breathe and become very anxious. Eventually the anxiety became so great, he would break off the engagement. However, because of his need to master the fear, he soon became engaged again. When Dan came to see me, he had been engaged eleven different times!

In treating Sally and Dan, I used Fear Control Training methods very successfully. However, the important thing in each case was that both Sally and Dan were brought to realize *their behavior was counterphobic*. Without identifying the core phobia, treatment would not have been possible.

SPOTTING THE SUBTLE PHOBIAS

Many fears are obvious. You know when you're scared of the view from the fortieth floor or getting cancer. Other fears aren't so easy to identify. And, although you may realize you have problems, you don't realize these stem from your attempts to cope with a phobia. I call these "the subtle phobias." Most of them fall within the "interpersonal and social fears" category. You must be able to recognize this kind of phobia as well as the "thing and place" phobia. All the situations given below came up in my private practice or at the Payne Whitney Clinic, The New York Hospital. In taking the quiz, assume in each instance that some fear is involved.

SPOT YOUR PHOBIC BLOCK QUIZ

1. Your mother-in-law calls and tells you about the wonderful, elegant luncheon she attended that day. Do you:
    a. Ask what the hostess served, making some

mental notes for yourself as you hear about the menu.

b. Begin to feel uncomfortable and terminate the conversation as quickly as possible, thinking to yourself, "She always tells me what a wonderful time she has at other people's houses."

c. Say, "That's why you wouldn't go shopping with me." An argument starts.

2. You have a good middle-management job. One task: a weekly report on your department's current activities. This makes you very nervous. In previous jobs where you handed in a similar report to your immediate superior, you experienced only mild difficulty. Here you bring the report personally to the president (a very nice guy) and discuss it. This makes you nervous and uptight. Your procrastination over the weekly report has become so bad that your position is threatened. Do you:

a. Start looking for another job.

b. Try to rearrange the job situation so that personal discussion isn't necessary.

c. Increase your contact with the president in all kinds of different situations.

3. You keep getting involved in close relationships. The more involved you become, the more resentments you feel until the relationship just has to break up. You realize that this happens because as you begin to feel tender to the other person, more and more you say what would please him/her and are careful not to make waves by voicing what you really think. Do you:

a. Keep berating yourself for your lack of ability to work through a relationship and dwell constantly on what may be wrong with you as a person.

b. Work harder at trying to say the "right" thing.

c. Starting with trivial things, more and more you attempt to say what you feel.

4. You're at a social event where there are a number of attractive and interesting members of the opposite sex. Do you:

a. Start talking to the people you find most interesting, making yourself as pleasant as possible.

b. Talk to the interesting people but find you have little to say.

c. Avoid the interesting people and gravitate toward guests whom you find less interesting and attractive.

5. There's tension in your marriage because your partner enjoys travel to new places whereas you will only go to familiar places or spots where you have friends or family. Now your spouse, who has been through a pressureful work year, wants to take off on a cruise to some remote Greek islands. Do you:

a. Flatly refuse to go and insist on visiting your parents in California.

b. Say, "We'll visit my parents this year and go to Greece next year. Mother hasn't been feeling well."

c. Agree to go and set up a project of planned reading about Greece.

6. You're in a job rut. You know you have the ability to produce better work, be more creative, get attention and the promotion you crave. However, whenever the opportunity to do something original comes up, you find a dozen reasons for not doing it. Now there's a staff meeting to discuss a problem and you clearly see the perfect solution. Do you:

a. Build up all the possible objections to your proposed solution and use these as reasons for not saying anything.

b. Think through in your mind just what you want to say and how you'll express it—and concentrate on doing this at the meeting just the way you planned.

c. Tell your idea at the meeting but in a halting, stammering way that fails to convey the meaning clearly.

7. You and your partner have been having sexual problems. It has gotten to the point where you feel uncomfortable about any expression of affection that has the potentiality of leading toward sex. Now you're

spending an evening together and you feel a tension and distance from your partner. Do you:

a. Give in to the pressure to make sexual advances that you know will lead to another experience of sexual failure.

b. Call up close friends and invite them over for a drink.

c. Difficult though it may be, discuss the situation with your partner and decide what you would both be most comfortable in doing that evening.

8. You have many friends and acquaintances and you constantly keep in touch with them and do things with them. This social activity leaves you little time to read books you want to read or even perform necessary house chores. The chores have piled up. To do something about them will take a full weekend of work without distraction. Do you:

a. Clear the decks and do the job.

b. Call in an old favor and ask a friend to come and help you clean.

c. Start doing the operation clean-up, but begin to procrastinate, start telephoning friends, and eventually end up spending the weekend visiting and entertaining.

9. You have a fear of heights. There's a person you like very much who lives on the twenty-fifth floor of a high-rise. You have turned down a number of invitations to visit this person, to the point where it is embarrassing and tension has started to develop. Now X calls you with a dinner invitation. Do you:

a. Find another flimsy pretext for declining.

b. Accept. Go to the dinner party and once there complain of "having a headache" and leave early.

c. Frankly tell the person about your height phobia.

10. You're female, good at work, and have been offered a big position in a different firm. You really want the job. Do you:

a. Take it, welcoming the challenge, and do the best job you can.

b. Refuse it, saying to yourself, "Things are just fine the way they are now in my marriage and my job. Why change?"

c. Take the job and then begin to make all kinds of mistakes. You don't perform as well as you know you can.

ANALYSIS OF ANSWERS

1. Phobic block: *fear of criticism.* Right answer: (a). Here, instead of seeing criticism where your mother-in-law intended none, you give a response that leads to sharing of feelings and obtaining of information that might be helpful when you entertain. In (b) you practice straight avoidance behavior and in (c) you react in an inappropriate and disruptive way. You see criticism where none was intended.

2. Phobic block: *fear of authority figures.* Right answer: (c). You're trying to do something about your phobia through increased exposure to the authority figure. Planned exposure to phobic situations often reduces tension—if only for the reason, in this case, that you learn that an authority figure isn't necessarily an ogre. Answer (a) is a straight cop out. In (b) you try to set up the job so that you can function in it but you don't come to terms with your phobia.

3. Phobic block: *fear of hurting or upsetting someone to whom you're close.* Right answer: (c). This is right because by making statements that express what you feel (good lines: "I don't like it when you're a half-hour late and keep me waiting" . . . "It isn't fair that we always do what you want to do" . . . "No, I don't think that's a good idea"), you stop avoiding the problem and increase your exposure. *Note:* It is important here to figure out how you would handle your partner's responses. In this way you increase your command of the situation and so the phobia decreases. In

(a) you fall into the trap that the phobia has to indicate something is deeply wrong with you and can't be changed without resolving your unconscious conflicts. In (b) you continue your phobic pattern, making the false assumption that the more you avoid the basic problem, the more successful you will be.

4. Phobic block: *fear of rejection by the opposite sex*. Right answer: (a). Here you are willing to risk rejection in order to make social contact with people you may learn to care about. In (b) you're caught up in a self-fulfilling prophecy. Your anticipation of rejection is so strong that you act as if you've already been rejected. This makes the phobia stronger. In (c) you minimize the risk of rejection because you think that there's less chance of the uninteresting people rejecting you than there would be with the interesting. Besides, rejection from the former wouldn't make you feel as bad.

5. Phobic block: *fear of novelty (of strange places and people)*. Right answer: (c). Here you expose yourself to the fear but, at the same time, by doing a lot of reading, you may take some of the strangeness away. Even more important, in the course of your research you may develop feelings of interest and excitement about the trip that will serve to counter your phobic reaction. In (b) you're trying to make your avoidance behavior appear reasonable both to yourself and to your partner. In (a) you continue the same phobic pattern you've had all your life. This way you'll never get over it.

6. Phobic block: *fear of looking foolish*. Right answer: (b). By concentrating on the task rather than the fear, you're more in control of the situation. In answer (c) you try to handle the situation but you let the fear take control. In answer (a) you rationalize your avoidance behavior. This may make you feel more comfortable but you don't achieve your career goals.

7. Phobic block: *fear of sexual inadequacy*. Right

answer: (c). By taking a beginning step, you recognize that the phobia has generalized from actual intercourse to any expression of tenderness between you. By speaking up and doing something you're comfortable doing (which may be something as simple as just sitting close together), you start to reverse the generalization process. In (b) you escape from the phobic situation and in (a) you indulge in counterphobic behavior. Without changing your attitude or actions in any way, you're repeating the phobic situation.

8. Phobic block: *being alone.* Right answer: (a). You do your chores and go through whatever disturbance you feel from being alone. You'll find you live through it and eventually will feel an increased sense of self-command. In answer (b) you increase your comfort but the phobia is still in command. In answer (c) you practice a very common form of avoidance behavior which many phobics mislabel as procrastination, often blaming themselves for being lazy.

9. Phobic block: you have two—the obvious one is *fear of heights* but the *secondary subtle one is the fear the other person will think you're crazy.* This is a common secondary fear based in part on the reality that others just don't understand your irrational fears. Many people suffer in silence and hide their fears as long as they can. Right answer: (c). You face your secondary phobia directly and do some reality testing. Even though the other person may not understand your heights phobia, at least he/she will know you want to be friends. There's some chance of salvaging the relationship. In (b) you practice both escape and avoidance behavior. You do get yourself into the situation but when your anxiety builds up, you run away from the situation (escape) and give a false explanation (avoidance of the secondary phobia). You avoid explaining "I'm afraid of heights." In (a) you exercise avoidance behavior with both phobias.

10. Phobic block: *fear of success.* Right answer: (a). You have the opportunity for professional growth

and you take it. In (b) the answer is wrong if you make the decision because of your need to avoid the fear that success might bring rather than on the basis of its being the correct professional step at this time in your career. Under certain conditions it might be the right answer for you if you base your decision on choice rather than fear. In (c), as you become closer to success, your anxiety mounts. Your judgment becomes impaired; your mistakes accumulate. Your fear of success is taking over.

The above should get you started in determining your own subtle phobias. Write out your own problem situations, offer alternative ways of behavior (including what you did or might do in the situation) and see if you can determine whether any specific phobia is involved.

SETTING YOUR FEAR CONTROL TRAINING GOALS

1. *If you have a mild phobia that causes you little annoyance, you don't have to do anything about it.* Some people think any phobia, no matter how minor, signifies deep unconscious unresolved conflict. For example, if you fear mice, phallic implications must exist. Your fear must mean that you have a basic fear of penetration—in your unconscious you do not want any man to enter your vagina. Forget all those symbolic meanings. Get an exterminator.

2. *Don't try to make your fear look reasonable.* Stop making statements like, "I did fluff my last talk" . . . "People didn't act nice to me at the last party I attended" . . . "My friends will see how nervous I am and think less of me." Concentrate on what sets off your fears and your reactions, not your rationalizations.

3. *Check with your family doctor.* Sometimes fears stem from physical conditions. For example, low blood

sugar can often give you feelings of dizziness and weakness that you interpret as an anxiety reaction.

4. *Make a list of phobias you've had in the past and recall what happened to them.* You've probably been going in and out of phobias all your life. Many disappear on their own. Some don't. Childhood and adolescent fears usually offer the clearest examples of this. A few of my own:

•Fear of dogs. Even though I had a terrier for a pet for a short while, as a child I was always terrified of most dogs. This continued until late adolescence when I got a summer job on a farm. Part of my job was to care for a variety of dogs. Because I needed the job, I had to face my phobia. I did. Now I have no fear of dogs.

•Fear of being hurt by a baseball. This was particularly strong when I was nine years old and played baseball every day after school. I was especially scared during practice when lots of balls were flying around and my turn would come to bat. As I gained competence in baseball, my fear diminished. However, once I began high school, I stopped playing baseball. Some remnants of this fear still remain. When I walk by a baseball game in an open park, I experience a wariness and a desire to get out of the ball's range.

•Being alone in the woods at night. The first time I camped out in the woods at night, I couldn't sleep. Every thump and rustle signaled "danger." Since it was a weekly summer camp assignment, I had to do it. With repetition, the fear completely disappeared. I now enjoy camping out alone in the woods.

5. *Think through how giving up these fears will improve your life.* List the things you'll be able to do that you can't do now, the talents you can use, the life-style changes you can effect. Put this list in some place where you can see it every day. It will help motivate you to keep on if the going gets tough.

6. *Be sure you diagnose the correct fear.* Sometimes you think you feel fear of one thing when it's really

something else. There are two mixed-up fears I have found to be very common: (a) people who claim they're terrified of elevators when their phobia is really heights; (b) people who have a series of fears relating to bridges, tunnels, crowds, traffic when, in actuality, they fear a panic reaction.

CASE

Jennie had a sailboat phobia, which was causing many marital problems. Her husband was a sailing buff, but Jennie flatly refused to go near his cherished sloop. Even in winter they would fight about his hobby, with Jennie hurling accusations like "You have no right to leave me alone so much." She explained it to me very logically: "I have a fear of the boat tilting and heeling before the wind."

As long as we treated it as a fear of sailboats, we got nowhere. It was only after failing to cure it that we tried to reevaluate what it might be. Originally I had asked Jennie, "Do you swim?" She had answered, "Yes." Now I asked, "Are you afraid of deep water?" She answered in the affirmative. I followed up with, "Are you afraid of drowning?" She thought a moment and said, "That's it. I'm afraid of drowning. It's not sailboats at all." She had developed the fear as a child, rationalized it by deciding "I don't like to swim," and confined herself to sunbathing ever since. We got rid of Jennie's fear of drowning. Then she started to like sailing.

7. *Realize that getting rid of one fear doesn't mean you won't develop another.* As life situations pose new problems you may develop new responses to some of them. Or you may discover a deep lurking fear you never knew you had.

CASE

Frank W., a thirty-two-year-old unmarried artist, had spent years painting in a loft. Eventually he had a very successful exhibit. Reviewers hailed his work, and, within a week, all his pictures had been sold. His dealer immediately scheduled him for another exhibition a year later. Suddenly Frank found he couldn't paint. In great distress, he came to me.

In our sessions it turned out that Frank had had phobic reactions to the fear that (a) he wouldn't be able to get enough pictures done in time for the upcoming show, and (b) his second exhibition wouldn't be as good as the first and his dealer would be contemptuous of him.

Using a series of graded exercises, we worked on this second fear. For example, I would make the very type of remark that Frank feared the dealer would say: "I figured you were only a one-shot guy." Frank would practice both relaxing and possible retorts. We also worked on his inability to paint. In his studio he commenced a series of simple tasks to get him started. For instance, he would prepare a canvas for painting. Again, here the aim was to maintain a state of relaxation while doing this so that the actual painting would not be so frightening.

The techniques worked. Frank started painting again. The exhibition turned out so well that Frank received invitations to give lectures, courses and participate in art seminars. Suddenly, he realized he had a public-speaking phobia and came back to me to work on that. If Frank hadn't gained success as an artist, he might never have realized the public-speaking problem.

8. *Always keep in mind the two basic Fear Control Training goals:* You want to decrease the intensity of your fear reaction and increase your sense of self-com-

mand over the fear. Accomplish this and the fear must go.

Do not expect Merlin at your side. You are going to have to make yourself do things you may be frightened to do. You may have to endure the scared feelings you experience when you do these things. You may have moments of discouragement when—even though you have carried out your fear assignments— you still feel "I'm afraid—of that elevator, that plane, that he/she may reject me." Know this. If you work hard at the Fear Control Training program, you have an excellent chance to conquer your fear and perhaps, in the process, change your life. It has happened to others. It can happen to you.

CHAPTER 3

AGORAPHOBIA

Fourteen years ago Mary W., age twenty-nine, was standing in line waiting to get into a movie. Suddenly— "as if some Thing attacked me"—she had a panic attack. Her heart palpitated; her knees quivered; she felt completely isolated from the world. From that moment on Mary's entire life has revolved around two questions: "Will I get another attack?" . . . "What can I do to avoid it?" She has avoided any situation (like trains) that she couldn't escape from quickly, that might make her feel anxious or pressured. A secretary, she has refused several chances for promotion to office manager. Her fear of another panic attack has confined her life to ground-floor-apartment–job–apartment and greatly limited her marital social life. She has never been back to the movies.

Like a multitude of fellow sufferers, Mary has agoraphobia, the crippling condition in which the victim goes through an incapacitating fear away from the safety of home, particularly when in crowded or isolated places —anywhere the sufferer cannot make a quick getaway or get help immediately should her fears grow beyond her and the dreaded panic attack begin. It includes fear of traveling especially in a vehicle which she lacks the power to stop at will.

According to Dr. Isaac M. Marks of the Bethlehem Royal and Maudsley Hospitals, London, agoraphobia is the most common phobia. It differs greatly from other fears and phobias. With a fear of cancer, germs, mice, you fear the potential of the object to harm you. If you have agoraphobia you fear the feelings that will grow *within yourself*—the relentless feeling of panic that sweeps over you, incapacitating you and making you feel trapped, isolated, ashamed, reluctant to go anywhere.

If you are a victim of agoraphobia, you need not continue to be one. In the past ten years, thousands upon thousands of unhappy women and men have been cured, not by medicine or by digging into the "why" of this disabling condition but by learning to change their behavior. Think of agoraphobia as showing itself in three main ways: feeling (of fear), thoughts (about the awful things that might happen) and behavior (avoiding things). The way to start things moving is to change behavior. This will lead to changes in thoughts and feelings later on.

BASIC FACTS ABOUT AGORAPHOBIA

The things that frighten you.   Begin your cure by understanding the nature of your symptoms. Whatever your specific fear (being in a crowded place, traveling away from home either alone or even when accompanied by spouse or parent, entering shops, standing in line, being alone in the house), your *Main Fear* is that of having a panic attack and suffering the symptoms that come with it. This can include anxiety, weakness, heart palpitations, "jelly knees," dizziness, missed heartbeats, a feeling of inability to take a deep breath, blurred vision, aching muscles, an illusion of walking on shifting ground, a sense of isolation and unreality. Above all you suffer flashes of incapacitating panic and the yearning to "get back home where I will be safe."

People can get panic attacks anywhere and under any conditions. What happens is that they begin to associate attacks with the place where they originally experienced the attack: the movie, open street, crowded store, bus, train, elevator. They start to anticipate the attack and work themselves into a high state of tension before going into these situations and get into such a nervous state that they bring on an attack in the store, street, bus, train, elevator. The result: Either they train themselves to have attacks in these places or they avoid them completely.

They grip this fear with *Maintenance Fear,* which consists of one or more of the four basic feelings that keep the Main Fear alive and make the agoraphobic different from the normal person who also worries over stressful situations:

•"I'm going to have a heart attack and die."

•"I'm going to faint or fall." (This causes many agoraphobics to clutch handholds in the streets; they go from fire hydrant to lamppost. In another instance of this fear of falling, one woman couldn't wait for the elevator. On her hands and knees she climbed up three flights of stairs, all the time saying to herself, "Hurry, hurry, hurry.")

•"I am going crazy. They will have to take me away to a mental institution."

•"I will lose control. I will begin to yell, scream, or somehow make a fool of myself." (With this sometimes you have a conflict of feelings. You want someone you know to come along and help. On the other hand you're afraid someone you know will come along and see you in this state.)

You fear the Main Fear so much that you add the Maintenance Fears to it until the various fears feel like one and thus you keep the Main Fear going. You can't control the Main Fear. However, if you control and do away with the Maintenance Fears, *eventually the panic attacks will disappear.*

The point is that these occurrences—fainting, dying, going crazy, losing control—are extremely rare. Even if you do some inappropriate thing (like bolting from church in the middle of the service or suddenly getting out of the bus to take a cab home), you generally maintain your dignity and don't do anything really peculiar. *There is no more chance of anything really terrible or fatal happening to you than to the person who does not have your fears.*

What causes agoraphobia. Statistics show that agoraphobia usually begins in young adult life between ages eighteen and thirty-five. An agoraphobic attack can happen to almost anyone. It has no relationship to intelligence, education, occupation, socioeconomic status, religion or ethnic group. It's unrelated to other psychological conditions; you can be completely "normal" in every way and still get agoraphobia. It's no respecter of sex. Men and women get it with equal frequency. However, it's more apt to persist in women. Dr. Marks estimates that about 66 percent of all agoraphobics seen by psychiatrists are women. Dr. Claire Weekes reports that in her 1970 survey of 528 agoraphobics, 91 percent were female.

It's a very common condition. Various studies in the United States and Great Britain show that in severe form it's found in 6 of 1000 people. However, many victims never seek professional help or have milder forms. My own estimate is that 12 out of 1000 people in the United States suffer from this condition.

About three out of ten agoraphobics have a history of separation anxiety. For example, one agoraphobic had trouble going away to college because of fear of separating from her parents. When her father died ten years later, she couldn't "cope with life" and felt anxious and depressed. Today, at forty-four, she cannot go more than two blocks from her house without being accompanied by her husband. She constantly asks, "If anything happens to him, what will happen to me?"

Most people know where they experienced the first attack and can describe the conditions in detail decades later. Usually, they attribute it to some form of stress that had been taking place in their lives at that time: the physical stress of an illness, operation, even child-birth; intense psychological stress caused by the death of someone close, loss of a job, being jilted at the altar; less intense but longer-term stresses like an unhappy marriage or a series of personal difficulties like continuing lack of money; or an unfortunate shock (says one woman, "Twenty years ago a window cleaner fell from the top of a high building right in front of me. I haven't been able to go out on streets since"). Because of this, agoraphobia has won the label "calamity syndrome."

It *appears* that the attack stems from such problems. In actuality, professionals really do not know what sets off the first attack; why, under similar circumstances, some people get it and some do not; why it comes at that time and in that form. Once the panic attack has started, we do know what keeps it going and how to treat it successfully; we just don't know what sets it off in the first place.

It's always easy to look into someone's life and find stress. I've seen men whose first attack came after their wives had borne a child. I've seen several cases that seem to have been precipitated by a diabetic attack or by the smoking of marijuana. It can also "just come out of the blue."

For example, in his senior year at Harvard, David L. and a friend took a class with Arthur Schlesinger. One day the friend didn't show up. David felt "trapped in a row of people. . . . I felt my knees shake, my hands get clammy. I thought I was going to faint. I didn't go back to class the rest of the year." Now forty, divorced and working as a trade magazine editor, David goes everywhere by cab ("It's important to me to feel in control of the method of transportation. I hear of a subway getting stuck under a river and I start to shake"). David diagnoses his condition as claustrophobia, not recognizing it for the agoraphobia it really is.

The form of the panic attack. When the attacks occur, generally they are sharp and sudden. One minute you're all right; the next minute you experience the attack. Here are samples of notes reflecting the agoraphobic's agony from two patients.

CASE ONE: HOUSEWIFE. "By the time I am dressed I am already shaking and cold. Don't know if I am getting a new cold or if something is wrong with my metabolism. I'm shaking. It's getting worse and worse. I'm afraid to go outside. I have a feeling of fear about everything. Everything may slip away. I may faint the next time . . . drop dead. I have anxiety about the shaking—the feeling of coldness, feeling unstable—like no confidence in my body . . . may faint . . . may have an attack. I look for my sunglasses. I can't find them. I'm going crazy. I will never get over all this. It's hopeless."

CASE TWO: STOCKBROKER (MALE). "I go into a place [supermarket, bank, post office, office building]. I feel off balance as I walk and things don't look 'right' and sound different and the lighting may seem excessively bright or dull. As I start to transact my business I begin to feel more and more off balance and dizzy as if I am about to pass out. The floor is unsteady beneath my feet. My vision seems blurred; it's difficult to read or focus. My muscles feel weak and shaky when I move my arms. I get a feeling of fear that increases to panic proportions. I get a shock wave of dizziness in my heart. I break out in a sweat and I feel hot all over. I'm so afraid I'll pass out that I feel I must lean against something and am afraid to step into open spaces, away from halls or objects on which I can lean against. I feel I cannot stay where I am but must run out, and if people are in line in front of me, I feel angry and want to push them out of the way. When I leave, I still have all the above feelings and am afraid

I won't make it home. If I am far from home, I may think of going to a hospital instead of home.

"If the above is one of my 'clear-cut' seizure-type spells, then it ends with a feeling of the above symptoms flowing out of me, especially out of my head area, and I am left with a tired, relieved feeling."

Victims should know:
•The first attack is usually as bad as it will get. This is not a condition where the panicky elements get stronger and stronger. They may get lower or fluctuate around higher, but you have had the worst.
•You do not have a brain tumor, a heart condition or epilepsy. No evidence exists that connects agoraphobia with any of these three illnesses.
•Your basic fear is that of having panic attacks. In the new diagnostic manuals the very name *agoraphobia* will be replaced by the phrase *phobic anxiety state*.

The safety devices of agoraphobics. If agoraphobics go to a movie, theater or church, they feel less frightened in an aisle seat near the exit so that they can leave quickly in case of a sudden panic. A telephone near at hand affords similar relief. They prefer a ground-floor apartment to one many flights up to which access can be had only by elevators.

They use props for clutching purposes: umbrellas, shopping baskets on wheels, baby carriages. They prefer deserted streets. They can go more easily on trains that make frequent stops so they elect the local rather than the express. Agoraphobics usually find it easier to travel by car than by any other way and can drive themselves for miles even though they cannot stay on a bus for even one stop; however, they have to avoid heavy traffic. Some journeys are easier if they pass the home of a friend, doctor or a police station. It is the possibility of aid that helps them.

Many agoraphobics feel easiest in the presence of a trusted companion and become dependent on that person. Others become afraid of being alone or in any situation where they cannot reach safety with speed and dignity. In severe cases the need for constant company places enormous strain on friends and relatives.

Some can't tolerate confinement in a barber's chair or dentist's chair or at the hairdresser (sitting under the dryer) since the possibility of an immediate escape is blocked. This has been labeled the "barber's-chair syndrome."

Thus they set up the avoidance pattern. They learn to associate the panics with the situations where they've had the attack and begin to avoid these situations. Since they can get an attack almost anywhere, they begin to avoid more and more. Many housewives become completely housebound.

They also escape from the situations, thus further convincing themselves that if they had stayed in them, the worst thing they fear—going crazy or dropping dead—would have happened. One young woman, who worked for a home-furnishings organization, devised an original means of escape should she have a panic attack at the office. Before a meeting, she would hide her contact lenses in a "secret place" in the ladies' room. She says, "That was my excuse to leave the meeting. I couldn't say, 'I'm going mad.' I would say, 'I have to get my lenses.'"

The consequences.   There are many.

•You may be terrified to take any medicine. Many medicines cause side effects such as sweating or feelings of tiredness. Because agoraphobics are so sensitive to body changes, many, unless it is urgently necessary, refuse to take any medicine, including aspirin. Conversely, some agoraphobics become addicted to tranquilizers or alcohol in their attempts to keep the tension down.

•You feel depressed. This has two roots. One stems directly from the agoraphobic condition itself, but the other comes from the restricted life-style and loss of self-esteem that go along with the conditions. Says one victim, "I feel terribly isolated and depressed. I'm not like other people. There are all those other people walking around happily and doing things and I'm so helpless."

•You feel depleted. You have no energy. You can't mobilize yourself to do anything.

•You constantly make and break plans. Says one woman, "I can't plan in advance. If I feel tense or upset that day, I won't go."

•You feel other people don't understand you. One woman says, "My husband used to be helpful but now he's fed up with the whole thing." Agoraphobia usually has one of two extreme effects on spouses. Your mate can become very angry or annoyed. He resents that he has to be at your beck and call to take you places or that you will go to a movie but not a party full of people who might "see me make a fool of myself." Conversely, he may be very protective and caring. Even so, a big undertone of resentment exists. In rare cases, a husband may glory in his wife's condition. He likes her dependency. I had one patient who was making remarkable progress. However, as she improved, her husband began taking out other women. She stopped treatment, reasoning, "Why give up my agoraphobia if it means I lose my husband?"

•You restrict your life. You can't go to the supermarket, the department store, shop for clothes alone, go out socially alone. Many variations on the agoraphobic theme exist; you may be able to go out with a single friend but not attend a group luncheon.

•You go to great lengths to keep others from knowing about this "terrible thing." For example, Marjorie D., a very charming woman and active hostess, has not been out of her house by herself for twenty-five years. She can leave only if someone accompanies her. Marjorie is most creative in getting people to drop by to pick her up ("My car is acting up. Can you get me?"). If she can't get someone to call for her, she finds a plausible excuse for not keeping the date ("I can't . . . Jim has something very important that he wants me to tend to"). She won't fly because of her fear of a panic attack, but tells friends, "I love my summer house in Westhampton. I have no desire to go to Europe." Only her husband knows about her problem. Not one of her large circle of friends has any inkling that something is wrong.

•You are always asking questions: "What will happen if I get an attack?" . . . "Why did this happen to me?"

The "why" is unimportant. You are doing this to you. Psychoanalytically oriented treatment won't help. It does not work with the agoraphobic condition. For one thing, analysis begins to probe and thus stir up anxiety. This makes the condition worse. Furthermore, analysis tries to dig away at the "roots" of the fear, not to do something about it. With agoraphobia, the important thing is *doing something about it*. Many times an analyst sees a patient with acute anxiety which doesn't seem to change plus a pattern of growing phobias, seemingly unrelated to each other (both tunnels and bridges, open and closed spaces). Many times the analyst gives up or spends years looking for a linking clue in the patient's unconscious.

Behaviorally oriented treatment will help. Study after study reports successful results in 85 percent or more cases. In Payne Whitney we ran two groups for people who couldn't travel alone. At the end of seven weeks for each group, every one of the fourteen patients involved was able to travel around New York City alone.

In beginning treatment, your goal must be to get into the situations you fear and see the panic through. If you are prepared to let the panic do its worst without trying to withdraw from it, the panic will not mount. You will learn that you will not faint, have a heart attack and die, go crazy or lose control. When you learn that the panic will not destroy you, you will stop being frightened of it. Your goal: to stay in these frightening situations for longer and longer periods of time. In this way, the panic attacks will begin to decrease in frequency until they disappear.

Note: In our society the social stereotype is that men have to go out and work. Because they have to get to offices and job appointments, they are forced to go through the panic attacks, learn they can handle them and so the agoraphobia disappears. On the other hand, many women keep up the pattern of avoidance, never go through the panic reaction and so keep being agoraphobic. That is exactly why agoraphobia is found less frequently in men than women.

Remember, agoraphobia is a frightening condition. *It is not dangerous.* All your symptoms stem from a single cause: fear. You can get rid of your fear.

TREATMENT OF AGORAPHOBIA

Take the case of someone who knows how to swim but is afraid of deep water. You throw her into the deep end of the pool. She panics but manages to swim to the end of the pool. The panic is self-limiting. It has to pass unless she does definite things to prolong it. When she climbs out, you throw her in again. This time she experiences less panic and quicker recovery. You do this a number of times, until she experiences no panic. This essentially is the treatment for agoraphobia. It is called *Flooding.*

Agoraphobic Agenda

The idea is to get yourself into the situation. These steps will help.

1. *Make a list of Treatment Targets.* This means all the things you want to do but have been avoiding doing.

Everything on the list must be specific: "Going shopping by myself" is too vague. Try "get groceries at the supermarket" or "buy stockings at Lamston's."

Do not forget the trivial: This means the situations that frighten you only slightly. For instance, it might be going down three flights in the elevator alone, driving your car to the filling station just one block away, sitting on a bench in front of your house. You will need these trivial (they must be trivial to *you*) situations as starting points.

CASE

Rosalind T. set as her first goal "to get to Saks." She lived forty blocks away and thought she could make it. But she couldn't. Unable to get her to even stand outside of Saks and look at the window, I concluded that the situation was too hard. I pressed her to seek an easier beginning step. She insisted there was none. We were at an impasse.

One day Rosalind mentioned that she had started walking to Saks, and after a few blocks, panicked and fled home. I asked, "Why the long walk in seven-degree weather?" It turned out she had not been on a bus in years. She was so used to walking places in Manhattan that it never occurred to her to take the bus or even mention that she couldn't. She also had been too "ashamed" to tell me that she could not walk more than four blocks from home. At this point, I discovered she had been coming to my office with a friend who left her with me, went for coffee, and picked her up forty-five minutes later.

For Rosalind we found a simpler starting point: to go five blocks from home and remain there for an hour.

With agoraphobics every Treatment Target plan varies. However, here are some suggested practice situations which should aid you in making up your list. Be sure to write the list in your Fear Control Training workbook.

Beginner:

•Stay outside your front door—a half hour, one hour, two hours.

•Walk to the corner. Stay there a half hour, one hour, two hours. Do *not* leave until your assigned time is up. Read, look at windows, etc.

•Make a map of your neighborhood streets that you have been avoiding. Go to different points: the church three blocks down LaSalle Street, the post office four blocks down Grand. Mark in red where you have been able to venture. With each new place extend the red marks. Your aim: to cover the entire map with red.

•Stay home alone—one hour, two hours, three hours. *Note:* Some agoraphobics are frightened at the idea of being alone. They obsess, "What will I do if I get a panic attack and I'm by myself?"

CASE

One married woman, whose mother lived in the next block, could stay alone provided she knew she could contact either her spouse or parent. No one else counted. Whenever her husband left his office, he had to telephone Lorraine, tell her his destination, how long he'd be there and provide the phone number. If mother went out to the supermarket, beauty parlor, even the corner coffee shop, she had to do the same thing. Both husband and mother had to coordinate their schedules so that when the former was en route home, mother remained by the telephone. Conversely, if mother went out, the husband had to be by his phone. Furthermore, if the mother went out she had to call Lorraine every half hour.

We set a task for Lorraine. The next Friday when her husband went out for a business appointment and lunch between 11:00 A.M. and 1:00 P.M., he would not leave any telephone number. Her mother would also make it her business to go out, leaving no number. At that time, I would also be out of my office. Both were to call her at 1:00 P.M. and Lorraine would check in with me at 1:15 P.M. When she called me, she reported that several times during this "no phone" period, she felt panic attacks coming on—the very same feelings of anxiety and shortness of breath that would have sent her running to the phone in the past. This time, with no one to phone, she had to let the feelings run their course. To her amazement, she did not get a panic attack and started to learn that all such feelings do not signal oncoming panic. She had made a tremendous step forward toward freedom from agoraphobia.

•Go to a nearby park and sit there—one hour, two hours. Again, do needlepoint or take something along to read.

•Stand by a bus stop for a half hour.

•Drive in your neighborhood for a half hour.

Intermediate:

•Cross a wide street with two-way traffic alone. (Many people say, "What if I collapse in the middle of the street?") Go back and forth six times . . . ten times . . . and twenty times as the lights change.

•Stay on the first floor of a department store—a half hour, one hour, two hours.

•Stand by a train or subway platform. Do *not* take the train or subway. Choose a time when the station is neither crowded nor empty (a deserted platform may stir up other fears and these may be realistic).

•Walk a downtown street window-shopping at 10:30 A.M. or another relatively uncrowded time.

•Ride up and down on an elevator for a half hour.

•Take a point you have been avoiding (areas of traffic, city streets, highways), choose your difficult situation and drive there.

Advanced:
  • Walk along a major shopping street at lunchtime.
  • Go to the upper floor of a department store.
  • Take a two-hour bus or train trip and return.
  • Drive your car in very heavy traffic (or whatever frightens you the most).

2. *List the different items in order of the difficulty of getting yourself into the situation.* Again, pay a lot of attention to the easier situations you'll use as starting points. As a rating device, one patient estimated how many wild horses it would take to drag him into the situations. Standing at the bus stop for a half hour took one small Shetland pony, so that's where we started.

You may have to defer ranking the more difficult ones. At this point you can't even imagine yourself riding to the third floor of a crowded department store. Or it may be so many years since you've done this that you can't even think about it and thus can't estimate the difficulty. If that's your case, put off rating the really difficult situations until later.

3. *Put yourself into each situation and stay there.* In principle, it would probably be best to go into the most difficult situation, get your panic attack and stay with it for two, three, four hours until the panic leaves. However, that's theoretical. Even when working with a therapist, it's very difficult to get yourself to do these assignments. *Get yourself into the situations you can make yourself go into and stay there a predetermined time—the longer, the better.* The starting point depends on what *you* can get yourself to do. *Note:* Emphasize what you do, not how you feel while doing it or what you can do comfortably. If you can make yourself do it, do it.

CASE

This is the program we worked out for Lydia A., a married agoraphobic who was unable to travel alone.

•The first time Lydia came to see me, she had her sister call for her at home and they came by bus.

•The next time the sister did not pick Lydia up. Instead she waited at the bus stop, which was one block away. Then they came together.

•The sister waited at the bus stop. Lydia sat in back of the bus so she could watch her sister in front.

•They switched seat positions. Lydia sat in front of the bus where she could not see her sister.

•The sister got on the bus one stop after Lydia.

•At this point Lydia felt she could take a giant step. As long as the sister waited at the other end, Lydia felt she could take a bus trip by herself. Lydia chose a time of day when there would be little traffic (the more traffic, the slower the bus). Lydia made several expeditions. In the course of them she had a few panic attacks during the trip, but saw she could control them *without getting off the bus.*

•She came the thirty-block distance to my office by herself.

•She took the hour-and-a-half bus trip from midtown to Fort Tryon Park in Manhattan with her sister and then gathered the courage to do it alone. Again, during these trips she did get panic attacks, but there were also periods when she forgot all about her agoraphobia.

However, by now she knew she could take these panic attacks without getting excited, control the urge to escape from the bus, and could sit and "just calmly watch the panic attack subside." With her new confidence one day she reported that she had gone by herself to Lord & Taylor, experienced a panic attack in the shoe department, but had stayed on to buy two pairs of sandals. The agoraphobia had really started to break up.

4. *Practice every day.* If you don't, you can't make progress. I tell my patients, "Look, I'm in poor physical condition. I exercise every day. Each day that I exercise I'm in better shape. But on the days I don't exercise, I don't merely stand still. I slide back a little." The same principle applies to agoraphobia. Each day you do something on your Treatment Target List, you get stronger. On the days you don't, you slide back. You must practice every day.

Note: At the Max Planck Institute, Munich, Germany, they hospitalize the agoraphobic for a two-week period. Prior to the hospitalization, the patient has to prepare a list of situations where she/he gets panic attacks. During the hospitalization she stays in her self-assigned situations for two-hour stretches, going into four situations a day for a total of eight hours of treatment. To accomplish this, the therapists have a contract with each patient. If a patient refuses to go into even one of the situations, she/he is out of the program and gets discharged. Planck professionals report that following two weeks of this intense exposure practice *all* of the patients can do their assignments even though most of them still undergo panic attacks in the situations. As they keep doing the activities, within weeks or, in some cases, months after discharge, the panic attacks stop.

In carrying out your practice, keep two points in mind:

•*Do not become dependent upon tranquilizers or alcohol.* Neither will stop the panic attacks. They might lower your tension so that you can get yourself into the situation. You might also start to drink too much or become dependent upon drugs. If you feel tranquilizers will help, use them only with your doctor's permission. By the third time you go into the situation, either cut the dose or, better still, do without.

Medications do exist that, in a large majority of cases, will stop the panic attacks. These are mainly antidepressant medications and professionals disagree over which works best. Some prefer tricyclic antidepressants like Tofranil. Some opt for the monoamine oxidase inhibitors such as Nardil. *However, if you do not place yourself systematically in the situations, chances are that when you discontinue the medication, the panic attacks will return.*

•*If you get the panic during practice, the whole idea is to go through it calmly.* You are not trying to stop your panic reaction but to learn from it that you will not fall, faint, die, or get carted off raving like Ophelia. Once you learn this, the panic will stop.

TEN COMMANDMENTS TO REMEMBER DURING A PANIC ATTACK

i. It does not matter if you feel frightened, bewildered, unreal, unsteady. These feelings are nothing more than an exaggeration of the normal bodily reactions to stress.

ii. Just because you have these sensations doesn't mean you are very sick. These feelings are just unpleasant and frightening, not dangerous. Nothing worse will happen to you.

iii. Let your feelings come. They've been in charge of you. You've been pumping them up and making them more acute. Stop pumping. Don't run away from panic. When you feel the panic mount, take a deep breath and, as you breathe out, let go. Keep trying. Stay there almost as if you were floating in space ("Floating" is the term used by Dr. Weekes). Don't fight the feeling of panic. Accept it. You can do it.

iv. Try to make yourself as comfortable as possible without escaping. If you're on a street, lean against a post or stone wall. If you're at the cosmetics department of the department store, find a quieter counter or corner. If you're in a boutique, tell the salesperson you don't feel well and want to sit for a while. Do *not* jump into a cab and go home in fear.

v. Stop adding to your panic with frightening thoughts about what is happening and where it might lead. Don't indulge in self-pity and think, "Why can't I be like all the other normal people? Why do I have to go through all this?" Just accept what is happening to you. If you do this, what you fear most will not happen.

vi. Think about what is really happening to your body at this moment. Do not think, "Something terrible is going to happen. I must get out." Repeat to yourself, "I will not fall, faint, die or lose control."

vii. Now wait and give the fear time to pass. Do not run away. Others have found the strength. You will too. Notice that as you stop adding the frightening thoughts to your panic, the fear starts to fade away by itself.

viii. This is your opportunity to practice. Think of it that way. Even if you feel isolated in space, one of these days you will not feel that way. Sometime soon you will be able to go through the panic and say "I did it." Once you say this, you will have gone a long way toward conquering fear. Think about the progress you have already made. *You are in the situation!*

ix. Try to distract yourself from what is going on inside you. Look at your surroundings. See the other people on the street, in the bus. They are with you, not against you.

x. When the panic subsides, let your body go loose, take a deep breath, and go on with your day. Remember, each time you cope with a panic, you reduce your fear.

5. *Be prepared for side effects and setbacks.* As you go through the agoraphobic treatment procedures, two things may happen:

•*Even after successful experiences, you may get feelings of depression and depletion.* These are common side effects with this kind of treatment. Know that they are temporary reactions and will disappear.

CASE

Susan A. was coming along nicely with her Treatment Target program. Then she ventured a big step and took an hour train trip to visit a friend in Westchester County. This was the first time she had done anything like that—either by herself or with someone—in eight years. At home that night she felt like a conquering heroine. The next morning she awoke with the feeling of depletion (absolutely no energy). This frightened her so that for two weeks she refused to go out of her house (something she had mastered two months before). If she had expected that sensation of depletion, which is not uncommon after a successful practice experience, she would have been able to overcome it more quickly.

•*Panic attacks will recur.* For example, you've mastered riding to work on the bus. For weeks you've been doing it comfortably. Suddenly, one day you get a full-blown panic attack and flee from the bus like an Olympic sprinter. Keep your cool. *Get back on that bus as soon as you can.* Remember, setbacks commonly come under three conditions: (1) you're overtired; (2) you're worried or tense about something; (3) you're not feeling well physically. For many women the last panic attacks to disappear are those that come during their premenstrual period.

SOME SPECIAL ADVICE
FOR FAMILIES OF AGORAPHOBICS

Families of agoraphobics often think of the victim as "terribly selfish." They resent the demands of time and energy made on them. Often they feel manipulated. You must realize that her suffering is real. Even though she causes enormous strain in the household, this is not her intention. Her actions stem only from her concern to get any relief she can from her distressing symptoms.

Your aim: to do anything you can to help her. This means making yourself available. If she can only go out of the house with you, allocate time to take her shopping, for walks, to a restaurant, etc. Suggest additional activities like museums and galleries, but do not pressure. Pressure creates tension.

Be sure to encourage small steps that may seem minor to you but will be major for her. In carrying out the steps, think about more than the doing of them. You want to give her a feeling of trust in you. For instance, you agree to meet at the A&P at 2:00 P.M. Make it a point to get there ten minutes early. Or if you say you'll wait outside a department store for her while she spends her assigned time on the main floor, wait where you're supposed to wait. Don't cross the street to window-shop at another store. In case she bolts from the store, you want to be in the agreed-upon spot. If you promise to stay by your phone while she performs a task, stay there. Keep the line clear. If anyone calls, say, "I'll call back."

If the agoraphobic is housebound, try to think up a program of activities for her. Exhortations like "You can fight this," "Pull yourself together" and "Stop this nonsense" don't help. If she could "stop this nonsense," she would. Instead be constructive. If she likes crossword puzzles, bring home a book of them. If she has a passion for needlework, buy some new kits and present her with them. By building up her activity within the home, you begin to counter some of her depressiveness and you may be able to get her out of the house.

Find the fine line between encouragement and pressure. For example, you ask, "Do you think you can manage to get to the corner and back today?" She says, "No." Don't give up. Ask, "What can you do today that you haven't done?" In this, you must recognize the importance of trivial-to-you accomplishments to the agoraphobic. Something as simple as going to the basement laundry room by herself may possess great significance to her.

Above all, give her the feeling that you understand, have sympathy and compassion, and that you know if she makes the effort, she will get better.

6. *Sometimes overcoming a reality life situation will help the victim to master agoraphobia.* Under extreme emergency people mobilize themselves. During World War II in the concentration camp of Theresienstadt, in Nazi-occupied Europe, in which 120,000 people (86 percent) died or were sent to extermination camps, phobic symptoms either disappeared completely or improved to such a degree that inmates were able to work.

CASE

"My dream is to go to the fourth floor at Bendel's and buy everything I can afford." That was the first thing Margy A., a tall, long-legged woman from the Midwest, said to me on her initial visit. Margy had come to New York at twenty, held a series of jobs which she always lost because of her panic attacks ("I'd feel that unreal feeling, grab my bag, press the elevator button, leave the building and not come back for three hours"). The fears spread to elevators ("I can go up but I can't go out on a floor. I panic that the elevator won't come back and I'll be trapped there. I can't breathe. Others will stare at me and think I'm berserk").

Now Margy, a free-lance artist, has programmed her life so that she rarely goes out. She has made some progress. For the first time she has a boy friend ("I always avoided one-to-one relationships before because I felt so inadequate"). He manufactures dresses, and Margy feels "terrible because I can't shop the stores with him."

We started on the Treatment Target program and were making great advances at her initial goals: to get out of the house, into the street, and in and out of elevators. Then an unfortunate incident occurred. One of Margy's targets had been to get her hair done. One day, gathering her courage, she went up to the fourth floor of a brownstone in the East Fifties to have a shampoo and set. Freshly "done," and feeling very elated at her accomplishment, she got on the elevator. It stopped at the second floor. A youth yanked her out, grabbed her handbag and raped her. During this experience, Margy—who five weeks before had been virtually unable to walk more than a block from her front door —kept her cool. She even picked up the scar marks on his shoulder which later enabled her to identify him out of a police lineup.

That night I saw Margy for an emergency 11:00 P.M. session. But she was not in a panic. She told me, "I thought agoraphobia was a real fear. It is. But now I know what real fear is as opposed to my fearful fantasies." She had managed and she was proud.

The following week Margy shopped the fourth floor at Bendel's (a small store so it was easier for her), the fifth floor of Bloomingdale's and comparison-shopped at Lord & Taylor with her boy friend. It is too soon to know whether she has won a complete victory over her condition, but Margy knows she has a choice: She can give in to the agoraphobia and again avoid things or she can do things despite it. The rape experience triggered her confidence. She says, "Now I know I've got strength. I'm not inadequate."

7. *You can overcome a lengthy pattern of agoraphobia.* Through adolescence and college Lois M. had a mild history of fears and anxiety but nothing serious. She married a college classmate, eventually got pregnant and after four months had a miscarriage. Two weeks later she had her first agoraphobic attack in the supermarket. Terrified, she left her basket full of groceries in the aisle, rushed home and called her doctor. A cardiogram showed nothing was wrong with her

heart. Thereafter, Lois had constantly recurring panic attacks until she couldn't leave the house alone.

Psychoanalytic therapy didn't help. Initially her husband was sympathetic, but after several years of accompanying her to the doctor three times a week and seeing Lois become increasingly difficult to live with, he thought, "I don't need this" and divorced her. Lois moved back into her parents' suburban home. She wanted to get her master's degree in social work but this wasn't possible; she couldn't even go out of the house for a family wedding. This went on for years. At thirty-two, this pretty, bright, charming woman was a recluse. In desperation, she came to me.

We worked out a program that took a year and a half to complete. Initially she took small steps. She stayed in a chair in front of her house for two hours at a time. She drove the family car around the block for a half hour at a time. She drove with her mother to the local supermarket. The mother would come and get her in an hour. Eventually, Lois did the supermarket routine by herself. She also carried out the same procedure at a local shopping center twenty minutes away.

We moved on to intermediate steps. For example, she visited a cousin who lived a half hour away, at first accompanied by her mother and then alone. She went to church with her parents. After several successful experiences, she then attended a church singles group that met on Monday nights. Her aim was to stay a half hour, but she met many old school friends and stayed longer. She had a real ego trip; the men liked her. But when they called for dates, she couldn't accept.

We forged ahead with more advanced steps. Lois visited an aunt who lived fifty miles away in New Jersey. She took a photography class in the local high school (she cared little about cameras; her aim was to sit through the class). She began to establish a social life and began to go into the city alone. Finally she won admittance to one of the top social work graduate programs in the country. She felt totally confident that she could sit through the classes and, if she had a panic attack, she could stay in her seat calmly until it was over. At last report Lois was studying hard, dating frequently and had her own apartment. She still gets occasional panic attacks. She says, "I think of them as waves in the ocean. The waves wash over me but, eventually, the sea gets calm again. By facing the panic attack, I've learned that I can carry on despite them."

If she can do it, you can too.

CHAPTER 4 _____

FEAR CLINIC

Learning to cope with fear is like preparing for combat in the army. First the army gives recruits basic training. In this you learn such fundamentals as how to take orders, march, care for your rifle. These techniques serve as a basis for the more specialized skills you need on the battlefield itself.

The same principles apply to Fear Control Training. Certain basic exercises serve as the basis for the actual fear confrontation.

In this chapter we will give you your basic training for handling: (1) the feeling of helplessness that so often paralyzes you; (2) the anticipation of the fear situation; (3) the fear reaction itself. As you decrease any one of these three, your control of fear increases.

Learn the techniques and use them.

OVERCOMING HELPLESSNESS

Fear reactions vary in intensity, ranging from small, gnawing discomforts and slight muscle tension all the way to anguish, terror, panic. Whatever the magnitude, persistent fears all have in common the feeling of helplessness. You feel you cannot do anything to keep the fears from happening—except to keep away from the things or events that bring them on. Once the fear starts, you can do nothing to lower it. Unable to limit it, you feel it will grow until you lose complete control of yourself. This sense of helplessness produces secondary anxieties that increase, prolong and maintain your automatic fear reactions.

EXAMPLE ONE: You got on the elevator but became so frightened, you had to get out before you reached your floor. Feeling inadequate, you berate yourself for both your helplessness and your fear reaction. You start to dwell on future occasions when you'll have to use that same elevator. This triggers even more helplessness, and you convince yourself that the only solution lies in complete avoidance of elevators. In this way your elevator phobia grows.

EXAMPLE TWO: A salesman, whose job required much driving, had been under work tension. Feeling helpless to do anything that would relieve his feelings of tension, he became frightened of anything that might increase it. Noting that the tension always increased when he drove in heavy traffic, at great inconvenience he rearranged his schedule and driving routes to avoid heavy traffic. The fear grew until he stopped driving on crowded highways during weekends and vacations. Now the very idea of driving in traffic at any time brings on both fear and the defeating sense of helplessness. He describes himself to everyone as a "traffic phobe."

Deliberate relaxation serves as the key to conquering your feeling of helplessness. The ability to relax is not enough. You must be able to do it deliberately, to feel you have some command over it. People who can relax *even 10 percent* about a specific fear are usually in a better position to conquer the fear than people with a much milder reaction who cannot lower it at all.

Can you consciously relax? If not, why not?

RELAXATION QUIZ

1. *Do you have an inherited predisposition to tension?* Your nervous system may be a sensitive one. Because of heredity, you respond to stress more quickly, strongly and changeably than do other people. At one end of a scale you have the people whose emotions are stable and not easily aroused; they are calm, phlegmatic, even-tempered. At the other end you have people with easily aroused emotions; they are moody, touchy, anxious, restless. If you are at this latter end, you may have given up as impossible the task of learning to control these reactions. It's not. You may have just set the wrong goal. The goal is not to do away with your reactions but to gain the feeling of being in at least partial control of them.

2. *Do you have misconceptions about relaxing?*

•*Do you erroneously believe that high levels of tension make your work better or more meaningful?* While doing a job, you think that if you feel relaxed, you won't accomplish anything. For you, work—to be good—must be accompanied by stress.

•*Do you use tension as an armor?* Some people feel that if they allow themselves to relax, they will become vulnerable and be hurt.

•*Do you view tension as your insurance policy?* Some people use *magical thinking* and constantly say to themselves, "If I worry and suffer enough in advance, the thing I fear won't happen."

3. *Is the tension beyond your control because it stems from physical causes?* In despair over her inadequate social life, one young woman came to me. She also had a constant feeling of pain in her back, neck, shoulders, so I sent her for a physical. It turned out that she had a pinched nerve in her back that affected her neck and shoulders. The physical problem had set off increased psychological anxiety.

4. *Are your tensions a blind habit?* You have been through a difficult situation (divorce, death of a spouse, retirement, in-law trouble, financial difficulties, etc.) during which your tensions were appropriately high. Now you're out of the situation but your habit of tension persists and you do nothing to change it. For example, during a long period of unemployment, you became increasingly tense. This tension becomes a habit that endures long after you get another job.

5. *Do you lack relaxation skills?* You have never learned the skill of direct control of tension. Instead you have learned indirect skills: distraction (like watching TV or eating), task orientation (becoming involved in a diverting activity), rearrangement of relaxing conditions (taking a warm bath) and withdrawal from disturbance ("I just want to be alone"). These indirect methods can help but usually prove insufficient —especially in tense situations. To counter your helplessness effectively, you must be able to exert direct control over tension.

6. *Do you use Aristotelian rather than Galilean thinking?* According to Aristotle, something either was or was not. You either control your emotions or you do not. With this kind of reasoning, if you control 99 percent of your tensions, you interpret the remaining 1 percent as being out of control, become discouraged and convinced of your own helplessness. In Galilean-style thinking, things exist in quantity. You say to yourself, "I can control 10 percent of my tension. Now I'll try for 15 percent." Because you have a realistic recognition of what you can do and build on that, you increase your control and counter your helplessness.

7. *Are you helpless in the face of tensions?* Some people have the concept of doing something about their tensions and the skill to do so. However, because of their passivity, they do nothing. With such people, if you instruct them in the techniques of relaxation, they can often learn the active approach to tension control.

8. *Do you have a relaxation phobia?* Some people

have inordinate fears of relaxing. I have seen people so accustomed to the sensation of tension that when they relaxed and no longer experienced anxiety they felt they had lost their identity and became frightened. With other people, when they started to relax, feelings would flood in and they would begin to cry, feel angry, experience intense sexual desire. These reactions scared them. For example, in my office, I treated one man with relaxation techniques. Then, for the first time in his life, he began to cry. Because this strange, new feeling emerged, he immediately became frightened and began to build up tension again.

This fear of relaxation is usually a part of the fear of loss of control, a fear of "letting go" that perhaps serves as the most important core of the relaxation phobia. It is so common (at least, in mild form) that during my relaxation exercises, I keep repeating the phrase "Let it go" in hopes of bringing about some deconditioning at that point.

By evaluating your answers to these questions, you may start to understand why you avoid relaxation. This may lead to constructive action in reducing tension.

BASIC TRAINING FOR RELAXATION

The general aim of this program is to teach you to use deliberate relaxation under different circumstances. This will counter your helplessness. If you're like most people, you can learn the elementary technique of muscle relaxation that we offer in this chapter with the same amount of difficulty that it took you to learn to ride a bicycle. Furthermore, once you acquire the skill, you can invoke it instantly in the time it takes you to light a cigarette.

THE PROCESS
OF PROGRESSIVE RELAXATION

The rationale: When your autonomic nervous system sets off a disturbed response, this affects such involuntary muscle systems as your circulatory system so that your heart beats faster and your blood pressure rises. It also affects your voluntary muscles (the ones you can control), causing them to shorten and contract. It is these muscle tightenings you experience as tension and that relate to your feelings of anxiety.

You can reverse this anxiety process by eliminating these contractions. This is the technique of Progressive Relaxation, first devised by Dr. Edmund Jacobson, a Chicago physician, in the 1930s. Dr. Jacobson taught muscle relaxation through a series of alternate muscle tightenings and relaxations. These differ from other forms of relaxation (like TM) because you start to relax from a state of deliberately heightened tension. This builds up a momentum so that the relaxation proceeds much further than it would have if you started from a lower tension state. The muscle tension has an additional advantage: It lets you become aware of where and how you experience your tensions. This awareness can serve as a signal for deliberate relaxation on your part when tension occurs in life situations.

By using Progressive Relaxation, you treat anxiety directly and deliberately. As you learn to relax your muscles you will calm down your autonomic system, eventually influence the involuntary systems (for example, your blood pressure will go down) and replace your subjective feelings of anxiety with those of relaxation and a sense of peace.

The procedure: In Appendix I you will find the Full Relaxation Exercise and the Intermediate Relaxation Exercise. Basically, these training exercises consist of three parts: (1) muscle tightening and relaxation, (2) deepening the state of relaxation, and (3) conditioning relaxation to a neutral pleasant scene or the word *calm*.

Warning: Do not expect magic. These are training exercises. As with any skill, some will learn quickly, others more slowly.

PERFORMING THE EXERCISES

1. *Learn the Full Relaxation Exercise and do it every day in a lying-down position until you feel you're in control of your own relaxation.* Here are some tips that may help.

•Estimate your tension level with a sud scale (this is an acronym for subjective units of disturbance).

0	25	50	75	100
completely relaxed	very relaxed		very tense	complete tension

Zero means you have no tension whatsoever. At the far end, 100 means complete tension—the most disturbed you can imagine yourself. At the moment you cannot be at either extreme. The very fact that you are holding this book and reading this page means some muscle tension, so you cannot be at zero. If you rated your tension at 100, you would not be able even to read these directions. The aim of the Full Relaxation Exercise is to enable you to be closer to, or at, zero upon completion.

•Keep a relaxation record in your Fear Control Training workbook. Take a page and rule three columns down it. The first shows the date, the second your starting tension level, the third your tension level at the exercise's end. Over a period of time you should be able to lower your sud level and the written results of accomplishment should encourage you.

•You will find all the necessary instructions for the Full Relaxation Exercise in the Appendix. You will have to make a tape. You read the script into a tape machine, play the tape and follow instructions. When recording, use a soothing, relaxing tone of voice. Hold the muscle tensions seven to ten seconds and then allow time for relaxation before you give the instructions for tightening the next muscle group. The Full Relaxation Exercise should take you slightly over twenty minutes to do.

•In the exercise I ask you to imagine a "pleasant scene." This should be a neutral one, meaning that it contains no disturbing elements. Some people see themselves at the beach or in the country. Tailor your own scene. If you have any trouble visualizing a scene, just think or imagine the word *calm*. This usually works just as well.

•Make yourself comfortable and avoid distractions. Loosen your clothing. Lie down in a comfortable place (bed, couch, relaxicisor chair, floor). Dim the lights. No TV. Be alone—no other people or pets allowed.

•During the exercise, try not to fall asleep. Admittedly, this kind of relaxation training serves as one of the best behavioral treatments for insomnia. However, if you allow yourself to fall asleep, you defeat one of the exercise's major purposes: to attain deliberate control of relaxation. You cannot be asleep and in command at the same time. Even if you use the exercise to help you get to sleep, try to stay awake until you complete it.

2. *Once you achieve fairly deep relaxation (perhaps 10 or lower on your sud scale) with the Full Relaxation Exercise, go on to the Intermediate Relaxation Exercise*. This takes seven minutes. Make a second tape and follow the same procedure.

3. *Wean yourself from the tapes*. Learn to relax in a lying-down position without using either tape. Eventually you want to be able to imagine your pleasant scene and then achieve the relaxed state in a minute or two. Some people find it helpful to first tighten their muscles and then imagine the pleasant scene.

4. *Carry over your newly learned skills into real life situations.* Some transfer will occur spontaneously. However, the following method will help.

INSTANT RELAXATION EXERCISE

•Take a deep breath through your mouth. Hold it.
•Say "Hold it" to yourself four times, timing it so that you hold your breath for about seven seconds. Practice with the second hand of a watch until you get the rhythm right.
•Let your breath out slowly.
•As you let it out, think of your pleasant scene and deliberately relax your muscles.
•Use this every hour on the hour. It takes only seven to ten seconds. Also when you approach any frightening situation, be alert for any signs of tension and use this exercise to counter it.

5. *Look for opportunities to practice relaxation.*
•Make deliberate relaxation part of your everyday life. Be especially alert for the first signs of low-level tension and immediately counter them.
•Concentrate on even the most trivial signs of progress. Remember to use Galilean, not Aristotelian, thinking.

CASE

One secretary felt miserable because her boss always looked over her shoulder when she typed. She had told him, "I get nervous when you do that." His response: "It's my right." Every time he performed his over-the-shoulder routine, Margie's head and shoulders tightened up and her stomach contracted. She also got headaches and made typing errors. She tried relaxation when her boss did this and reported back to me, "It doesn't work. I'm still tense and making mistakes." When I pressed her for details, I discovered she had achieved muscle relaxation in her shoulders and arms. By getting Margie to concentrate on the success she could achieve, she was able to build up a momentum of increasing relaxation until eventually she mastered the situation.

•Use relaxation to counter and conquer your helplessness in fear-provoking life situations. For example, one business executive feared speaking up in conferences. Before every meeting, he experienced so much anxiety that by the time he arrived he was as jittery as a Presidential candidate on election night. So he took relaxation action. Prior to any conference, he told his secretary he would take no phone calls. For ten minutes he relaxed himself at his desk. Walking down the corridor on his way to the meeting, he again went through the relaxation routine. By reducing his preliminary anxiety in this way, John estimated that he lowered his anxiety at the actual meeting by 75 percent.

OVERCOMING ANTICIPATORY ANXIETY

Jane grips the seat in the plane and hysterically says: "I'll go down in flames."

As the elevator races upward, Mark closes his eyes and waits for the crash when the cage falls from the eightieth floor.

Allison looks out of the fourth-floor window and panics, screaming, "I'll fall out . . . spatter in the process . . . die."

But Jane isn't on a plane. Mark isn't on the elevator and Allison isn't on the fourth floor. All three are victims of waking nightmares in which they *anticipate* disaster. Because of this anticipatory anxiety, they brainwash themselves to an inevitable fear reaction. For many the numbing, agonizing fear reaction stems primarily from the anxiety they experience in advance. *You become vigilant.* Sensitive to anything that suggests the feared area, you notice factors others would ignore.

EXAMPLE ONE: Husband says, "The Smiths said they're inviting us to dinner."

Wife with fear of elevators: "What floor do they live on?"

EXAMPLE TWO: A friend calls and invites you to lunch. Your claustrophobic reaction: "I bet you've picked one of those small dark restaurants."

EXAMPLE THREE: Someone tells you of a good job possibility. Your first thought: "Will they expect me to fly?"

You build up your reaction. Remember, your fear reaction doesn't begin when you're in the situation. If you fear flying, it may start when you buy your ticket—two months ahead of the actual trip. At the first thought of the dreaded situation, you start to mull about it, build up the dreadful things that might happen, figure how you can get out of it. With other fears, the very words *tunnel, elevator, doctor, rat* increase your tension. The closer you get to the fear event, the worse your fear becomes. Thus your thoughts make you more prone to phobic reactions and make these reactions stronger.

You rehearse your phobic reaction. For example, you fear job interviews. For days before one you keep imagining that you're tense during the interview, say the wrong thing or go blank and can't think of anything to say. Because in your imagination you rehearse your upset over and over, you become better and better at being upset. If you can bring yourself to have the job interview, you do just what you've trained yourself to do; you sit there and get increasingly disturbed.

Your anticipatory thoughts seem to take on a life of their own, separate from the fear itself. The result:

Even when you know your fear reaction is gone, your anticipatory anxiety may continue to exist and lead you to avoid the situation. For example, Eleanor fears she might panic if she rides a subway or bus. When she actually does, she is fine. Yet her anticipation of an anxiety attack is so strong that she can rarely get herself to use either form of transportation.

If you learn to control your thoughts and images, your anticipatory anxiety will decrease and you will be in a better position to cope with the frightening situation itself. You can do this in three ways:

Thought Stoppage: You keep yourself from thinking dire thoughts.

Thought Switching: You practice thinking "I will cope" thoughts instead of "I will fail" thoughts until the former become so strong that they replace the anxiety thoughts.

Success Rehearsal: You change the images from scenes of failure to scenes in which you manage the feared situation successfully.

Thought Stoppage

With anticipatory anxiety, your thoughts can become very detached, persistent, creative. They can also produce a kind of self-fulfilling prophecy. If you constantly say to yourself, "If I fly, I'm bound to have hysterics in the middle of the flight," you run the risk of starting to act in certain ways that fulfill your prophecy. One point of leverage: to break the chain by *stopping* your thoughts.

EXERCISE IN THOUGHT STOPPAGE

Aim: To break the habit of fear inducing anticipatory thoughts.

STEP ONE: Sit in a comfortable chair. Bring to mind one of the thoughts you want to control. Most people have a whole series of such anticipatory thoughts. Choose a single one to concentrate on or use a different one at different times when you perform the exercise. Make it come. Making the thought appear is one form of control.

STEP TWO: As soon as you begin to form the thought, break it up by giving yourself the verbalized command STOP! Then say "Calm," deliberately relax your muscles and divert your thoughts to a pleasant or neutral topic.

•You don't have to scream STOP!, but it should have the clipped, compelling quality of a drill sergeant's command. Try barking it.

•To be effective, the STOP! command must produce at least a momentary break in the anxiety thought. If your barked command does not achieve this effect, make the disruption stronger. For example, as you say STOP!, simultaneously slap a table top or your thigh. Do it hard enough so that you feel a sting and so that the action makes a sharp noise. If this doesn't prove strong enough, put a rubber band around your wrist and snap that as you say STOP! You can also add visual images to increase the power of the STOP! Imagine the word STOP! in flaming letters or as a policeman's upraised hand in front of your face.

•It's a good idea to think of the "pleasant or neutral topic" before performing the exercise. Plan your next vacation. Review the next steps for the bookcase you're building. Avoid any thoughts connected with the fear situation.

STEP THREE: During each self-training session, repeat the procedure:—Thought–STOP!–"Calm"–Muscle Relaxation–Diverting Thought—five times. The process usually takes between thirty seconds and one minute. Be certain that each time you get that momentary break in the anticipatory thought. The number of training sessions you will need depends on the intensity of your anticipatory anxiety. Sometimes you can bring your thoughts under control in a single session. I've also seen the other extreme where people had to train themselves for weeks to get results.

STEP FOUR: You must use this method in life situations whenever your anticipatory thoughts start to zoom. In using Thought Stoppage, the two rules are *as soon as* and *every time*.

As soon as you have one of these anxious anticipatory thoughts, go through the STOP! routine, say "Calm," relax, and think of something pleasant. If you give the thought a chance to gain momentum, it becomes harder to control. If the thought comes back in two seconds, two minutes or two hours, *as soon as you get* it, repeat the procedure.

Every time you become aware of having the disturbing thought, STOP! it. In this way you practice the habit of stopping the thought and relaxing rather than practicing the habit of thinking the thought and increasing tension. With practice, your control increases.

CASE

David S., a recent Ph.D. in the experimental area of psychology, had a core fear that his colleagues would discover "I don't know all they think I know." During his doctoral examinations, he had felt fortunate because the professors asked no questions about "the long list of things I don't know." Now David was looking for a teaching position. This meant interviews with members of psychology departments where these potential faculty colleagues, sometimes singly and at other times in groups, would explore his areas of knowledge. David had gone through college with excellent grades and even been accepted into Sigma Chi, the graduate honor society, but, facing the job hunt, he could think only of lengthy lists of questions he might be asked where he couldn't give satisfactory answers. His anxious thoughts set up so much tension that he failed to show up for a single scheduled job interview.

David came to me, and we embarked on a Thought Stoppage program with the aim of getting him into the interview situation. As soon as he became aware that he was having one of those phobic anticipatory thoughts ("What if one of my journals is late and there is an article in it that I should know and haven't read?"), he would tell himself STOP!–"Calm"–Relax. A disciplined person, David practiced this systematically and rigorously. In two weeks he had his thoughts under control and found himself spontaneously mentally quizzing himself and answering in areas where he possessed competence. He managed to set up a series of interviews. Before each one the thoughts started to come back and he had to use STOP!–"Calm"–Relax with machine-gun rapidity. He must have handled the interviews well. Even in the current competitive job market, he landed the job of assistant professor at an eastern university.

Thought Switching

When you think, imagine, ruminate, daydream, fantasize, you often give yourself a set of instructions that ensures your acting in a phobic manner. These instructions become habits. Again, one way to break up a habit is by setting up a more powerful counterhabit. Here the counterhabit we aim to achieve is that of instructing yourself not to be fearful. With Thought Switching you do not try to stop your anticipatory thoughts of doom directly as you do with Thought Stoppage. Instead you (1) determine a series of counterthoughts and (2) deliberately strengthen these thoughts until they become strong enough to override or replace the anxiety thoughts. The following exercise is adapted from a method devised by Dr. Lloyd Homme, a California psychologist.

EXERCISE IN THOUGHT SWITCHING

Aim: To replace your fear self-instructions with competent self-instructions.

STEP ONE: Recall the anticipatory anxiety connected with the fear area on which you are now working. List the self-instructions you give yourself (the small, detailed ones as well as the big, overwhelming ones) in your Fear Control Training workbook. For example, here are the self-instructions an elevator phobe gave himself.

1. "As I enter the building, I will start thinking about all the terrible things that can happen to me on the elevator."

2. "When I enter the building, I will strain to see if any people will be getting on the elevator with me."

3. "I will look around to make sure there is a staircase—what if I get stuck up there and I can't get back down!"

4. "I will make myself notice whether it's an express elevator or not. I will begin to wonder what if it gets stuck in the part where there are no openings."

5. "When I'm in the elevator, I will stand near the front (or the back). I will tighten my muscles and make myself think of all the bad things that might happen."

6. "I will pay attention to the slightest sound or vibration and deliberately make myself think of them as signals that things might be going wrong."

STEP TWO: For each of these self-instructions set up a list of coping self-instructions. Your aim: to set up the opposite habit of thinking that you will be able to handle whatever comes along. Here is the list that the elevator phobe worked out:

1. "As I enter the building, if I start thinking about

the terrible things that might happen, I will tell myself that very little chance exists that anything bad will happen."

2. "If I find myself noticing whether people are getting on the elevator, I will tell myself that it really doesn't matter if other people are on the elevator."

3. "If I find myself searching for the staircase, I will tell myself that even if I'm nervous about coming down in the elevator, I will be able to cope with it."

4. "I will start thinking that there is very little chance of anything bad happening."

5. "When I'm on the elevator, I will deliberately relax my muscles and think about something pleasant."

6. "If I hear an unusual noise, I will tell myself that even if something goes wrong, at most it will be a minor inconvenience."

STEP THREE: Put each of the new self-instructions you have worked out for yourself on a separate card. The order doesn't matter. Carry the cards with you or stick them in a convenient place—in your purse, on top of the night table, by the telephone, etc.

STEP FOUR: Take a class of actions you perform fairly frequently every day: drinking coffee or soda, changing channels on the TV set, running a comb through your hair, washing your hands, making a phone call. Each time, *just before* you do one of these high-frequency acts, take your topmost card, read it carefully and say the instruction to yourself. *Then* take your first sip of coffee, change the TV channel or run the comb through your hair. *Alternate way:* Say the new instruction before you do something that gives you pleasure—read your mail, eat cake, have a cocktail.

STEP FIVE: When you're in the real-life fear situation, deliberately repeat the instructions and try to follow them. It may take several weeks, but your anticipatory thoughts should change and your anxiety decrease.

STEP SIX: After using your self-instructions for a while, you may think of better statements. Don't hesitate to switch, but don't change too often. You want to get enough practice with each new self-instruction so that it starts to take hold.

CASE

Anne E., a young woman who worked as an administrative assistant for a large corporation, had attended a two-year college, maintained a high B average, and won an associate of arts degree. Her firm offered Anne a chance to return to school on company time and expense to get her B.A. The thought of taking exams threw her into a panic: "If the company pays for my education, that means I must get an A average; if I don't, I'll be cheating the company. The bosses there won't think I'm worthy of promotion." However, if she turned down the chance, Anne knew she'd feel humiliated. Her conflict increased to the point where the only solution seemed to be another job somewhere else.

Anne and I worked on antithetical coping statements: "I've gotten a high B average before and I can do it again; it's certainly a respectable grade" . . . "I'll be able to keep my cool during exams" . . . "All the company expects of me is to do my best." Anne typed her new thoughts on index cards, put them inside the cellophane of a cigarette pack. Just before she lit a cigarette, she would read the topmost card to herself, then light the cigarette, and put the card at the back of the pack. She performed this act roughly twenty times a day, usually when other people were around. At the end of ten days, she discerned that she was having more optimistic thoughts about school. The whole chain of anticipatory thoughts had started in June for courses that would begin in September. By the time Labor Day arrived, Anne was looking forward to her adult education program.

Success Rehearsal

With anticipatory anxiety, you imagine being overwhelmed by anxiety in the feared situation. You rehearse being frightened. In the following exercise (based on a method devised by Dr. Alan E. Kazdin, associate professor of psychology, Penn State University), you rehearse handling your fears. You do this by creating scenes *in imagery* in which a model copes with his/her fears in the situation that so terrorizes you.

In devising your scenes follow two rules: (1) The scenes must be something you can expect yourself to do with a little practice. If the model is too far ahead of you, you'll think, "It's impossible for me to do that" and give up. (2) As a result of the model's act, a positive consequence must result. For many of us a picture is worth a thousand words. This holds true even if the picture exists in your imagination.

EXERCISE IN SUCCESS REHEARSAL

Aim: To change your anticipation of helplessness by replacing your imagined fear rehearsals with imagined coping rehearsals.

STEP ONE: Make up twelve to fourteen scenes showing a model in the feared situation. Each scene should be realistic, easily imagined and relatively simple. The model should be roughly your age and of the same sex. In each scene you should have the imagined model face some anxiety and cope with it. The model should verbalize his/her feelings. Each scene must have a positive outcome. Before practicing them, write down the scenes and make sure each follows the rules I've noted in this paragraph.

SAMPLE SCENES RELATING
TO A FEAR OF HEIGHTS

SCENE ONE:

Content: Model walks toward a fifth-story window and stands by it looking down.

Coping: Model verbalizes, "I am starting to feel a bit dizzy and tense but I will relax it out." Imagine model looking tense. Then imagine him/her taking a breath, letting it out. Picture the model's body relaxing.

Reinforcer: Imagine the model looking pleased and saying: "I did it."

SCENE TWO:

Content: Model is driving on a raised ramp.

Coping: Model verbalizes, "I am very aware of the height of this ramp and it is starting to make me tense. I will gain control of the tension." Imagine the model deliberately relaxing.

Reinforcer: Imagine the model driving along the raised ramp with the tension under control. The spouse, who is sitting alongside, looks admiringly and says, "I really like the way you're getting the fear under control."

In doing this exercise, you want to choose scenes that fit your specific fear. Have the model's tension be just like the one that you experience. Be sure the reinforcer is reinforcing for you.

The above illustrations demonstrate two rules you should follow in creating your own scenes.

•The first scene demonstrates a *coping* rather than a *mastery* model. It shows the model coping with anxiety rather than going through the situation with no anxiety. With this exercise, using a coping model yields better results. Of your twelve imagined scenes, only the last two should be mastery ones (such as standing by the window with complete comfort).

•It shows the model giving himself/herself instructions in which he/she counters customary helplessness in the feared situation with successful self-command. In each of the scenes you want to have the model give herself an order and carry it out successfully.

STEP TWO: Imagine the scenes as you have written them. Hold each image about fifteen seconds. Make each image as clear as you can before you go on to the next. The exercise usually takes from five to ten minutes. Do each scene once a day for a period of one week. Then check over the scenes and make whatever adjustments seem to be necessary. Repeat daily for another two weeks.

STEP THREE: Place yourself in the feared situation. Take that elevator ride. Get on the subway. Enter that crowded room. Then deliberately try to act just the way the model did in your imagined scene. Give yourself the same verbal self-instructions and follow them.

STEP FOUR: Keep practicing both in imagery and life. As your self-command increases, usually a steady decrease in anxiety follows with a concomitant reduction of your fear reaction.

CASE

Henry M., a thirty-year-old lawyer, was under consideration for a junior partnership in his firm. If he got this, it would mean trial work. Henry was afraid he'd be nervous, stammer, make a bad impression in court. He imagined himself looking at the jury and judge, not knowing what to say or what to do with his hands. One scene he rehearsed over and over: While questioning a witness, he couldn't find the specific paper he wanted and so looked foolish. In actuality, Henry had no reason to believe any of these disasters would occur. He had done trial work, and, except for some mild anxiety, he had had no problems. His difficulty lay completely in his irrational anticipation.

As our first Success Rehearsal step we had Henry go to the courtroom several times to watch actual trials. His assignment: to pay particular attention to lawyers whose styles resemble his and whose work he admires. He selected one lawyer as his model. Here are some of the scenes Henry then used for his Success Rehearsal:

•The model stands up to address the judge. Henry visualized the model tensing up, and then imagined the model saying aloud, "I am getting tense. I will deliberately relax myself." Henry imagined seeing the model relax and then talk to the judge in just the way he would like to be able to do.

•He pictured the model addressing the jury. In the image the model stammered and seemed to be blocked. Henry imagined the model saying out loud, "I'm starting to block; I will relax myself." He observed the muscle relaxation in the model and then imagined a scene in which the model spoke fluently and smoothly to the jury, knowing just what he wanted to say.

We had nine such coping scenes, followed by two mastery ones. In the latter Henry imagined two situations where the model handled himself well: (1) Completely at ease, he spoke to the judge about a point; (2) sitting in his chair, listening to the procedure, attentive but relaxed.

For two weeks Henry went through all eleven scenes three times a day. At the end of that period when he came for his session, he turned to me, saying, "I don't know what all my worrying has been about. Of course, I can do it."

How do you know which of the three suggested exercises—Thought Stoppage, Thought Switching or Success Rehearsal—to use first? In a clinical situation, the therapist would do a detailed analysis of anticipatory behavior and make a professional decision of which exercise would yield the best results. You're too close to the situation to have the necessary perspective to do this. I recommend you start with the one you think easiest for you. The reason: You want some kind of success to begin countering your pattern of helplessness. If it doesn't help enough, switch to one of the other exercises. Don't do more than two simultaneously. You'll just get confused.

You may find out that your fear no longer exists. For example, Elaine had flown but once in her life—twenty years ago. This frightened her so much that for the next two decades she refused to get on a plane. Finally, her husband convinced her to fly to Mexico for vacation. Once on the plane, Elaine found she wasn't upset at all. Somehow, during the long years of flying avoidance, the fear had just disappeared. In thinking about it afterward, she decided that over the years watching pleasant TV commercials about flying and hearing friends speak so casually about their own plane trips had countered her fears.

The mere reduction of your anxiety may enable you to cope with your fear.

CASE

Mona L., a very personable and ambitious public relations executive, was terrified of business parties. She knew she had to attend one the forthcoming Monday. The previous Friday she began to agonize: "I'm sure I'll be wearing the wrong thing and everyone will notice" . . . "It will be a big room full of people I don't know" . . . "If I go up to someone I don't know and start a conversation, he'll probably just walk away" . . . "I'm going with my boss, but I just can't cling to her. If I leave early, she'll think I'm no good at business parties." Mona went to the party and because she was so tense, stayed just ten minutes and bolted.

Several weeks later she had to attend another business party. This time she used Thought Stoppage. Although she still felt nervous, this time she was able to talk to people and even found herself enjoying the friendly crowd and the chance to make contacts. She left that party feeling good with herself.

REDUCING THE FEAR REACTION

In the situation itself, your fear reaction has two parts: (1) the reaction itself; (2) the things you do to magnify the fear reaction and make it more frightening. The most common and almost universal way of intensifying your fear reaction is through *hyperventilation.*

Hyperventilation

As you become anxious, your breathing changes and you begin to take in too much oxygen, thus causing a whole series of body changes (like dizziness, heart pounding) which makes the situation frighten you even more. These symptoms are caused by hyperventilation. When you become anxious, your breathing changes so that it becomes more shallow. Just as when you pant during physical exercise, this builds up excess oxygen in your blood. During heavy exercise, you use up this excess oxygen; during your fear response, you do not use it up. As a result, it changes the acid-alkaline balance in the blood and consequently brings on the changes of body feeling—the dizziness, heart palpitations, feeling of weakness in the knees. These intensify the fear reaction and may prove a source of fear in themselves. Many times people with these symptoms believe they are having a heart attack and rush off to the emergency room of the nearest hospital.

To test whether you hyperventilate, when you have the fear symptoms, deliberately try to build up the carbon dioxide in your blood. One simple way of doing this is to cover your nose and mouth with the opening of a paper bag and breathe in and out into the bag for about three minutes. *Do not use a plastic bag!* A second method that's almost as good: Hold your cupped hands over your nose and mouth and breathe in and out into them for about three minutes.

In many situations, the above procedures might be too conspicuous. If so, then you might try pressing your lips firmly together and breathing through your nose for two or three minutes.

As these techniques build up the carbon dioxide in your blood, if you are truly hyperventilating, you should experience noticeable lessening of the physical symptoms.

Once you have demonstrated to yourself that hyperventilation plays at least some part in magnifying your symptoms, you can train yourself in a rather simple habit. Each time you begin to experience the fear reaction, simply keep your mouth tightly closed and breathe through your nose. If necessary, press the palm of your hand over your mouth. Keep doing this until the symptoms start to fade.

Systematic Desensitization

Three-year-old Billy Jones fears the ocean. Wisely, his mother doesn't force him to go in the water. Instead she takes him by the hand to the fringes of the approaching waves and lifts him up when a wave nears. After Billy feels comfortable, Mrs. Jones encourages him to dip a foot in the wave, then an ankle, and eventually by degrees to wade in. By starting in a situation where he felt little anxiety, approaching his core fear (probably submersion) in stages, and, at each stage, conquering any anxiety before he went on to the next stage, by degrees, Billy mastered his fears.

Without realizing it, Mrs. Jones was teaching Billy through the technique of Systematic Desensitization, a major method for curing fears.

Systematic Desensitization takes the premise that you have learned to react automatically and irrationally with fear to some sort of stimulus—whether the closed door of an airplane, looking out of a high window, driving in traffic. It aims to retrain you to respond without fear to the airplane door, the high window, the traffic. Once this retraining has taken place—when you have experienced the terrorizing situation a number of times without having a disturbed reaction—you will no longer be frightened.

Systematic Desensitization requires three things on your part:

1. Knowing how to relax deliberately. You cannot be relaxed and anxious at the same time. Keep on doing the muscle relaxation exercises from Appendix I until you can achieve relaxation at will. With practice most people can manage instant relaxation by imagining a "pleasant scene" like lying on the beach and feeling the sun soaking into your body.

2. The working up of a graded series of anxiety-producing practice situations which we call a hierarchy. You must start off with a situation that produces merely the slightest twinge of fear (looking out of a first-floor window, if you fear heights). You do not set the top of the Empire State Building as your first training situation—if you do, the odds are you'll never get there. That's your last step.

In selecting situations for training, you have two choices: (a) You can use real ones that you can actually get into. You can actually look at a picture of a crawling insect in a book, stand next to a third-story window, ride one stop on a subway. This is *Systematic Desensitization in Reality*. (b) You don't have to stand by that window. You can imagine standing by it and use that image as your training situation. *This is Systematic Desensitization in Fantasy*.

3. Whether you use fantasy or reality desensitization, you go through your graded situations, *relaxing after each one and mastering each one before you go on to the next*.

Systematic Desensitization does not attempt to reason you out of your fear, provide you with insight or uncover deep, unconscious conflicts. It is a straight-forward training procedure that teaches you to respond with no fear to situations that may have paralyzed you for many years of your life.

A form of the desensitization method was described in the 1940s by Andrew Salter, a leading New York psychologist. The systematic method, using the graded series of anxiety-producing situations that serves as the bases of current clinical practice, was developed and tested by Dr. Joseph Wolpe, now of Temple University School of Medicine, during the 1950s. Since that time Systematic Desensitization has been the subject of more scientific experiments than any other psychotherapeutic method (several hundred studies involving over ten thousand fearful people). Experiment after experiment shows that the technique does lead to actual changes in the life situation and that *these changes last*.

PREPARING FOR SYSTEMATIC DESENSITIZATION

1. *Pick the fear you're going to work on.* As a start-er, it should be the least anxiety-provoking of your "meaningful" fears. For example, if you fear being trapped in a plane, tunnel and elevator but feel least anxious in an elevator, use that as a takeoff point.

2. *Make the decision of whether you prefer to de-sensitize yourself in reality or in fantasy.* This is a mat-ter of individual choice. Some people want to go through the actual fear situations while remaining re-laxed. Others prefer to use the imagined situations, gradually building up the confidence to go try the anx-iety-producing situation in real life. Others combine the methods, using the imagined situations for training and then going out and doing it in life. In the next chapter we're going to show you how these techniques have worked for individuals who had spent their life in fear.

3. *Construct your hierarchy.*

    a. In forming your hierarchy, you'll need some method to estimate the amount of disturbance each situation would set off. Use a Fear Thermometer. This thermometer has zero and 100 as end points. Zero is when that situation brings on no increase in disturbance at all. For instance, you have a fear of heights but it does not really start until you reach the fourth floor. Looking out of a second-story window (or imagining doing it) brings on no increase in disturbance. Your Fear Thermometer registers zero.

One hundred is when your fear shoots sky high to utter terror. You are as disturbed as you can imagine yourself becoming. Many fears, even severe ones, do not reach the 100 mark. Readings of 80 or 90 are bad enough.

Every disturbed reaction must be somewhere between zero and 100. By estimating where on the Fear Thermometer your reaction to each of a number of situations falls, you can devise the graded series of situations you need for your hierarchy.

b. List a series of situations involving the fear you are working to reduce. You should have from twelve to twenty items. These can be situations you have been in, might be in or fear being in. Keep each situation relatively uncomplicated and select ones that set off differing amounts of disturbance. For example, if you fear electric shocks, turning on the radio might be Fear Thermometer 0. Putting a cord in an electric outlet might be 75. Getting a small shock might be 90. Apply your Fear Thermometer to estimate the amount of disturbance.

When you have the Fear Thermometer readings for each situation, arrange them in order from lowest to highest on index cards. You may find you have to think up several additional situations to fill gaps in the hierarchy.

Check the hierarchy to make sure it meets the following requirements:

•It starts at a low level. Below 20 make a deliberate effort to find a situation for every five points.

•There are no big gaps. Between any item, there should not be a spread of more than 10 points. If it is a very fearful area, have an item every 5 points.

•It should go through the core of the phobia—the very worst that can happen. This is the thing that most frightens you: the plane actually crashing, your dying slowly and painfully of cancer, the rabid dog knocking you down and tearing at your throat, sitting alone in your room with not a single friend or acquaintance in the whole world.

The fear of heights provides a clear-cut example of hierarchies that illustrate these points. Here is one I used with an insurance salesman whose income suffered severely because he couldn't personally visit potential clients who lived above the fifth floor. The core of his fear was that he would fall out and "smash to the street below." Heights were one of the things that set off the fear. The lower signs of the fear started at about the third floor where he believed there was a reasonable chance of getting killed if he fell from that level. Above the fifteenth floor the fear did not increase ("You get just as squashed from the fifteenth as you do from the fiftieth"). The size of the windows, whether he was on a terrace, whether he was leaning out, all increased the chance of falling and increased his fear.

In the actual case, we used fantasy scenes. However, essentially the same hierarchy could have been used for reality desensitization. He probably would not have been able to find these exact situations (he might not have had access to a fifteenth-floor terrace) and probably would have started at the second floor because reality items bring on more disturbance than fantasy ones. And, of course, he would not perform the very last item.

Hierarchy Item	Fear Thermometer Rating
1. Standing on a third-floor terrace	10
2. Looking out of a fourth-floor window	15
3. Looking out of a fifth-floor window	20
4. Looking out of a sixth-floor window	25
5. Standing on a sixth-floor terrace	30
6. Looking out of a seventh-floor window	35
7. Looking out of an eighth-floor window	40
8. Looking out of a tenth-floor window	45
9. Looking out of a twelfth-floor window	50
10. Looking out of a fifteenth-floor window	55
11. Same but a big window with a very low sill	60
12. Standing by the railing of a fifteenth-floor terrace looking down	65
13. Same but leaning over railing	70
14. Same but starting to slide over railing to street below	75

Following desensitization to scene number 8, for the first time in years he visited people on the seventh floor. He reported some initial discomfort which soon died out. After completion of the entire hierarchy, he was able to go everywhere, but sometimes with discomfort that did not dissipate. At a six-month follow-up, his discomfort had disappeared completely. A holiday card two years later stated, "Only problem is that it's getting harder to remember what used to frighten me."

c. Some helpful hints for hierarchy construction:

•For a starting point, find one you can do. For a reality hierarchy, if you're terrified of injections you may be able to look at an advertisement with a picture of a hypodermic needle. For a fantasy hierarchy, use a vicarious scene—imagine someone else in the situation.

•You may have gaps to fill. For example, looking out of a fourth-floor window gives you a Fear Thermometer reading of 20 and looking out of a fifth-floor window provides you with 40. Fill the gap by looking out of the fifth-floor window with a trusted friend standing by you or do it early in the day when you feel rested.

•In forming your hierarchy, whenever possible, *quantify*. Some possible ways:

Distance: you are 100 yards from a dog . . . 50 yards . . . 10 yards. You are 100 yards from a snarling dog . . . 50 yards . . . 10 yards . . . etc.

Time: you are taking a half-hour bus trip . . . an hour trip . . . a two-hour trip, etc.

Size: the vehicle in the lane alongside you is a compact . . . a sedan . . . a pick-up truck . . . a huge trailer truck.

Height: the bridge is just over the water . . . 10 feet above the water . . . 30 feet above the water.

d. Personalize your hierarchy. You must individualize your treatment so that it gets completely to the core of *your* fears. For example, two people with fear of elevators may have completely different fantasy hierarchies.

ELEVATOR FANTASY HIERARCHY I

Tim J. was a salesman who had to call on customers in tall buildings with elevators. Often he would walk up fifteen to eighteen floors. On one occasion he walked up sixty-seven floors. His core fear was that he would suffocate in a small space (claustrophobic people often experience anxiety as a pressure on the chest, feel difficulty in breathing and a consequent fear of suffocation —which never happens). Tim felt especially fearful about the lack of openings in the elevator ("whether there's a grating or a window"), the size (the smaller the elevator, the more fearful he felt), number of people in the elevator (it was easiest for him in a self-service elevator when he was alone; each other person in the elevator took away some space and made him anxious). He wasn't bothered much by the age of the elevator, any lurchings or clanking noises or the length of time he spent in it.

In our hierarchy we used an elevator with no openings of any kind. We systematically reduced the elevator and we also systematically introduced more and more people into the elevator. In addition, we paced off the size of each elevator so that he could get a fairly accurate image.

Hierarchy Item	Fear Thermometer Rating
1. In an elevator 8' by 10' alone	
2. In an elevator 6' by 6' alone	
3. In an elevator 5' by 5' alone	
4. In an elevator 4' by 5' alone	
5. In an elevator 4' by 4' alone	
6. In an elevator 4' by 3' alone	
7. In an elevator 4' by 3' with a child	
8. In an elevator 4' by 3' with an adult	40
9. In an elevator 3' by 3' alone	40
10. In an elevator 3' by 3' with one adult	45
11. In an elevator 3' by 3' with two adults	50
12. In an elevator 3' by 3' with three adults	55

Hierarchy Item	Fear Thermometer Rating
13. In an elevator 2′ by 3′ alone	60
14. In an elevator 2′ by 3′ with one adult	65
15. In an elevator 2′ by 3′ with two adults	70
16. In an elevator 2′ by 3′ with two adults and one child	75
17. In an elevator 2′ by 3′. Tim is squashed in with all the people the elevator can hold	80
18. In an elevator 2′ by 3′ with all the people it can hold. It is very stuffy and Tim has difficulty breathing	85

ELEVATOR FANTASY HIERARCHY II

Mary F., a graduate student, avoided going places alone if an elevator was involved. Her core fear: that the elevator would get stuck and she wouldn't know what to do and would panic. If someone she trusted (like her boy friend) was in the elevator with her, she wasn't frightened. She also felt very little anxiety if a uniformed man or someone she thought "competent," like a policeman, was there. She felt frightened by older elevators, clankings that signaled "We are going to get stuck" and spending a lengthy amount of time in an elevator. She had no fear of heights.

Hierarchy Item	Fear Thermometer Rating
1. In a moderately old elevator with creaking and jolting but there is an elevator man	5
2. In a moderately old self-service elevator with policeman as fellow traveler (she feels some tension because she doesn't know when he'll get off)	10
3. In a rickety self-service elevator with policeman going to same floor	15
4. In an old rickety self-service elevator with policeman as fellow passenger. Elevator gets stuck. Policeman calmly says, "Just relax. They'll get us out"	20
5. In stuck elevator with boy friend, who looks a little worried.	25
6. Alone in elevator which lurches, creaks but keeps moving at moderate speed	25
7. Alone in elevator which lurches, creaks and moves very slowly	30
8. In a stuck elevator with strange man, who looks a little worried	35
9. The only other passenger gets off and the elevator door is very slow to open	40
10. At her floor doors open just enough for her to squeeze out	45
11. Alone, just got on. Elevator takes a long time starting out	50
12. Alone, between floors. Elevator stops briefly but then continues	55

Hierarchy Item	Fear Thermometer Rating
13. Alone, stuck between floors, alarm bell ringing, she hears people working on the elevator	60
14. In an elevator, alone, stuck between floors with no sign of action on the outside	65
15. In an elevator alone, stuck between floors. A very long time passes with no sign of action and she has no idea what she can do	70

e. Put the finishing touches on your hierarchy. The previous examples and those in Appendix II may trigger you. Don't despair if your first hierarchy isn't perfect; the first is the hardest. When you have your completed hierarchy, list each situation on a separate index card. Put the least anxiety-producing situation on top and the one with the highest Fear Thermometer reading on the bottom. Now you are ready to start your Systematic Self-desensitization Process.

SELF-DESENSITIZATION IN REALITY

Whenever possible, you want to work on your fear in the real-life situation. By doing this, you experience the true fear feelings and you also get that feeling of confidence that comes from actually having mastered an actual life problem. You feel good because you actually got on a subway, bus, train, or plane.

EXERCISE IN
REALITY SELF-DESENSITIZATION

Aim: To use your hierarchy as a training process to teach you a non-fear response in the fear situation.

STEP ONE: Take the lowest item in your hierarchy and put yourself in the situation.

STEP TWO: While in that situation, practice relaxation. When you feel calm, leave the situation.

STEP THREE: Repeat the process (like going to the fifth floor on the elevator) several times. You can do this immediately, at different times on the same day, or several days apart—but not more than two or three days apart. Repeat it over and over until you feel completely comfortable in what previously has been a frightening situation.

STEP FOUR: Go on to the next hierarchy item and repeat the process. Keep going, relaxing yourself at each step until you complete the entire anxiety hierarchy.

STEP FIVE: You may have problems. Go back an item or two in your hierarchy if there has been a big time lapse in your practice sessions; you have had some sort of bad experience which makes your fear worse; or you aren't making progress with the current item.

CASE

Martha D., a homemaker and mother of three, lived in Great Neck, a suburb some twenty-five miles from New York. She didn't drive, and the only way she could get to New York was to take the Long Island Railroad. However, Martha had a lifetime fear of trains ("What if there's a wreck?"). We worked out a program that went like this.

•The next station stop after Great Neck en route to New York was two minutes away. Martha's first assignment: to take that short trip, relaxing out any tension she felt. No matter how good she felt when she got to that stop, she was to get off the train, walk to the cab stand and take a taxi back home. It took three to four trial runs until she felt comfortable doing this.

•She would go to the next stop, get off, cross the tracks and wait there for the next train going back to Great Neck and take it. She did this once a day for five consecutive days. At this point Martha noticed a marked decrease in fear.

•Martha skipped several stations and rode five stops to Jamaica. Again, she crossed over and rode back. Now Martha reported that instead of each clank of the train signaling impending disaster, she found the clanks had a lulling effect.

•We decided to try the trip to New York. This proved too difficult. She got to Manhattan but was so frightened that she took a costly taxi back to Great Neck. "My fear is back in full force," she told me.

•Starting with the brief trip to the next stop and the cab ride home, Martha *repeated the entire hierarchy.* This time she added an item. After the Jamaica item in the hierarchy, she added a stop at Woodside before continuing to New York and "the trip under the East River that scares me so." She repeated the trip to the Woodside station seven times.

•She tried New York again, and this time it worked. The entire process took five months.

SELF-DESENSITIZATION IN FANTASY

To bring about change, research has proven you don't have to be in the life situation. Also it is not necessary for you to have *experienced* each situation included in an anxiety hierarchy. If you imagine being in the fear situation and counter it with relaxation, the systematic desensitization in fantasy method proves just as effective.

To use it, there are three musts: (1) to be able to relax yourself deliberately; (2) to imagine the scenes in your hierarchy, to get the feeling that you are there; (3) to be able to experience and recognize the small increases in fear as you imagine the ascending items in your hierarchy. Look for small muscle tightenings anywhere in your body, feelings in your throat, chest, gut. Or look for changes in subjective feelings such as discomfort, fear or irritation. Some people can experience tension while actually in an elevator but not in imagery. If you fall in this category, you cannot use the fantasy method.

When I do imagery desensitization in my office, I have the patient lie down on the couch. I dim the lights and turn off the phone. I go through the Intermediate Relaxation Exercises. When he/she is relaxed, I start with the first item in the hierarchy we have worked out. I read it to him. I tell him to imagine it. When he has that item clearly in his mind, I ask him to signal me by raising his finger. After he signals that the image is clear, I ask him to hold the image for five seconds and then, using his finger, he signals me whether he has experienced any increase in uptightness while imagining. He also signals a rough approximation of how much increase there was, I then instruct him to switch to his "pleasant scene" or the word "Calm" and spend thirty-five to forty seconds giving him relaxation instruction. When he is relaxed, I repeat the disturbing scene. When he is able to imagine the scene two successive times without any increase in disturbance, I move on to the next item in the hierarchy.

In actuality, a therapist is not necessary. Here, *for the first time in print for the layperson,* are directions for doing Systematic Self-desensitization in fantasy.

EXERCISE IN SYSTEMATIC
SELF-DESENSITIZATION IN FANTASY

STEP ONE: Get yourself in a comfortable position— lying down or in a relaxicisor chair. Dim the lights. Arrange things so you will be undisturbed for a half hour. Have your hierarchy index cards at hand.

STEP TWO: Get yourself completely relaxed. You must be totally relaxed before you visualize your first hierarchy scene.

STEP THREE: Imagine your first scene (the one with the lowest degree of tension).

STEP FOUR: At the first sign of any disturbance, push the scene from your mind and concentrate on relaxation. Continue until you are again relaxed.

STEP FIVE: Repeat your scene. There will come a time when you can hold the image of the fear scene for roughly five to ten seconds without feeling any increased disturbance whatsoever. At that point again push that scene from your mind and relax. When this occurs on two successive trials, consider that item mastered and move on to the next higher one in the hierarchy. Do this with each card in your hierarchy.

Some cautions:

•Limit each training session to a half hour. This includes your relaxation period. With longer periods too much chance exists that you'll lose your concentration or fall asleep.

•Aim for two or three training sessions a week.

•Do begin each new session by imagining the last mastered hierarchy scene from your previous self-training session.

•Be certain to imagine the situations exactly as you've worked them out for your hierarchy. Do not change them during the exercise no matter how good the idea you get seems to be at the moment. If it seems important enough to merit immediate change, discontinue the exercise and reformulate your hierarchy. You may realize that you have omitted an important clue.

For example, one woman couldn't get rid of her fear of sitting under the dryer. Finally, she saw she had left out an important item—the feeling of heat from the dryer which she associated with her fear of being trapped. Once she added that, she got good desensitization results which carried over into real life. Also as relaxation counters the tension, you may gain a different understanding of the fear situation. For instance, you may realize that it's the elevator vibrations you feel through the soles of your feet and not the noise that triggers your fear. If this happens, make changes in your hierarchy, but not while you are doing the exercise.

There is no predicting how many times you will have to repeat the scenes. You may find that because of the previous scenes you've mastered, by the time you get to a specific scene, the fear may be all out of it. Or you may have to repeat a scene fifteen to twenty times before you get the tension out of it. As long as the tension keeps going down, stick with the method.

•If, with a number of repetitions, the tension evoked by a particular item in the hierarchy does not go down, consider several things.

Are you getting sufficiently relaxed between scenes? Check your tension level. You may only require some additional time for relaxing.

Did you get *all* of the uptightness out of the preceding scene? Go back and repeat it several times and then try the difficult situation again. This time your tension may start to go down.

Is there too large a difference between that scene and the one preceding it? You may have to bridge the gap with a new scene.

If none of these suggestions works, assume there is something wrong with the situation you've formulated. Probably it is too difficult. Discontinue it. Either get another situation or reformulate that one to make it easier.

Because of the many details and the importance of timing, this kind of Systematic Desensitization requires hard work on your part. Some can do it with no problems. Others would perform better if they received a constant stream of step-by-step instructions, just as they would if they were actually working with a therapist. You can give yourself these ongoing instructions by using a tape recorder. As an aid for people who want to use this method I have prepared a script for a Systematic Desensitization in fantasy tape. You will find this in Appendix III. Make your tape simply by reading this script into a recorder.

You know your imagery desensitization is working if you can feel the tension going down in a specific scene each time you repeat it, or find that you can hold the scene for longer and longer periods before you get any fear reaction.

Of course, you must carry over the reduced fears from the fantasy desensitization into life. That's the point of the whole procedure.

CASE

"Every day I lived with fear. The smallest thing—like trying to shop for groceries—was terror-ridden for me. I had dizziness, heart palpitations and felt totally isolated. If I went out on the street, I felt I'd lose control in public, start to scream, that I was floating in space while I was walking. The feeling started in my knees and spread. I couldn't go to the corner comfortably. If I went out of the house, I was afraid I wouldn't get back."

That's the way Carolyn A., today forty and a successful New York attorney, describes her life in 1972, when her agoraphobic fears had reached the point where she could not work, was terrified in buses, subways and elevators, virtually housebound in a second-floor apartment, afraid to go "almost anywhere" without her husband.

She had taken the first step to recovery on her own. She decided to go to law school ("If I didn't stop vegetating, I'd go batty") and selected it on the basis of elevators ("The one I went to had old elevators with operators and railings for me to clutch, but I almost always used the stairs"). Unable to take public transportation, for three years she drove back and forth to classes. Having passed the bar exam, she faced a root problem: "I can't walk in a street or get in a modern elevator. I'll have to work on the first floor of a building in the sticks." Her first job appointment was with a famous firm on the fifty-fifth floor of a steel skyscraper! Desperate, she came to me, begging, "I have this appointment in a month. Can you get me to it?"

With Carolyn the core of treatment was to get her to stop being frightened of having a panic attack, to have her go through it and learn that it was frightening but not dangerous and that she would not die or make a fool of herself in public. We zeroed in on the elevator because Carolyn had that appointment which meant so much to her. The preappointment treatment for Carolyn had four parts:

•*Relaxation.* I taught her the relaxation exercises and put them on tape for her so she could practice them at home twice daily. The point: to give her a method with which she could deliberately relax at will, one that would provide some feeling of control in the elevator situation.

•*Systematic Desensitization in fantasy to riding in an elevator and her anxious thoughts about elevators.* Purpose: to lower the intensity of her fear. In my office Carolyn imagined various situations in ascending fear order: "Tomorrow I have to go in an elevator" . . . "I'm walking into a building and see a blank stainless steel door on an elevator" . . . "I'm stepping into an elevator" . . . "I'm stepping into an elevator with nothing to hold onto" . . . "I'm in an elevator alone." After each frightening thought, Carolyn would relax. Until she could imagine the situation with no fear, she could not go on to the next.

•*Life exposures.* No more stairs. Carolyn's assignment: to go up and down the elevator in her building several times a day.

•*Systematic Desensitization in fantasy to her core*

fear of panic attacks and body sensations. Carolyn worked on imaginary hierarchies of "I'm dizzy" . . . "My knees feel weak" . . . "I'm going to panic," again relaxing and conquering each paralyzing thought before she went on to the next.

Interview day came. Carolyn's appointment was for 9:30 A.M. At 9:20 A.M., she called me hysterically, saying, "I'm in the lobby. I can't get into the elevator!" Over the phone I gave her relaxation and then commanded, "Now walk to the elevator and get in."

Carolyn recalls, "I did it as though I were hypnotized. [It wasn't hypnosis; she had been conditioned to a state of relaxation.] All the way up I clutched a crack in the elevator. I was dizzy and thought I'd collapse. But I did it! When I arrived on that fifty-fifth floor, I wanted to kiss the receptionist."

Carolyn didn't get that job. However, two weeks later she landed the one she now holds with a prestigious law firm located on the fortieth floor of a midtown skyscraper. For two more months she continued treatment, following through on Systematic Desensitization (she eventually conquered her most paralyzing thought, "They'll find me with my eyes staring and my hair totally white!"). She also carried out such "approach behavior" assignments as taking a bus to and from work instead of a taxi, going to crowded stores, staying home alone for two-, three-, four-hour periods.

But the elevator trip was the turning point. Because of it she lost her major fear of panic to the point where she could put herself in any situation where panic might occur.

Carolyn still doesn't like going into an elevator alone, but she does it. She says, "Overcoming my problems has made me feel very brave. I feel like a human being instead of a second-class citizen."

CHAPTER 5 _____

THE FEAR OF "THINGS"

When you have a fear of "things"—tunnels, elevators, planes, animals, insects, heights and other objects and places involving no interpersonal relationships—you know it.

You recognize exactly where you get the fear reactions (in the elevator, the subway), what triggers them (the vibrations, the number of other passengers), what the feelings do to you. Often you know the worst that can happen ("The elevator may get stuck between floors" . . . "I'll crash"). Even if you don't ("I only know I'm terrified"), you have no doubt that it's the elevator that sets off your fear, in extreme cases crippling your activities and confining your life.

Because you know exactly what frightens you, you can change "things" phobias more easily than any others. The very clarity of your knowledge makes for the ease and success of treatment.

THE COMMON FEARS OF "THINGS"

•*Fear of being in certain places:* elevators, escalators, tunnels, big rooms, small rooms, tall buildings, bridges. Varying degrees of claustrophobia affect many people. Some react with panic or stress; others can't bear to think of being in the situation. The fear comes out when you're in any small, enclosed place where you feel severely hemmed in or trapped. Closed doors make the situation worse. Usually claustrophobic anxiety attacks are characterized by a tightness in the chest that appears to make breathing difficult and leads to a fear of suffocation. Some claustrophobics are extremely uneasy in a room where they can't open the windows, are below ground level, when a piece of clothing is too tight. Even in some open spaces, some victims can get the trapped feeling. I've seen it with people riding on limited-access parkways, because they feel if something goes wrong, they're trapped and can't get off until the next exit.

Some claustrophobics do lose control. For example, one woman, riding in a car on a narrow road surrounded by mountains in Wyoming, suddenly lay down on the car floor, screaming, "I'm going to die!" However, as with most fears of places, the thing victims most fear rarely happens; as with agoraphobia, you rarely experience complete loss of control, suffocate, faint or die.

Whether on a plane or on steep stairs, many heights phobics are terrified at being more than three feet off the ground. Their reaction is marked by dizziness, the feeling "I'm going to fall" or "I'm going to be sucked out." The dizziness may be strong enough to make "things seem unreal." Out of the situation, their symptoms disappear. The heights phobia can be very specific; some people fear heights in buildings but not on planes. Some fear heights only when there's no railing or enclosure; otherwise they can look out of a tall building with no discomfort. Some are afraid only when they look down, not when they look out.

With escalators, sometimes the victims fear heights, but many times it's the fear of falling or other people falling on you and knocking you down. One woman felt comfortable on an escalator only when she rode facing upwards. She did this whether she was riding up or down, believing that if anyone fell, she would have time to brace herself or sidestep.

Often phobics misdiagnose their fear. For instance, you think elevators scare you but you really fear the heights to which the elevator takes you. Or you think you fear bridges but in actuality, you fear the height of the bridge over the water.

•*Fear of conditions:* darkness, fire, different weather conditions like thunderstorms, lightning, heat and cold. In one case an older woman had arthritis, and the doctor advised "lots of heat. During the summer, get out into the sun a lot." Terrified of heatstroke, she refused to follow her physician's orders and always stayed in an air-conditioned room. When her husband had to make a business trip to Greece in July, she refused to go ("It's too hot there"). Another woman says, "I worry that below-freezing temperatures will do me some physical injury. I avoid going out when the weather is cold and in winter often spend several weeks away from work."

Some people live in constant dread of fire. Indoors, they're uncomfortable because they think the house or apartment will catch fire. Some have only to hear the noise of a fire engine and they react, "My house is burning up."

Fearing darkness, many adults sleep with a dim light. Often this fear started during childhood and has lingered on.

With thunderstorms, the basic fear is either of the noise of the thunder or of being hit by lightning. Thunder phobes often have a safe room (a small room without windows) where they hide to get away "from doom hanging over me." Some hide their heads under a pillow. Others use earplugs to cut the noise. One woman covered the plugs with candlewax and topped this with earmuffs. She still felt terrorized because, with all the ear coverings, she didn't know when the storm was over.

Thunderstorm phobes possess an uncanny knack of

predicting when there will be a storm. Many claim superiority to the local weather bureau.

•*Fear of animals and insects:* This type of fear usually starts in childhood and carries over into adult life. Most common fears: dogs, cats, mice, reptiles (snakes particularly), animals running loose (skunks, squirrels, raccoons), birds, bats. Various kinds of insect fears exist. You can fear insects in general or have a specific fear of spiders; flying, stinging insects like bees and wasps; crawling insects like ants and roaches. One woman was driving on the Montauk Highway when an insect flew in the window. Stopping the car in the middle of the crowded highway, she screamed "Tarantula!" She recalls, "I almost killed everybody and myself."

Most animal-insect fears can be set off by the sight of them or even pictures of them. With most the core fear is: (1) coming into contact with the creature; (2) physical harm: being bitten by a dog, scratched by a cat ("They jump on a table and you never know what they're going to do"), stung by a bee, poisoned by a spider, that the bat will get tangled in your hair, bite you or even suck in your blood. Says one woman about snakes, "I don't fear the snake killing me. It's the feeling that it's going to wrap itself around me, the evilness of it touching me."

Usually people with such fears have for years successfully avoided animals and/or insects. According to one survey, most animal fears occur in women. Until adolescence they are common in both boys and girls, but after this time they usually persist only in girls.

•*Fear of transportation:* planes, buses, trains, subways, elevators. Many times these fears possess claustrophobic elements, but more often there has been a specific, traumatic life incident involving some upsetting experience. This may have happened to you, to a friend, or someone you've read about. Vehicular accidents make news. You hear a lot about them (a plane crash that kills five hundred people, an automobile collision in Memorial Day traffic). The who's-in-control factor matters. Some people are fearful when they drive; others when someone else drives.

People with transportation phobias practice tremendous amounts of avoidance. When they are forced into the frightening situation, their reaction is often characterized by racing thoughts of disaster, feelings of jumpiness and nervousness and sometimes such physical reactions as nausea and vomiting.

•*Fear of illness and/or medical procedures:* You may fear specific illnesses like cancer, venereal disease or a heart attack. With this phobia, victims become very sensitive to any bodily change that may signify the appearance of the disease. Says one woman, "Every little ache and pain I get, I know it's cancer." These disease phobias differ from hypochondria in that usually they involve fear of only one specific illness, rather than fears of many. The fear of dying sometimes underlies the phobia, but more often it is the fear of physical pain, becoming helpless or deformed (many women live in daily obsessive dread of mastectomy).

People can also be phobic to medical procedures: the fear of injections, the physical discomfort induced by medication, the doctor poking around, internal examinations like proctoscopy. Some fear the sight of blood. With these fears, the victim may actually faint at the doctor's office.

The thought of vomiting terrifies many. For example, one young man had cancer, but of the kind that responds well to chemical treatment. However, some of the medications used would bring on nausea and vomiting. He traced this fear to the fact that, as a boy, whenever his ill-tempered father would yell at him or hit him, he got sick to his stomach and often vomited.

Now he can't bring himself to go to the clinic to get the shots he needs to save his life.

•*Unusual phobias:* Almost anything can be conditioned to set off a fear reaction. For example, I have now treated six people with a fear of chewing gum. One patient got so upset when she saw someone in the street chewing gum that, to prevent herself from screaming, she would bite her hand until the blood ran.

You can fear firecrackers exploding in the distance. One patient was terrified they'd start coming closer. Oddly enough, he wasn't frightened when they were close.

You can fear dolls (pediophobia), beards (pogonophobia), flowers (anthophobia), going to bed (clinophobia), trees (dendrophobia), writing (graphophobia), sitting idle (thaasophobia). There are even more bizarre phobias: balloons (they might suddenly explode), traffic lights, looking in a mirror, buttons, the color pink and seeing anyone cut his/her fingernails in front of you. The grandmother of the late James Thurber feared empty electric bulb sockets; she could "feel" the electricity pouring out.

Who Gets These Phobias

The victims of "things" phobias are some of the strongest, most self-sufficient and creative people. To be afraid of cats, injections and high buildings doesn't mean you're crazy. Some of the world's most famous people suffer or have suffered from these very same fears.

Spencer Tracy had a fear of flying. So did Judy Garland, who was also afraid of appearing on stage and entering crowded stores or cars. Albert Camus was phobic about driving a car; ironically, he died in a crash when a friend was driving. Freud himself had a fear of travel. Reputedly Mamie Eisenhower has always had drivers go miles out of the way to find bridge routes instead of tunnels.

Many years ago, the late J. Edgar Hoover, director of the Federal Bureau of Investigation, made a trip to California. While making a left turn, his chauffeur-driven car was struck by another car from behind. The director, who had been sitting on the left seat behind the driver, was shaken up. From then on he refused to sit on the left rear seat any more (he called it "the death seat") and forbade all left turns on auto trips. Henceforth his aides had to go through the most complicated arrangements to get Director Hoover from place to place without any left turns.

Just as the director of America's major law-enforcement agency was reduced to a mass of nerves at the thought of making a left turn, the adventurous traveler, who jets fearlessly all over the world, may panic at the thought of driving in the traffic of a Los Angeles freeway. The assertive businesswoman may tremble if she has to ride on an elevator over the third floor.

Coping Procedures

To deal with fear of things, you have developed various coping methods. You note devices that may reduce your fear (for example, you clutch the handrail in the elevator); you arrange your life so that you don't have to do what you're frightened to do.

CASE

Ellen P., an attractive, fortyish book buyer for Larson's, a major, southwestern department store frankly confesses to a fear of heights. She doesn't know its origin ("I grew up in a small town and never saw a skyscraper until I moved to the big city at twenty"), but now finds she arranges many of her social and professional activities to avoid heights. She works on the fourth floor in an office without windows. She lives on the second floor of an apartment building. If a date wants to go to a restaurant on top of a building, she says a firm no. She admits, "For work purposes I can usually get up to the twentieth floor, but if I go into an office that is all windows, I start to shake. When I have nightmares, the dream is always about a high building."

To deal with her fear of heights, Ellen has worked out a resourceful system of "alternatives." For example, when she goes to New York and meets with a public relations contact at Doubleday & Co., where the office is on the thirty-fifth floor, she refuses to go up. Ellen says, "The p.r. girl meets me in the coffee shop. I can get away with it." With hotel reservations she specifically requests the lowest floor possible. Once she had to go to a famous Atlanta hotel with an open elevator in the lobby. Ellen took one look and marched up to the registration desk, declaring, "I have to have a room on the second or third floor, or I won't register." The clerk responded sympathetically with, "Frankly, it's no problem. We always keep three or four rooms for people with a fear of heights."

Recently Ellen went to Chicago to attend the annual American Booksellers Association convention. At cocktail time, she headed for a publisher's party to be held in the Mid-American Club, located on top of a skyscraper.

She recalls, "As badly as I wanted to meet the guest of honor for professional purposes, I took one look and tried to get the cab back. When I couldn't, I stood there on the street for what seemed like hours, trying to decide whether or not to go to the party. It was important for business for me to attend, so finally I walked into the lobby and got into the elevator. As it rose, I thought the building was tipping and that I'd die of fright. When the door opened, the publisher's public relations man was in the hall. I was so shaken and pale that he greeted me with, 'What's wrong with you?' I couldn't even answer. At the party I just wanted to flatten myself against the wall. My hands shook so much that I couldn't even hold a drink. I stayed, but the p.r. man had to go down in the elevator with me. I couldn't have made the return trip alone."

Ellen's story reveals not only her helplessness and awareness of what triggers her fears, but the methods she has learned to help her cope.

•*The pattern of creative avoidance:* Because she possesses an active rather than a passive orientation to life, Ellen carries out highly creative attempts at avoidance. She makes advance reservations on the second floors of hotels and has business contacts meet her in ground-floor coffee shops. She is still at the mercy of her phobia but uses her creativity to minimize exposure to it.

•*Actual coping:* When she cannot avoid, she does what she can to minimize her fear of heights. For example, she gets someone to accompany her down in the elevator. Devices like this are familiar to all people with fears. Some practice the *blackout* technique, a little game that virtually ensures insensitivity to phobic cues. Most usual method: to have four martinis before boarding a plane and go through the trip in an alcoholic daze. Others use tranquilizers before going into the fear situation. Drinking and drugs may help you get through the immediate situation but, since they are both basically means of avoidance or escape, in the long run they perpetuate the fear. They confirm your helplessness; if you use them, you feel bad about doing so.

•*The use of the discomfort-desire balance:* When her desire outweighed her fear, Ellen was able to make herself go up in the elevator to the party. Many people with fears utilize this discomfort-desire balance. To get something they want badly, they will endure their worst fear reactions. For example, a thirty-four-year-old divorced man, living in Philadelphia, fears all forms of transportation. His seven-year-old daughter lives in Urbana, Illinois. Gregg manages to fly there "because I want to see my daughter."

Others refuse to enter the fear situation. Actress

Maureen Stapleton wouldn't go to the Rainbow Room, sixty-five floors atop Rockefeller Center, to receive an award for her acting accomplishments. They had to bring the award down to her.

Still others will place their very lives in jeopardy rather than risk the fear reaction (for example, you have some very real and frightening symptoms, but you cannot bring yourself to see a doctor).

Using Ellen's experience as a guide, try to analyze your own pattern in dealing with the fear of "things." It may prove helpful to write the answers to the following questions in your Fear Control Training workbook.

1. What is your own avoidance pattern? What specific things have you done to minimize your exposure to your fear situation?

2. In the fear situation, what kind of things do you do to help you cope? Do you ever use the black-out technique?

3. What is your discomfort-desire balance? Under what conditions would you make yourself experience the fear reaction?

Answering these questions may take some of the mystery out of the fear and provide clues to help you face the things you fear.

The Origin of Your Fear

Many people know just how their fear began.

Says one claustrophobic: "When I was eight, I went with my family to a hotel in the Berkshires. We were all stuck in an elevator for ten minutes. Ever since I've had this fear of being enclosed."

Says an ornithopobic (*fear of birds*): "My older brother used to flutter the dead birds at me that my father had shot. Since then the sight of a dead bird terrifies me. I'm afraid to swim; I may find a dead bird in the water."

Says a pyrophobic (*fear of fire*): "When I was six, there was a fire drill at school. They took us out by a different door. I got lost. Ever since I've been terrified of fire. I'm even scared by the sight of a match."

Although many people gain great personal satisfaction from knowing how their phobia began, I repeat, this knowledge really makes no difference in treatment.

Reactive phobias serve as an excellent example of this. You may have had a bad experience, like being in an automobile accident. Thereafter, you become phobic to riding in cars. You have no doubts about how your phobia began. Yet, despite this knowledge, the phobia keeps growing in a rather typical pattern. You become aware of its onset about two weeks after the traumatic experience. Usually, you have a fairly mild initial reaction and you experience surprise at this fear reaction. With each exposure to cars, during the next few months, your fear gets worse. Your avoidance and escape patterns build up; a general state of tension may develop. In these instances, knowing the cause of your phobia may heighten it. Over and over, you review in your thoughts the worse parts of the trauma and so increase your fear.

THE TREATMENT OF "THINGS" PHOBIAS

Systematic Desensitization serves as the best way of treating "things" phobias. In this, you approach the feared situation a step at a time, each time countering the tension with relaxation before you go on to the next. Experiments have shown that the Systematic Desensitization method has an 80 to 90 percent cure rate with "things" phobias.

Systematic Desensitization in Reality

It is always a good idea to try first for a reality desensitization: (1) Because "things" phobias are so specific and concrete, you can often devise good reality hierarchies. (2) You eliminate a step. When you do it first in imagery, you still have the additional step of taking over the desensitization to the life situation. Besides, mastering a real-life situation often gives you greater satisfaction and more confidence. *Note:* Whether you opt for the reality or imagery method, use your Fear Control Training workbook to keep careful record of your progress. As with all FCT exercises, the people who keep notes make the best progress.

1. *To come up with a workable reality hierarchy, sometimes you have to use ingenuity and know your surroundings.* With people who fear escalators, I know that the very short escalator at Bloomingdale's in New York is a good place for the first step and that the long, steep escalator at the Fifty-third Street subway station often serves as an effective final step. For people with the fear of traveling over bridges, I often used the following hierarchy items:

- The Harlem River bridges like the Third Avenue Bridge (it's small and short)
- The Fifty-ninth Street Bridge to Queens (it's longer)
- The Manhattan/Brooklyn bridges (still longer)
- The George Washington Bridge (longer still)

With buses and subway trips you can predetermine the length of the trip.

Search around your local area for appropriate stops, bridges, windows, etc.

CASE

Martin E., a twenty-four-year-old assistant professor, felt terrified of heights. His panic reaction always started on the third floor of a building, where he would get the sensation "There's nothing under me. I'll fall."

Beginning his reality desensitization on the third floor of a building, Martin did three things. First, he found a spot with *no windows,* usually a corridor. He would relax himself and leave. He repeated this until he was able to be on that floor, not near the window, with no anxiety. Second, he raised his tension. He would stand on a third floor, *near a window,* and practice his relaxation. After four or five repetitions he was able to do this comfortably. Third, on the third floor he would *open a window,* lean out a little and practice relaxation until he could swing this act with no anxiety.

Martin repeated this same threefold process on fourth, fifth and sixth floors, using offices, friends' apartments and classrooms. He couldn't find an available seventh floor, but he did locate eighth and ninth floors. From these he progressed to the eleventh, twelfth, fourteenth and fifteenth floors.

Then he located a skyscraper and gave himself the task of going to the men's rooms on alternate floors and looking out of the windows. Because the windows in these lavatories were sealed, he couldn't lean out, but he did manage to get up to the forty-fourth floor.

This process took about four months. At the end of this period Martin tested himself. He rode up 107 floors to the Windows on the World Restaurant at Manhattan's World Trade Center. Martin didn't have the money for the costly dinner, but he wandered around looking out of the windows. He had some initial feelings of discomfort, but managed to relax them out. After about twenty minutes these feelings stopped. Martin left, knowing he had licked his phobia.

2. *Use time and/or distance as factors in forming your hierarchy.* These have special uses in dealing with "thing" fears. Not only can you set up different situations, but you can increase the amount of time you stay in each one.

CASE

Pam had claustrophobia. She could go into many small rooms but only with tremendous anxiety. Lately she noticed she had started to avoid elevators, subways, even going to the hairdresser because she couldn't face having the robe around her neck. She also observed her increasing discomfort in her own home when a door was closed. In the bathroom, she had started to leave the door open.

In treatment, we first ranked the rooms in her apartment. She experienced the least anxiety in the living room (it had big French doors), then the bedroom, the bathroom, and finally in a tiny pantry, half the size of the bathroom, with a door but no windows.

First she stayed in the living room with the door closed, until she felt disturbed. With a stopwatch she would note the amount of time she had stayed there and then step outside the room and relax. She stayed in the living room increasing amounts of time until she experienced the first signs of anxiety. When she could remain there with the door closed for twenty minutes, she progressed to the bedroom. She repeated the same procedure there, then in the bathroom, and finally in the pantry. When she handled the pantry successfully, she found her new freedom from fear had spread to other situations. She could go in the subway, elevators, and, best of all, have a weekly appointment at the hairdresser's.

3. *Use pictures and artifacts to help you get started on your reality program.* Many times pictures and objects that remind you of the fear situation do produce a definite fear reaction. For example, one man with a cancer phobia used to get terribly upset when he saw ads for the American Cancer Society. Another with a fear of medical procedures would become terrified by the smell of medications; to begin his reality desensitization we used small drug samples.

CASE

Joan was terrified of spiders ("If one starts toward me, I just stand there shaking"). This affected her life because her husband loved the country but Joan would never leave the city ("I might see a spider"). Using pictures and artifacts, we worked out a program.

•Her husband cut out a series of pictures with spiders from nature magazines, mounted them on cardboard and arranged them in order of disturbance. Joan was too scared to do this herself. The photo that set off the least anxiety was a cartoon of a spider from a children's book. She took the picture, looked at it until she felt the first signs of anxiety, turned it face downward and relaxed. When she could look at it for three to four minutes with no anxiety, she went back to the cartoon and this time, instead of just looking, she actually touched the picture. At first, she could just flick her finger in the air over it before the fright came on. Eventually, she could keep her hand on the cartoon for several minutes. In this same way she went through the whole stack.

•In a novelty store her husband purchased several different models of spiders. She followed the same procedure as with the pictures. First she looked (her husband gradually brought them closer and closer). Then she touched.

•Her husband managed to buy mounted specimens of actual spiders. First Joan looked at them in the glass case until she felt comfortable, then out of the glass case. Finally she touched them.

•Because of the difficulty in getting live spiders, her husband tied a string around one of the specimens. He would jerk it around the table. First Joan watched, then she tried to touch it. This became a game. He tried to keep her from catching the spider.

At this point they went to visit a friend in the country, something Joan had avoided for years. I gave her the instruction, "Look for live spiders." She didn't see any on the first expedition and felt disappointed. On their second outing, she saw a spider and found she no longer felt terrified.

CASE

Very much in love with her fiancé, Pauline R. couldn't get married. Terrified of hypodermic needles, she was unable to take the required blood test. In treatment, first she looked at pictures of hypodermic needles cut from medical magazines. Next a doctor friend loaned her a hypodermic needle which she first looked at, then touched, then handled. Next her fiancé found a trick hypodermic needle (it didn't really penetrate). Pauline watched Joe apparently stab the needle into himself, then she did it to him, then he to her. Finally, the same doctor friend arranged for her to sit in a clinic and watch blood being drawn. From this clinic experience Pauline learned something very important: that other people felt nervous about injections but they could control themselves and go through it. For her this served as a coping model. Finally, she went through the blood test and was able to get married.

4. *Sometimes you don't need a formal hierarchy.* Some situations lend themselves readily to reality desensitization. For example, I have a mild fear of heights. A few years ago I visited the Uxmal ruins in the Yucatán peninsula of Mexico. Holding on to a chain, I had climbed to the top of one of the pyramids when suddenly my lifetime fear of heights took over and I felt terrible sensations of dizziness. I decided to desensitize myself to that fear.

Cautiously, I backed down the pyramid. When I got to the foot, I put myself through the Intermediate Relaxation Exercise, and then started a return climb up the pyramid, making a point of continuously looking down. I had managed to get one-third of the way up when I started feeling dizzy again. I stopped and kept on relaxing myself until I was able to look down without any signs of anxiety. This took about four minutes. Then I resumed my climb until the next signs of a fear reaction. Again, I went through the relaxation routine. Eventually, making five or six stops, I got to the top. At this point I was able to do what I had been unable to do forty-five minutes earlier: to stand on the ledge and look down without any feeling of panic.

Note for residents of and visitors to Manhattan: I am completely convinced that the Guggenheim Museum must have been built to cure people of a fear of heights. There's a winding ramp that goes up and up and from any point you can look straight down. One acrophobic art student just kept climbing until he felt the signs of anxiety. Then he would relax himself and follow the reality desensitization procedure. Eventually he got to the top.

5. *Make use of friends and relatives.* They can serve three functions.

•To help provide samples of the feared object as did the husband of the woman in the spider case.

•To accompany you into your self-assignment situation and thus help reduce your anxiety. For example, one woman had a fear of elevators. Her first hierarchy item was to stand outside an elevator door but not enter. Her second: when the door opened, to put one foot in and quickly take it out. Roz couldn't bring herself to do it. That little space between the elevator and the door loomed as an impenetrable barrier. She got her boy friend to help. He stood with one hand in hers for reassurance and the other holding open the door of the elevator. With this as a confidence-builder, for the first time in years, she got into the elevator. He went through the entire hierarchy with her. Then she went back and did it alone.

You can use this technique in your own home. For example, if you're claustrophobic, ask your spouse or a close friend to stand outside the door while you close yourself inside for longer and longer periods of time.

•To serve as a reinforcer. Encourage your spouse,

lover, friends, co-workers to praise you each step of the way as you move toward your goal. For instance, in the case of Martha, the woman with a train phobia, her children served as a source of reinforcement. They kept a record of her progress, and her eight-year-old son started to give her slips of paper with gold stars on them. When she had a setback and had to start all over again, her ten-year-old son comforted her with, "Don't worry, Mommy; you'll be able to do it." After she made the final successful hour-long ride, he gave her a drawing of a train, with an arrow pointing to one of the windows and an inscription: "That's Mommy."

6. *Note that reality desensitization can cause inconvenience in terms of time and money.* You have to get to the place where you can practice and spend time in practicing. This can prove a big stumbling block.

One man with a terrible fear of having an auto accident on a hill, especially the steep hill near his home, found a solution to the time problem by using his three-week vacation for Fear Control Training. He took a series of twenty different hills and divided them into five groups, according to the anxiety they caused. Number-one group caused the least, four was "very bad" and the steep hill with the traffic light near his home was the worst. During the vacation he would do no driving except for his reality desensitization assignments.

He drove up the number-one hills four times daily; this took him four days to master. Within ten days he had progressed to the terrible number-five hill. First he tried it at 5:00 A.M., when there was little likelihood of another car. He did this three or four times every morning. Then he switched the time to 6:30 A.M., then to 2:00 P.M. and finally to 5:00 P.M. rush hour. By the end of his vacation he had cured his hill phobia.

In another instance a harassed Wall Street executive with a fear of animals scheduled his practice time as if he were going to a therapist twice weekly. He figured out what each session would cost, gave himself a cut rate (he was a businessman!) and spent the money on cab rides to the Bronx Zoo.

Systematic Desensitization in Fantasy

Reality desensitization has certain disadvantages. You may not be able to get into the right situation to reduce your fears. You may not be able to set up the right graded steps—for instance, you can't always produce a thunderstorm when you need it. It can be inconvenient; you can't practice when you want to.

Because of these factors, fantasy desensitization some times proves more effective. You can imagine exactly the amount of lightning you want, the exact length of the tunnel, or the doctor probing and pushing. The following examples should serve as models for you in using imagery desensitization for your own fears.

1. *You can call up the fear at any time; you don't have to wait for it to occur.*

CASE

Maryann L., a woman in her early forties, was terrified of thunderstorms and spent a great deal of time scanning the skies for black clouds. Her core fear was the noise of the thunderstorm. Rumbles of unseen trucks could cause startle reactions. She couldn't travel anywhere without her earplugs. The fear was worse in the country than in the city. In imagery, we worked out various steps for her.

•She's at home watching a TV show and the actress says, "I think it's going to storm."

•She looks at a newspaper headline that reads, "Severe storm in Midwest."

•On the radio news the weatherman says, "There's a twenty percent chance of thunderstorms tonight."

•At home with her husband, she hears thunder rumbling in the distance, but the storm is almost over.

•She's with her husband at a country hotel and she hears loud thunder rumbling in the distance.

•She's at home alone and hears a medium clap of thunder.

•She's at home alone and hears a loud clap of thunder followed by a second. This lasts about five seconds.

•She's in the country and hears loud claps of thunder directly overhead. They seem to go on endlessly.

While carrying out the desensitization, Maryann noticed she was paying less attention to weather reports ("Suddenly, I stopped being a barometer") and was more relaxed generally because different street sounds didn't startle her. Several months after we completed treatment Maryann was riding in the country with her husband. He commented, "It looks like rain." Said Maryann, "Oh, it really doesn't matter."

2. *With imagery desensitization you can prepare yourself ahead of time for something that's coming up and that you can't accomplish with reality desensitization.*

CASE

In chapter 1, I told about Roger, who got his M.D. but was so frightened of taking his medical boards that he worked as an insurance salesman for ten years. During this period, he studied continually but could not take the exam. Extremely depressed, he came to me. Roger had two core fears: (a) that he would get a failing grade on the exam; (b) that he would look at the examination questions and be unable to answer them. We worked out the following hierarchy.

Hierarchy Item	Fear Thermometer Rating
1. Studying medicine four weeks before exam	5
2. Studying medicine three weeks before exam	10
3. Studying medicine two weeks before exam	15
4. Hearing about a classmate who had failed the exam the year before.	20
5. Studying medicine one week before the exam	25
6. Leaving the exam room and he's fairly certain that he passed	30
7. Gets notice in mail that he passed the exam but barely	35
8. Studying the day before the exam	40
9. The exam room—he's looking at the questions and thinks he can answer most of them	45
10. Looking at the exam questions and several seem difficult	50
11. Getting up on the morning of exam day	55
12. Has notice in the mail that he passed part of the exam but has to retake part	60
13. He's walking into exam room, settling himself in his seat	65
14. He's looking at the exam questions and most seem beyond him	70
15. He's looking at the exam questions and there isn't one he can answer	75
16. There's a notice in the mail that he failed the exam	80

Hierarchy Item	Fear Thermometer Rating
17. The notice says he failed the exam so badly that under no circumstances will he be allowed another chance to take it	85

Roger and I worked together for five months. Exam day came and he took his boards and passed. Today he's working as a physician and feels good about himself. He had overcome this fear, so crucial to his life, entirely by coping with his anxiety in imagery.

CASE

With her first child Emily W. had experienced a difficult and painful delivery. In the delivery room something had gone amiss and the doctors and nurses didn't pay attention to her or provide her with proper medications. Three years later Emily became pregnant again. She wanted the baby but could think only, "Will this delivery be as painful and prolonged as the first?" This fear caused so much tension that she consulted me.

In imagery we went through a number of scenes introducing increasing amounts of pain. For example, "You're in the delivery room and you feel contractions with a tiny amount of pain" . . . "You feel contractions with a moderate amount of pain but it passes" . . . "You feel contractions with a moderate amount of pain and the pain is lasting."

As we went through the hierarchy, her concern for the delivery lessened. This was obvious not only to her but to her doctor and husband. In real life when Emily felt the first contractions, she telephoned her husband at his office. He ordered, "Take a taxi. I'll meet you at the hospital." Emily wasn't at all scared. In fact, she was so relaxed that she had the baby in the cab.

3. *You can be frightened of something that may not happen.*

CASE

Everyday Norman lived with the fear of cancer. At any little sign (a freckle on his forearm, a slight cough), he ran to his doctor. He was always in a state of anxiety ("I know an operation wouldn't be successful; the cancer would just turn up somewhere else"). At one point a friend died of cancer. Hearing of this, Norman went home and started to scream. Because we couldn't do reality desensitization for this fear, we tried imagery.

•In conversation he hears mention of a stranger having died of cancer.

•In conversation he hears about someone having been hospitalized for cancer, but the doctors think they caught it in time.

•The doctor tells him, "It looks a little suspicious. You'd better take some tests."

•The doctor tells him, "You've a little tumor but it looks benign."

•He's in the hospital and getting medication for cancer.

•He's in the hospital, following an operation for cancer, and he feels weak and full of pain.

•He's in a hospital bed, wasting away from cancer. He knows the chemotherapy hasn't worked and that the end will be soon.

This imagery desensitization worked. Norman stopped being so terrified at the idea that he might possibly get cancer. When his brother-in-law got cancer of the liver, Norman maintained enough cool to give his wife the emotional support she needed.

4. *You can tailor-make the situations in exactly the way you want them.* With reality situations you can't always do this.

CASE

Ken, now in his forties, had feared dogs since child-hood. Now the fear was getting worse. On his way home from work, the direct route took him past a pet shop with puppies in the window. To avoid this, Ken would go a block out of his way. His imagery desensiti-zation:

• He's at the Museum of Natural History looking at a mock-up of a dog with real hair but no teeth. He imagines putting his hand in the statue's mouth.

• Same scene but the statue has teeth. Ken puts his hand in the statue's mouth and feels the teeth.

• Series of scenes with dog a block away. He started with a small dog and kept making the dog bigger and more ferocious looking.

• Series of scenes, bringing the dog closer yard by yard in imagery.

• Final scene—huge, growling dog jumps on him, knocking him down.

Following this, Ken was able to walk past the pet shop without fear. He visited a friend with a dog and for the first time was able to pat it. At our next session he said to me, "For the first time I realized how much bigger I am than that spaniel."

Combination Desensitization

Combining the reality and imagery techniques serves as a powerful method of fear reduction.

EXERCISE IN
COMBINED DESENSITIZATION

STEP ONE: Make up your reality hierarchy. You will do it first in imagery, then in reality.

STEP TWO: If there are any gaps in this hierarchy which you are unable to fill with reality situations, use imagery scenes. For example, you may be able to get to a second-floor window but have no practical way to get to third-, fourth- and fifth-floor windows. Your Fear Thermometer reading shows that the gap between the second and sixth floors is too great (more than ten units). You need some intermediate steps. You can fill in these gaps through imagery: You imagine being at the third-, fourth- and fifth-floor windows. Thus your fantasy hierarchy will have all the items of a reality plus additions.

STEP THREE: Either using the cards or your tape, do each step in the hierarchy first in imagery. After you have managed the situation in imagery with no fear reaction, then do it in life. Keep the reality desensitization two or three steps behind the imagery desensitization. For example, if you are going to do item three of your reality hierarchy, wait until you have mastered item five in fantasy.

If you experience difficulty in mastering the reality situation (even with repetition, you can't lower your tension), do it again in imagery. Sometimes you can have two separate parallel hierarchies.

CASE

My wife, Jean, mentioned in chapter 1 that she married me because I was "the one man who didn't criticize" her driving. She knows how to drive but hates to do it. Some years ago I mistakenly said to her, "If you're so frightened, why drive?" So she stopped.

Recently I had some eye problems. In August, I knew that when my current driver's license lapsed at the end of December, I would not be able to get it renewed until the eye condition cleared up. At that point Jean decided she had to get more confident behind the wheel and asked me to desensitize her. We were spending the month of August in Rowayton, a small Connecticut village by the sea.

Jean's core fears are of the people honking at her from behind, turning left at intersections, driving over thirty miles an hour and driving in the dark (she never had). We made up the following fantasy and reality hierarchies. You'll note that in each of these she is driving with me. I wanted her to put in items about driving alone, but she retorted, "I'd break the Fear Thermometer!"

Fantasy Hierarchy	*Reality Hierarchy*
1. Drive with Herb to village of Rowayton	
2. Drive with Herb to shopping center in Darien	
3. Driving with Herb on thruway in mid-day (little traffic)	1. Drive to Rowayton, a distance of about a mile, and back
4. Driving with Herb on thruway with pick-up truck in next lane	
5. Driving with Herb on thruway with bus in next lane	2. Drive to Darien (three miles) and back
6. Driving with Herb on thruway with big trailer truck in next lane	
7. Making the left-hand turn to get onto the thruway	3. Make left turn at intersection
8. Driving on the thruway. The car behind honks and starts to pass	

Fantasy Hierarchy	*Reality Hierarchy*
9. On the curvy two-lane road, a car is behind her	4. Make left turn onto thruway at 10:00 A.M. and 2:00 P.M. (low traffic times). Drive back and forth between Rowayton and Darien on the thruway.
10. Two cars are behind her on a rural road	
11. A line of cars is behind her on a rural road	
12. A line of cars is behind her on a rural road. All honking	5. Drive to home of Anita Berke in Weston (twelve miles) via the thruway and back country roads. Drive back
13. The line of cars is behind her, honking. She has to make a lefthand turn at an intersection. She'll have to stop and hold up the line.	
14. Driving on the thruway at night with every car going fast	6. Drive to Rowayton at night
15. She's driving on a two-lane country road at night with traffic. She sees the lights of a car coming toward her.	7. Drive to Darien at night Drive to Anita's at night
16. She's on a country road at night. A car is coming toward her and there's a line of cars behind her.	

During August Jean managed to get through half of item seven in reality, but she could not make herself drive to her friend Anita's at night. She always said, "You do it. I can't." In December we rented the house again for the period between Christmas and January 2. I would be losing my license at the end of the year and on New Year's Eve Anita was giving a big party. If we were to attend, Jean would have to get us back.

The entire week Jean practiced relentlessly, alternating between confidence and "How will I ever get us back . . . that awful left turn . . . that dark country road where the cars honk at me." On December 31, she spent the day deciding on possible routes, feeling she must drive us there or she couldn't drive back. As we left, I had to remind her about the lights; in her nervousness she forgot where the switch was.

We got there. Jean regaled all the guests with her triumph as if she had won the Nobel Prize for literature. Driving back she ran into a problem—sleet that turned into a big snowstorm. But she got us home even though she got stuck on the hill in front of the rented house and had to park right under a "no parking" sign (she got a ticket). Running into the house, she danced around the living room, screaming, "I did it. I did it."

The next day she triumphantly started writing new hierarchies, beginning "Drive *alone* to Rowayton." But she did something even more important. Jean has written many nonfiction books and articles. For years she had an idea for a blockbuster novel. Even though editors have given her enormous encouragement, she's afraid to try it. "I'll fail," she says.

After writing her new driving hierarchy, Jean said to me, "There's something I want to do," and disappeared into the bedroom until dinnertime. She emerged with a sheaf of copypaper. In a rather offhand way, she handed the papers to me, saying, "I just thought I'd start my novel. After all, Herb, if I can drive back from Anita's at two A.M. in the middle of a snowstorm on the thruway, I certainly ought to be able to do something as comparatively simple as writing a novel."

Overcoming one fear had enabled Jean to conquer still another fear.

CHAPTER 6 ─────────

SOCIAL FEARS

Of all the fears that affect human beings, social fears are the most camouflaged. These fears may run your life—even ruin it—and you may not be aware of their existence, influence or power.

You may be very well aware that difficulties occur in your social life. You know you come on so strong that you push others away, that you fight a lot. You may realize that you are lonely, shy, constantly exploited, that your life lacks closeness and love.

You attribute these fears to "neurotic needs," an unhappy childhood, the faults and shortcomings of other people. You fail to understand that many (not all) of these difficulties stem from specific social fears.

CASE ONE: Bob, a lonely man, has few friends, fewer dates. Occasionally, friends will call him but he rarely makes an overture. At the limited number of parties he attends, he can make charming small talk only if someone else starts the conversation. Bob admits frankly, "I don't make overtures because I'm afraid of rejection." Seemingly candid, he does not understand that his fear of rejection represents a true social phobia, responsible for his entire unsatisfactory social pattern. Just as people with "things" phobias have to avoid elevators, dogs or doctors' offices, Bob must keep away from any situation where the slightest chance of rejection exists.

CASE TWO: On the other hand, Mary has a very active social life. Her problem: a series of unsatisfactory relationships with men. Her pattern: She meets a new man; they date intensively, and, within a short time, begin living together. However, within weeks the relationship starts to deteriorate, and, in two or three months, they break up. Mary goes through a few weeks of intense anxiety, but within a month she commences a new relationship. The cycle starts again.

Mary understands that when she is alone she becomes nervous. She speaks at length about the "painful loneliness" of an only child whose parents "didn't care." However, Mary's current problems spring from far more than memories. She is phobic to being alone. This brings about her peripatetic social life and brief, unhappy involvements. To her, men are not partners, mates or lovers but represent merely a means of avoiding solitude. With this as a base, a good relationship cannot develop. Her entire social life has but a single aim: the goal of avoiding the fearful situation of being alone.

SOCIAL FEARS ARE DIFFERENT

Social fears are similar to other fears in that they too cause automatic Robot Responses to specific situations, people, events. If the possibility exists that the dreaded situation may arise, you try to avoid it. If you can't escape from it, you become tense and even more fearful. However, social fears are also different from other fears. It is these differences that make your fears hard to recognize and that allow them to have such a clutch on your life.

•*Social fears produce a wide variety of disturbed reactions.* Besides the fear response, the reaction can be guilt, anger, resentments and depressions. All these reactions lead to avoidance, escape and/or disruption and can influence your whole social life. You can change these in exactly the same way you change the automatic fear and anxiety reactions.

•*Your human fear object responds back to your behavior, complicating the situation.* No matter how frightened or jumpy you are, the elevator, plane, small room stay the same. However, with social fears, people react to *your reaction.* The result: Many times you needlessly bring on the very thing you fear will happen.

EXAMPLE ONE: Because you fear rejection, you do not reach out to people. Soon they stop reaching out to you, and you are rejected.

EXAMPLE TWO: Your parents always criticized you. To avoid that "naughty boy/girl" attack, you always reacted by being docile and good. Now this has become an automatic response. In your marriage, when your spouse criticizes you, you are always placating and supernice. Thus you reinforce the criticism and, in essence, train your spouse to criticize more.

Because people do react back, even mild, disturbed reactions may have big consequences. They tend to snowball. Your mild discomfort may communicate itself and make the other person uncomfortable. In turn, this makes you still more upset, and, before you know it, a little incident has assumed major importance.

•*Even low-level disturbances can become pervasive.* Social situations are complex. Even with the simplest, you can experience an array of feelings. One or several of these feelings may be anxious ones. As long as you experience the other more positive feelings along with anxiety, you can keep the anxious feelings in perspective and remain in command. You can act to reach your specific interaction goal, such as to express an opinion, enjoy a party, negotiate a disagreement. When low-level anxiety reactions spiral, they spread and mask other feelings. Your disturbances influence your actions.

Situation: You're going to a cocktail party that will be full of strangers.

•*Constructive approach:* You walk into your neighbor's living room feeling tense, but you're also aware of a feeling of excitement at meeting new people, curiosity about who'll be fellow guests, the hope you'll meet someone "special." Keeping your tensions in perspective, you call on your social skills and begin to talk to various people. Soon you find someone who shares your interest in travel, skiing or rebuilding old barns. You become more spontaneous and the tension disappears. To a greater or lesser extent (depending on the party and the people), you begin to enjoy yourself.

•*Destructive approach:* You focus all your attention on your mild tension and lose sight of your feelings of excitement, curiosity, hope. Because you are aware only of being disturbed (even though this may be mild), you begin to anticipate disaster even before you get to the party. As you circulate, you concentrate so much on your fear reactions that you can't use the social skills you have. Your spasmodic attempts at desultory conversation don't work. Your error: Instead of aiming at having a good time, you have made it your goal to minimize your anxiety.

As a first point in change you must pinpoint the specific social fears you want to eliminate.

COMMON SOCIAL FEARS

In interpersonal relationships you can be anxious with authority figures, peers and subordinates; large groups and in one-to-one situations; same sex and opposite sex; old and young, deformed people, sick people, rich people, poor people, fat people, thin people. I have seen patients who had automatic anxiety reactions to tall people and others made fearful by short men and women. Despite this wide range, some fears are more prevalent than others. Here are the seven most common categories I see in my practice.

1. *Fear of being looked at.* Often this fear possesses no real content. Purely and simply, you become aware that another person is looking at you (not staring, just looking) and get frightened. For example, in a group conversation you utter some remark and the others start to look at you. You feel uncomfortable and stop talking. Next step: avoidance. In order to minimize the chance that people will look at you, you don't participate in conversations. Your fear may not confine itself to social situations. To avoid being looked at, you may hide behind a newspaper on trains or buses. Despite your continual avoidance attempts, people may still look at you. For this reason, in public places you continually go around in a high state of tension. This same fear sometimes leads to difficulty in public speaking.

2. *Fear of people seeing you are nervous.* Unlike the above fear, this possesses content. You show your nervousness with outward manifestations like hand trembling, blushing, tremulous voice. Afraid others will notice these signs, you refuse invitations where you know the hostess will serve coffee, tea, liquor. If you accept, you take the cup or glass, place it carefully in front of you and do not pick it up again. You agonize over the worst thing that could happen—someone says, "Your hand's trembling. How come you're so nervous?" With this fear, you don't have to show the outward signs. Even a subjective feeling of anxiety can trigger the upset reaction.

Note: Sometimes labeling the outward manifestation helps counter avoidance. For example, with patients who had the hand-shaking symptom, I suggested they explain it in terms of "tennis strain." At a party when they became aware of their hands trembling, they were to say, "I strained my arm at tennis." Whether they used it or not, having this crutch available helped get them to the party. For several other patients who had sweating as the outer manifestation, I came up with the label "sudorific allergy"—instead of stuffing their noses or making their eyes tear, this "funny allergy" caused them to sweat. While this labeling didn't solve the problem, it made it possible for them to get into the fear situation.

3. *The fear of being trapped in a relationship.* Victims often rationalize this as "not wanting the responsibility" or "not being able to do what I want to do." They believe they have no choice. In actuality, this fear is a social claustrophobia. Earlier in their lives many of its victims had a fear of being trapped in a small room. They overcame that, but the fear of being trapped generalized to interpersonal situations.

4. *Fear of being "found out."* You think if people "really know" you, if you are exposed for "what you really are," they will recoil and reject you. Many times you aren't even sure what qualities would be "exposed." However, some people can be quite specific: "They'll find out I'm stupid" . . . "silly" . . . "evil" . . . "inept." Even if to some extent you are these things, that doesn't cause your fear. Fears aren't that reasonable.

This fear leads to avoidance of closeness. Your tender feelings frighten you because they may lead to closeness. When you get close to others and share your feelings, the threat of social exposure grows. The result: The expression of tenderness and love by others as well as the expression of your own tender feelings may trigger the fear reaction and avoidance pattern.

5. *Fear of negative feelings.* Within this category fall a whole series of fears that can influence your whole life-style. Most important, it includes the fears of *anger* and *criticism.* You may fear expressing anger or criticism or having either directed against you. Your fear can be general or specific, involving authorities, members of the opposite sex, people to whom you are close. Says one sixty-year-old woman, "I've always

been so terrified of criticism that I've never done a thing with my life."

6. *Fear of doing things alone.* This fear is often associated with loneliness and depression. Usually it takes the form of a mild feeling of discomfort rather than intense feeling. For example, on a weekend afternoon you'd like to go to a movie or take a walk. But no one is available to go with you and you feel uncomfortable at the idea of going by yourself. Often you don't know what you're uncomfortable about, but you give in to the discomfort feeling. Rather than do something alone, you stay home. If you're depressed, staying home will make you more depressed. If you're lonesome, it will not increase your chances of meeting someone new.

In this fear area, if you start a new pattern of doing things alone and keep at it for a period of time, dramatic results often occur. Many people can't or won't do that. Instead they remain housebound with the thought, "Someone may see me alone and think I'm unpopular."

7. *Fear of not getting along with others.* This includes such fears as the *fear of being ignored* and the *fear of a lull in the conversation.* With the latter you get such a panic reaction that you actually may blurt out something completely inappropriate or start to avoid any conversational participation. There are many more such specific fears. However, within this category five fears merit special attention because they are so common and destructive.

•*Fear of not being liked.* This is the most common interpersonal phobia and the most destructive. Often when people dislike you, you respond with guilt, reasoning. "I did something wrong. There must be something wrong with me or they wouldn't dislike me." To avoid this situation, you become the patsy, the "always nice person." You do everything you can to keep people liking you, in the process often betraying yourself by suppressing your needs, not standing up for your rights and sacrificing your dignity. Closely allied and producing similar consequences is the fear of *inadvertently hurting others*. Any self-expression, any standing up for yourself does carry a risk that the other person may react with hurt. So you never stand up for your rights.

With both fears you shift your goals. You cease to act in terms of your own objectives and self-respect; you substitute the goal "to avoid being disliked"—one that is most difficult to achieve. Remember, you don't represent the center of another person's universe. He/she does not respond solely in terms of what you may say and do. He has his own needs, feelings, hang-ups, pressures. He may have just won a big, unexpected raise and he loves the world, including you—regardless of what you do or say. Or he may just have been unjustly fired and he hates the whole world, including you—regardless of what you do or say.

•*Fear of looking foolish.* The very thought of doing something that *others* may deem ridiculous fills you with fear. Concomitantly you can fear doing something *you* think foolish (most often you are a far more severe judge of this than your friends would be). Because anything you may say or do carries the risk of looking foolish to someone, you avoid doing more and more and your inhibitions build up. Because areas of spontaneity and creativity are far too dangerous for you, you stick to areas that are trite, stuffy and conventional—and thus turn yourself into a dull, boring person.

Closely linked to the above phobia is the *fear of being wrong,* which follows a similar pattern and produces similar consequences, though usually not as devastating. No one of us would deliberately choose to look foolish or wrong, but most of us will risk it and retain our spontaneity. The problem is when the fears take over.

•*Fear of rejection.* This fear does more than keep you from reaching out to other people. Like the fear of being disliked, it often causes you to placate people at the expense of your own goals and self-respect. It sensitizes you to the other person. Any fleeting facial expression or dissatisfaction signals potential rejection. You interpret any disagreement or disappointment with another person as rejection. Every rejection represents an overwhelming catastrophe and you can't cope with it.

Caution: Although social fears may be rather subtle and disguised to begin with, they can become even more so. This happens when they lead to *hypervigilant* and *counterphobic repetition* behavior. I repeat, with hypervigilance, you're so sensitized in the fear area that you see threats when they don't really exist—for example, you think your friend has criticized you when she has merely made a general comment. With counterphobic repetition, you keep putting yourself in the situation you fear and always set yourself up to fail— for instance, you're really frightened of "castrating" women, but you always get involved with one, and the relationship always goes wrong. Each of these behaviors can have a tremendous impact on your life-style, without your being aware that any specific fear is involved. Check yourself for these two behaviors.

EXERCISE IN
PINPOINTING YOUR SOCIAL FEARS

Aim: To see if specific fears produce your social problems.

STEP ONE: List several main areas of social difficulty. These may be difficulties in specific situations (parties, personal conversations), in performing specific acts (starting conversations, asking for a date) or in achieving specific goals (having close friends). You may do certain things but not like the way you do them or the way you feel while doing them. Or the list can include things you avoid doing.

STEP TWO: In each situation, try to figure out "What am I afraid of?" It may be one of the common social fears we've listed or one that for you has more significance. As an aid, check the Uptight Inventories in chapter 2.

STEP THREE: For each fear, answer the following questions in your FCT workbook.

1. Do you recall when you first became aware of having this fear?

2. Do you have any idea of how you might have learned that fear?

3. In the past has the fear led you to avoid or escape from certain situations to your own detriment?

4. Do you know anyone with a similar fear? How has it affected him/her?

5. In which of these situations would your fear tend to be more active?

   •personal_____impersonal_____
   •with same sex_____with opposite sex_____
   •in superficial relationship_____in close relationship_____
   •with authority_____with subordinate_____
   •in feeling situation_____in nonfeeling situation_____
   •one-to-one_____group_____

6. Before doing this exercise, had you been aware of this specific fear and how it influences you? If you were aware, what things did you try to do to conquer it?

STEP FOUR: Take what you believe to be your most important interpersonal fear. This may be one that goes through several social situations (for example, making a social overture to someone, inviting a member of the opposite sex to a party, and giving a party may all center around the fear of rejection). The fear you select should be the one that makes you feel "That's *me!*"

This is the interpersonal fear you want to work on. If two fears seem roughly to be of equal importance, choose the one where you'll have the greatest opportunity to practice overcoming it.

A BEHAVIORAL PLAN TO CHANGE YOUR SOCIAL FEARS

Correct Your False Beliefs

Many of your social fears come about because you do not properly understand the realities of social situations and interactions. In the course of growing up, you have acquired beliefs about the social world around you that are at least partially wrong and irrational. These incorrect ideas cause you to misinterpret what other people do and say and this distortion sets off your own fears and anxieties. Some common false beliefs:

•"If only I do the right thing, people will like me and be nice to me." Conversely, you think, "If people are not nice to me, I have done something wrong." With this false belief, you take a lifelong guilt trip. This kind of egocentric thinking puts you in the center of the universe. While it is true that most people do react to what you do, they exist independently of you and do not center their lives around you.

For instance, Jean had been quite friendly with the wife of an editor at a publishing house. Suddenly all contact stopped. She phoned. There were promises of "We must get together" but no return call or set date. Jean agonized, "I have done something wrong." From this false premise, she developed a whole series of logical-to-her beliefs: "He doesn't like me as an author" ... "He has forbidden her to get in touch with me" ... "He feels guilty because his firm spent so little money promoting my book." This led her to the erroneous conclusion "They don't want to be friends." Recently Jean discovered that the man had been walking a professional tightrope for months which culminated in his getting fired. He and his wife had been thinking about the mortgage payments and two children they had to put through college, not social engagements with Jean.

•"If I were a normal person, I wouldn't get so uptight in social situations." You make false assumptions: (1) You think other people know when you feel anxious or fearful, but in actuality, you can have these symptoms without showing any outward signs; (2) you look at other people, do not see any actual signs of tension, and conclude they feel perfectly comfortable; (3) you take it a step further and believe you *should* feel comfortable, and because you don't, something must be wrong with you. You are not "normal." However, in many situations—like going into a room filled with strangers—anxiety is a "normal" reaction.

•"The way my life is now is the way it always will be." You believe that if you get hurt, the hurt is forever. Hurt may leave scars, but the feeling passes and after a while you are stronger for it. It is the myth that things are "forever" that weakens you, keeps you from risking and results in a static life.

•There are many others: "If I'm not on top, I'm nothing" . . . "My value as a person depends on what others think of me" . . . "It's wonderful to be popular and famous; it's terrible to be unpopular and mediocre" . . . "In order to be happy, I have to be successful in whatever I undertake" . . . "Everybody must love me."

Recognizing your false beliefs is not enough. You have to do something about them.

•*Read.* Reading serves as a major way to change your inadequate understanding of the social world. Many excellent books exist. Some cover general social behaviors, others other specific areas like remarriage or adjustment after divorce or death. Ask your librarian for assistance.

You might try *I Can If I Want To,* by Arnold A. Lazarus and Allen Fay; *Conditioned Reflex Therapy,* by Andrew Salter; *How to Be an Assertive (Not Aggressive) Woman in Life, in Love, and on the Job,* by Jean Baer; *Don't Say Yes When You Want to Say No,* by Herbert Fensterheim and Jean Baer; *A Guide to Rational Living,* by Albert Ellis and Robert A. Harper.

•*Bring your irrational beliefs out into the open and actively work to change them.* Dr. Albert Ellis, a New York psychologist who is director of the Institute for Advanced Study in Rational Psychotherapy, has a method called Rational-Emotive Therapy in which he uses an A-B-C-D approach to changing personality.

A is the *activating* event that sets off your disturbance. It can take the form of going to a party, someone criticizing you, etc.

C is the *consequence* of the disturbance (you feel upset, depressed, dissatisfied with yourself).

B is the *belief system* that comes between the activating event and the consequence. This is the part that gives the meaning to the activating event and grants it power to set off a bad reaction. The belief system has two parts:

rB—*rational beliefs:* These are the beliefs that correctly mirror the actual reality of the situation ("If she turns down a date with me, I will be terribly disappointed. I hope it doesn't happen"). Such a rational belief allows you to see the situation in perspective and to make a choice of whether or not you are willing to take the risk of asking for that date.

iB—*irrational beliefs:* These incorrect beliefs turn a benign or at most uncomfortable situation into a terrifying one in which your survival or integrity as a person is at stake ("If she turns down a date with me, it really means that I am no good as a person and I will never be able to find a partner with whom I can be happy"). When you fuse this meaning onto the person's response of "I'm so sorry but I'm busy this weekend," your social fear of rejection grows.

D is *disputation.* You must dispute and challenge your irrational beliefs with both logic and action. Only in this way can you replace them with more rational understanding.

CASE

Susan E., a successful businesswoman, consulted me just after her thirtieth birthday because she wanted "a good relationship that might lead to marriage." Despite her many dates, she felt lonely and frequently depressed. She had a history of brief, intimate relationships. Her difficulties seemed to revolve around the fear of "being found out." Her family had had the tenet: The more people find out about you, the more they have to use against you. Thus Susan had the irrational belief that, at best, self-revelation could result only in contempt and, at worst, in being badly hurt. We decided to use the A-B-C-D technique.

Activating event: Out on a sixth date with a man she really liked, Susan listened to him speak very freely about his career plans and certain emotional problems with his parents. She wanted to speak equally candidly, but didn't. Instead, she told "charming anecdotes."

Consequence: Susan told me, "After the evening I felt very empty and that he was disappointed in me." He apparently was. He called only once after that and did not ask her out again. Susan lost the chance of developing a good relationship.

Once Susan saw the sad consequence of her *irrational belief* ("Anything I say can be used against me"), she *disputed* it by substituting a series of *rational beliefs:* "You can never be loved for what you are if you never let others see what you really are" . . . "True closeness is not possible if you don't let others 'find out' about you" . . . "While some people may use what you say against you, such people are few and many times, not always, you can spot them in advance of true involvement. In any event you must take the risk of self-revelation. You cannot give up your chance at love because of fear."

To help Susan see the reality of what happened when she let people "find out" about her, I gave her two action assignments.

1. To keep a tally of each time she deliberately avoided telling something personal about herself. In her Fear Control Training workbook, she was to note how she felt in that situation and immediately afterward.

2. To dredge up memories involving various meaningful reactions and experiences in her life and, one by one, tell them to different selected people. Again, she was to note in her FCT workbook how she felt as she told them and immediately afterward.

Susan soon saw for herself that the more she held back, the worse she felt and that the more she let people "find out," the better she felt. Now, on a date, if she has the urge to say something revealing, she can do it despite some small remaining twinges of anxiety. More and more she can make the statements spontaneously without giving a second thought to what she is doing. Thus she has overcome a lifetime pattern.

Use the case of Susan as a model for working out your own A-B-C-D plan. It may help if you keep in mind what the Roman philosopher Epictetus wrote in 500 B.C.: "What disturbs men's minds is not events but their judgment on events."

Directly Reduce Your Fears

Once you have identified your fears and the events that trigger them, you can decrease them with the same FCT methods you use for other things. Systematic Desensitization can be as effective with social fears as with the fear of "things." As I detailed in chapter 4, you approach the frightening situation gradually, a step at a time. At each step you counter the disturbance with relaxation until you feel no anxiety. Then, and only then, do you go on to the next step.

You can carry out this procedure in reality or imagery. However, reality desensitization can prove difficult. Social situations change. They are not predictable. You can't do the equivalent of going up to the third floor over and over until you feel comfortable.

Instead you utilize a *simulated reality desensitization*.

•As most of your social fears involve other people (what you may say to them or they to you), you will need a cooperative partner.

•Prepare a graded series of disturbing statements in your problem area (that's your hierarchy).

•Your chosen partner says the first statement to you. You deliberately relax. The partner repeats the statement until it sets off no disturbance. In this way you go through all the statements.

CASE

Philip W. came to me with a marital problem. He believed the fault lay entirely with him. At home he was moody, sullen and had occasional anger outbursts. He feared that if he spoke up and told what he really liked and disliked, his wife would become angry with him. His resentments had built up, bringing on the moodiness. Further discussion showed he had a general fear of women (not men) becoming angry with him.

We worked out this hierarchy:

•Woman says with mild annoyance, "I'm really annoyed at what you have done."

•Woman says with anger in voice, "How could you be so stupid?"

•With more anger and louder tone of voice, woman says, "You damned stupid moron. I don't see how you can live with yourself."

•Yelling and screaming, woman says, "You are the most uninformed person I've ever met. I don't want anything to do with you ever again. You are an idiot."

As a partner Philip chose a female cousin he trusted and with whom he felt very comfortable. As she said the first phrase, Philip had a strong anxiety reaction. He felt guilty and depressed. Then he relaxed. With repetition of the scene, his reaction changed to one of sharp anger. With continued desensitization the anger disappeared. When he completed the simulated reality desensitization, Philip had learned something about himself: It wasn't a fear of a woman's being angry at him that so paralyzed him but that of his expressing anger to a woman. His occasional uncontrolled anger outbursts had just strengthened that fear.

Realizing this, he and his cousin *reversed* roles. *He* would make the angry statements, relaxing after each one until he felt no inappropriate anxiety.

Next step: He carried out the simulated reality desensitization with his wife. First she played the angry woman; then they reversed roles and he played the angry man. Suddenly Philip noticed his moodiness was gone and that his marriage had markedly improved. For the first time he was able to express what was on his mind. Concomitantly there was an interesting side effect. His cousin, who had never felt she had problems in the anger area, reported to Philip that she felt more freedom in her own marital relationship and "more life in the marriage."

You can do this same sort of simulated reality desensitization if you have the fear of other people seeing that you are nervous.

• With your partner you simulate various degrees of nervousness: very minor hand trembling, rather obvious hand trembling, hand trembling so obvious the other person can't miss it, hand trembling so obvious that you can barely hold the glass, your hand trembles so that you drop the glass. With each situation, you simulate the nervous symptom and the partner notices. At that point you stop the scene, determine your Fear Thermometer rating, and relax. You do this until you have mastered all the scenes.

• You simulate a mild to moderate amount of trembling and have a graded series of phrases your partner might say. For example: "Is anything wrong?" . . . "Hey, your hand is shaking" . . . "Are you really that nervous?" . . . "Hey, you're terribly nervous" . . . "You ought to see a doctor" . . . (*looking at you with digust*) "Hey, you're really a kook." After each statement determine your Fear Thermometer rating, relax and repeat until you master your fear reaction.

In many cases, you may have to use imagery to desensitize yourself to social fears. As social situations tend to be complicated, you may need many scenes and *several hierarchies* concerning the same fear. For example, one twenty-seven-year-old man was terrified of being looked at. We used three hierarchies, starting with situations in public places (his fear was least there), working up to social situations and finally to the job area (his highest fear of being looked at).

As a result of imagery desensitization, you may get more than an immediate lowering of disturbance. You may find you get other new constructive feelings and more flexible responses as you lose your fear.

CASE

Carol J., a twenty-five-year-old grade school teacher, came to me because of her problems with men. She had a paralyzing fear of rejection. The core of her fear: that she might be rejected for another woman and that it would be worse if the woman were a personal friend of hers. Carol had no trouble calling a man she liked for a date. However, when she thought any chance of rejection existed, she couldn't call. To me she said simply, "I know something is wrong."

We worked out the following imagery hierarchy.

•Bob, a classmate, mentions he has asked her girl-friend Anne for a date.

•Steve, a guy she has dated a number of times, says he's so caught up in work that he can't chat on the phone that night. Carol had called him.

•Steve tells her he has a lot of work over the weekend and can't see her.

•She sees a guy she dated a few times several months ago walking down the street with a girl.

•She's in a restaurant with a casual date and he mentions how attractive a woman at a nearby table is.

•Steve hasn't called for a week.

•A female friend says she saw Steve having coffee with Anne.

•Steve says he'd like to be friends with her, but that's as far as the relationship can go.

•After a fight Steve storms out of her apartment, slamming the door loudly behind him.

•Stuart, another guy she has dated several times, takes her to a party but spends all evening talking to another woman.

•Stuart tells her he has decided to go steady with another woman.

•Steve tells her he has a girlfriend she doesn't know and is moving in with her.

•Steve tells her he is engaged to Anne.

We were making good progress with the fantasy desensitization when Carol related the following incident to me. The week before, she had met a new man at a local tavern. They exchanged phone numbers (she asked him for his). After waiting several days for him to call, she phoned him on a Wednesday evening. He wasn't in and she left a message that he should call her. He didn't. On Friday she phoned him again. This time she got him and they had a pleasant conversation. During it, Carol mentioned that she'd be at the tavern that evening. Henry said he'd join her. Carol got there at 9:00 P.M. Henry didn't arrive until 12:30 A.M.

In this incident there are a number of points that could be interpreted as rejection. Once Carol would have sulked when Henry didn't return her call, gone on an eating binge, gone into a blue funk at the tavern when he didn't appear and either have left or rejected him when he did arrive. Instead she felt disappointed when he didn't call but managed to call him again. At the restaurant she had a good time with her friends, and when Henry showed up, they had a good talk and went on to a coffee house. He made a date. The next day she felt proud of herself. Subsequently, she said to me, "That's the kind of person I want to be. If only I can keep it up."

Get Out in the Arena

1. *Set constructive goals.* Be task oriented. Concentrate on *how* to ask someone to dance rather than the false goal of how to keep from being nervous at the party. Here are some principles:

•Write down your goals in forthcoming social interactions. Your goal is the thing you want to make happen. It should be specific, positive and something you can reasonably expect yourself to do. For example, you fear rejection and you want to call an acquaintance you haven't spoken to for months. Your goals could be: (a) to talk in an interesting way about what you have been doing; (b) to encourage the other person to do the same; (c) to end up with an appointment to meet for a drink after work. Concentrate on these goals and figure out what you have to do to achieve them. Although this task orientation will lower the fear, it is the introduction of specific goals that combats the pervasive masking effect of your fear.

•Concentrate on your actions, not your feelings. Dwelling on your feelings will lead to paralysis and make your task more difficult and, if you make the phone call at all, lead to a less satisfying conversation. Emphasis on feelings will make the fear worse.

•Concentrate on what you do, not on what the other person may do. Of course, you take the other person into consideration, but your primary goal is not to change him/her. This is an area of minimal control.

You can never have a guarantee that he won't become angry, reject you, ignore you. You want to figure out what, if he does these things, *you* can do to move you toward your constructive goal and help you maintain your self-respect.

•Have a goal ready in case "the worst does happen." Think about it in advance. If that acquaintance really rejects you, what can your goal become? If you formulate each goal, you will feel less helpless in anticipation of the dreaded event and less paralyzed should it actually occur.

To help you get the feel for setting goals, take the following brief quiz. The exercise assumes there is a fear of criticism—the very thing that frightens you. Determine the constructive goal for each situation before you look at the answers.

CRITICISM QUIZ

SITUATION ONE: Your child's teacher asks you in for a conference and tells you that you create too much tension in getting seven-year-old Jimmy ready for school. He often arrives in tears.

SITUATION TWO: Your spouse tells you, "Sex with you is getting boring. You're just not adventurous enough. Maybe you ought to go into psychotherapy to loosen up."

SITUATION THREE: A close friend says, "There's something I feel I should tell you. Do you realize you constantly interrupt other people and it becomes very annoying."

Here are the answers. *Note:* You may come up with better or different responses but these should give you a frame of reference.

SITUATION ONE: The teacher.

Your goal: To help your child. To do this, you need more information.

What you might say: "He wasn't that way last year. Can you tell me why you think the cause lies in the home situation?" With this answer you give the teacher a chance to clarify her meaning and offer her suggestions.

Fear traps to avoid: Don't blame yourself ("He takes after me; we're both nervous types") and don't hit out at the teacher ("You have no right to tell me how to bring up my child").

SITUATION TWO: Your spouse criticizes your sex life.

Your goal: To establish that the problem concerns two people, not just you, and to think of a constructive action.

What you might say: "Yes, we have a problem there. What do you think we can do about it?"

Fear traps to avoid: Taking full responsibility ("It's all my fault") and nonproductive personality attack ("It's all your fault. You're still in love with your mother").

SITUATION THREE: The friend who tells you that you always interrupt others.

Your goal: To recognize that the friend means well and that often the most appropriate reaction to criticism is to think about it and do something about it.

What you might say: "Thank you for telling me. I never thought about it before. I'll keep my eye on it."

Fear traps to avoid: Defensiveness ("I'm just trying to make the conversation more lively") and counterattack ("At least I talk. You never open your mouth").

2. *Stop avoiding.* As with other fears, often the destructive consequences of your social fears stem from

the avoidance to which they lead, rather than the fear itself.

You avoid "offending" people, so you let yourself be exploited.

You avoid rejection by refusing to make social overtures and you end up Alice/Adam sitting by your own fire.

You avoid people looking at you by not participating in conversation. You settle for being a dull and uninteresting person.

Many times you don't even realize your avoidance pattern. You're too busy with rationalizations like "I feel tired" . . . "There are too many things I have to do." You may not even find out what the fear is until you stop avoiding and make yourself do things.

CASE

John E., a Philadelphia engineer, had few friends. He realized this was because he was a "poor conversationalist." Aware that he managed to avoid almost all conversations, he attributed this to a lack of social skills rather than a fear.

We set up a program. John's first assignment: to have lunch every day with a group of co-workers, something he had avoided because of his lack of small talk expertise. John discovered that as long as he wasn't the subject of it he could carry on a conversation. He became anxious and fearful when the talk turned to him. Then he himself identified the underlying fear: "If I talk about myself, other people will think I'm arrogant." He had never known he had this fear of being thought arrogant. Looking back, he realized the tremendous effect it had had on his life. For instance, he had refused to be president of the college math club. In the present his girlfriend always accused him of being "a cold, distant person" because he never spoke of himself.

As long as you keep avoiding, you cannot get rid of

fear or anxiety in the situations that frighten you. Fear assignments serve as a good way to conquer your avoidance and get yourself into the fear situation.

EXERCISE IN
FEAR ASSIGNMENTS

Aim: To deliberately expose yourself to fear situations you have been avoiding.

STEP ONE: Pick the fear you're going to work on.

STEP TWO: List situations in this area you have been avoiding. You might ask yourself some key questions. For example, if you fear rejection: Have you been avoiding any particular type of person: male, female, older, younger, bright, successful? At a party do you avoid certain types? Do you avoid asking certain people for dates?

STEP THREE: Consider each situation on your list as a fear assignment. Arrange them in the order you will do them. To do this, you probably will have to compromise between the difficulty of the task and your opportunities for performing it. It may be easiest to ask Barbara for a date. However, she's traveling in Europe and won't return for two months. To ask Margie is more difficult, but she is here. So, as your first assignment you ask Margie.

STEP FOUR: Do it. Note that the instruction is not to do it comfortably or without anxiety. The *instruction is do it.* Here are two sets of fear assignments carried out by patients:

Fear of Conversation
    •Say "good morning" and "good evening" to fellow residents of your apartment building.

•Without expecting a response, make comments to the person sitting next to you on the bus, on line at the movie, next to you at the concert. Your remarks can be simple: "Won't that bus ever come?" . . . "I hear it's a good film" . . . "I loved the sonata."

•Get in touch with a close friend you haven't seen for a long time.

•Go to a beach, swimming pool, exercise class. Converse with two or three strangers.

•Invite someone out to lunch—someone you have not eaten with before.

•Invite a long-lost friend over for a drink.

•Tell a close friend something meaningful about yourself that you've never told anyone before.

Fear of Doing Things Alone

•Take a walk through the park alone.

•Go to a movie alone.

•Go to a museum alone.

•Eat in a good restaurant alone.

•Take a weekend trip alone. (This patient visited a nearby city where she had never been and had a very good time sight-seeing.)

•Take a vacation alone.

No matter how good your intentions, you may not be able to bring yourself to carry out your fear assignments. If this is your problem, try the FCT Covert Reinforcement exercise, developed by Dr. Joseph R. Cautela, professor of psychology at Boston College and a past president of the Association for Advancement of Behavior Therapy. This technique uses imagery to reduce the avoidance. The principle behind increasing a given behavior is to reward the behavior you want to increase. In Covert Reinforcement, you take the behavior you want to accomplish; you imagine doing that act; you reinforce your performance of that act through *imagery*. It works like this.

EXERCISE IN
COVERT REINFORCEMENT

Aim: To reduce social avoidance through practicing and reinforcing doing what you want to do in imagery.

STEP ONE: Take the fear assignment that is giving you difficulty and the acts you have to perform in that situation.

STEP TWO: Break down the act into small parts. For instance, your major fear is being alone. You want to be able to handle one activity, like going to the local museum by yourself. The various acts involved:
   •At home putting on your coat.
   •Getting on the bus and going downtown by yourself.
   •Purchasing your ticket.
   •Looking at a painting in one of the galleries.
   •Sitting in the museum cafeteria and having coffee by yourself.
   •Staying at the museum for one hour looking at the pictures.
   •Sitting on a bench by yourself, resting.
   •Leaving the museum.
   •Going home on the bus.

STEP THREE: Select a reinforcer. You can use anything that evokes a feeling of pleasure when you imagine it. It does not have to possess any connection with the act you are trying to reinforce. It can be the image of swimming in the Pacific, eating a caloric parfait, hearing people say "You're wonderful," or winning the Pulitzer Prize. What works for one person doesn't necessarily work for another. As long as your reinforcer gives *you* a good feeling, use it.

STEP FOUR: Read the first item on your list and imagine it. When your image is clear, say to yourself "Reinforce," and immediately switch to your reinforcing image. Do this ten times and go on to the next item. Do the exercise daily until you can perform the behavior in actual life. If you do this ten times a day, seven days a week, this will give you seventy conditioning trials a week, three hundred a month. Before the conditioning works, it may take hundreds of trials. Don't expect magic and don't get discouraged.

STEP FIVE: When you have the opportunity, perform the act step by step just as you did in your imagination. In the life situation you can even use your reinforcing image. For example, you're at the museum looking at a Renoir. Do not let one of those "Someone I know will see me alone and think I'm unpopular" thoughts enter your head. Instead, continue to look at the painting, say "Reinforce" to yourself, and conjure up your pleasurable image.

STEP SIX: When you find this method decreases the avoidance with one behavior, select another and repeat the process.

3. *Program yourself for success:* Sometimes your fears are derivative. You simply don't have the skills to do what you want to do socially. My wife has confessed to me that until she was twenty-five she never attended a cocktail party without thinking "I'll die" and that often she bolted before entering the door. She never gave a dinner party until she was thirty. Today, she is an accomplished hostess and likes cocktail parties the way dieters like cake. Better than any therapist, she can give you some social skills training.

THE CONFIDENCE GAME

By Jean Baer

If someone were to say to me on a Saturday morning, "You must have twenty people for dinner tonight," I could do it. If I were to go to a cocktail party where everyone ignores me, I can make myself go up to a stranger and say, "Hello, my name is . . ." The reason: *I'm a thief.* I steal ideas that work for others and test them in my own life. The following is my Plagiarist's Guide to Social Security.

a. *Develop your conversational ability:* Talk, whether monologue, tête-à-tête, or group, takes effort and practice.

•*Prepare for conversation:* Develop small-talk know-how in just the way you perfect your skill at bridge.

•Read magazines and books so that you know what's going on in the world and can discuss it. With knowledge to back you up, you'll find it easier to say "I think." I guarantee that you can get through almost any awkward social situation by paraphrasing what Russell Baker wrote last Sunday in the *New York Times.* I collect small-talk items. For instance, recently *Town and Country* ran a story about the upper crust of Paris. The article revealed that "The ninety-two-year-old Duc de Lévis Mirepoix traces his lineage back to the family of the Virgin Mary. Indeed, he is still said to begin his prayers, 'Dear Cousin.' " I wrote the item down. Several evenings later, we were out with a couple when there was one of those ghastly lulls. I told the little story. Everyone roared and the evening got back on the right track.

    •Learn to draw the other person out: You do this not by asking offensive personal questions ("How much did you pay for that dress?") but with talk that will enable the other person to show something of himself/herself. Try lines like "The last time I saw you you were reading＿＿＿＿＿. Did you like it?" or "I'm not sure I agree with President Carter's policy on ＿＿＿＿＿. What do you think?"

    •Use self-disclosure: You don't have to tell the world about your nervous breakdown but you can make statements that reveal something about yourself: "I always feel a little shy at big parties" . . . "I just got a divorce and I'm sort of out of practice socially."

    •Prepare some good anecdotes: Rehearse them aloud at home. Watch yourself in the mirror as you tell them. Do you wave your hands too much? Can you cut your story and still make it interesting? I have two I use for conversational emergencies. One concerns the time fifty naked men serenaded me in Samarkand, the other my family cemetery in Belleville, Illinois. You'd be amazed at the number of cues that enable me to tell my cemetery story: the words *family, relatives, asparagus* (it's in the middle of an asparagus field), *Wuthering Heights* (it looks just like the scene where Merle Oberon runs around screaming "Heathcliff"), *expense, duty,* etc.

    Caution: Don't tell stories that don't interest most people. I come from a newspaper background. Most of my relatives went through life worrying about the coverage they'd get in the *Times* when they died. I have a wonderful story about my father's deathbed request: "Jean, don't let me go with three inches. Get me some space." I used to tell it all the time until I noticed it made most people uncomfortable. Now I confine the telling of it to newspersons who will identify with it and enjoy it.

    •*Learn to initiate conversation:* Don't be the intruder; stay away from two people deep in talk. Try to join one person or a group. Try to make some kind of statement that calls attention to you and through which the others will view you as part of the group and its ongoing conversation. For instance, they're talking about skiing in Switzerland. Grab your chance with "That reminds me of what happened at Vail"—and off you go. For big mixers have a couple of lines ready: "What a great shirt . . . tie . . . dress! Where did you get it?" . . . "Such a huge crowd. How does the hostess manage all the work?" . . . "Are you a good friend of the host? I work with him."

•*Learn to end a conversation:* Some good basic sentences: "The hostess is finally alone; let's go talk to her" . . . "I hear them talking about the mayoralty race over there; let's join them" . . . "Will you excuse me? A good friend has just come in and I'd like to say hello" . . . "I've enjoyed talking with you but I was asked to circulate. See you later." If you are bored, move elsewhere. Just wait till the other person pauses for breath and say, "That's really fascinating. I never knew that," and quickly follow up with "Let's join the Joneses." If you want to see the other person again, make sure he/she knows your name.

•*Learn to cope with put-downs:* In the course of interacting with others, you are bound to experience put-downs, whether others do them deliberately or inadvertently. Don't accept the put-down. You want to say something that will make you feel better about yourself—not something aimed at changing the other person. It helps if you have some lines ready for an emergency: "Boy, you sure are in a bad mood today" . . . "Was that a put-down?" . . . "Your own insecurity is showing. Are you upset about something?" You want to put it back on the other person. Above all, do not use the words *I, me* or *because* in the first sentence of your answer. Starting off with any of these makes you sound defensive immediately.

b. *Make a deliberate effort to expand your social*

life: You can meet people anywhere from apartment hunting and adult education classes to zoos (divorced fathers take their offspring to see lions and tigers on weekends). There is just one cardinal rule: know that you won't meet anyone by staying home.

•*Go places:* Pick activities you enjoy and follow through. Go to a coffee house. Attend cultural events. Play a musical instrument in a bar. Play games like bridge, chess, backgammon. Do group volunteer work like politics, fund raising, community projects. However, select your target groups with care. Go places where you have a special interest. If you're a tennis buff, spend your vacation at a tennis camp. If you're a lawyer, try a political club. Don't get into a group that really doesn't interest you; you won't be at your best.

•*Once in a group, try to be active:* You won't really be part of it unless you do. Pick the committee you'd like to be on and write a letter outlining your qualifications. This is what I did at the Overseas Press Club when I was a wallflower neophyte member. I wrote the head of the hospitality committee, and soon I was a hostess, feeling very secure as I went around passing trays of cheese. Having something to do made me less shy.

•*Renew your contacts:* Sometimes you let favorite people slip out of your life. Because I'm always on a deadline, I have a tendency to do this. Time passes and I think, "Oh, it has been so long. They've lost interest." What old friend would you like to see? Call him/her up and make a date.

c. *Recognize your rights and act on them:* You have the right to express your opinion, refuse a date, ask for things you want—like naming the restaurant you prefer, how you'd like to spend Sunday. You may know your rights but be afraid to voice them. Try expressing it to another person. The very act may reduce the fear. For example, I was brought up to believe that women should take a back seat to men. This is still one of my core problems. After my husband and I wrote *Don't Say Yes When You Want to Say No,* I got a letter from the women's editor of a Texas newspaper requesting an interview with me. That night I said to Herb, "We wrote the book together. You're the authority. I don't have the right to have the interview. I'll tell her to talk to you." The minute I said it, I saw how ridiculous I was being. I had the interview alone.

    d. *Learn the technique of going to cocktail parties:*

    •*Get there on time:* Be the first arrival—or at least the second or third. The hostess will have time to introduce you and you'll have the chance to meet the nucleus of the party. Later you can mix with ease and you won't have the petrified sensation that comes when you walk into a party at its peak and the hostess says, "Here's a drink. Introduce yourself around and make yourself at home."

    •*Don't speak only to your peers:* Try to develop a social circle that includes older and younger people. At one party I met a charming couple, older than my parents, who have become close friends.

    •*Mind your manners:* Call the hostess the next day and thank her. Do *not* make a date for lunch with someone you met at the party and exclude the hostess.

    •*Follow through:* Try to pursue a friendship with someone you met at a party and liked.

    e. *Entertain:* If you don't ask people to your house, they won't ask you to theirs. Buy the party props (glasses, dishes, etc.) that make entertaining possible. Learn three basic recipes. People have been eating the same thing at my house for years—it's always *paella,* chicken with grapes or *poule au pot.* If you can't cook, you have alternatives. For instance, once I was scheduled to give a party for thirty people when my boss commanded me to accompany her to Philadelphia the day before the party. I nearly died but averted disaster by taking my copper casserole to the neighborhood Spanish restaurant and buying dinner. When guests said, "How did you ever do it?" I responded, "Oh, it was nothing."

Important rule: Use entertaining as a means of widening your social circle. In any group of guests I have one-quarter old friends that make me feel very comfortable, one-half acquaintances that I know fairly well, and one-quarter new people that I want to know better. Incidentally, asking someone to your house can be a lovely way to start a close friendship. Years ago I had met a woman I liked at other people's parties. Shy, I hesitated to make any social overture. Finally, when I was giving a big party, I asked her and her husband. They came. Because of that overture, the friendship flourished. Now she is not only my literary agent but closest friend.

f. *Learn to travel alone:* The very thought of doing this seems to intimidate many people who are ordinarily not fearful. Some tips:

•*Go where you want to go, not where the travel agent says you should:* Read. You'll get ideas from the Sunday New York *Times* travel section, *Signature* and *Travel and Leisure.* But don't pick a resort on the basis of two-year-old information; the place may have become a tourist trap.

•*Before departure, try to get letters of introduction:* Better still, have your friend write her friend that you are coming and when. If it's a choice between Paris and Peru and you have introductions in Peru and none in Paris, go to Peru.

•*Use your work:* Does your company have an overseas office? One woman, who is personnel director for a major Ivy League university, planned a trip to England. She wrote seven personnel directors at British universities, asking to meet with them. All responded with invitations for lunch and tea.

•*Investigate what the various national tourist organizations have to offer:* Most have programs like "Meet the Dutch." When you're abroad, stop in at the tourist office and see what "meeting people" programs it provides.

•*If you're not twenty-one and gorgeous, stay at a*

big hotel: Frequent the major meeting-people places—restaurants, pool, bar and lobby. I met two people who have become close friends in the lobby of the Bristol Hotel in Paris.

•*Do things:* Staying in your hotel room and feeling lonely won't get you anything but the dubious pleasure of your own company. Go places. Take a day bus trip. Buy a ticket to Glyndebourne and ride there and back on the train. Go to the opera. Remember, you can be different on a trip. It's easier to be open and friendly without all your old friends around to watch you in operation.

•*Try to go to one offbeat place:* Hit the major capitals, if that's your wish, but do go to just one place that is "peculiar." All my best travel adventures have been when I did something like sailing down the Amazon and going to Samarkand. You know you're among kindred souls. Who else would be there?

In all these specifics, there's a core: You will respect yourself more if you try. One friend said to me, "I'm doing all these things and I'm still afraid of rejection. What good is it all?"

I answered her, "What you learn is to go out and get rejected and find it isn't so bad after all."

MOVING TOWARD CLOSENESS

When you move toward closeness, new social fears emerge. You become more exposed and vulnerable. When you love, you risk hurt. If you don't care, you won't get hurt as much. Yet most people crave closeness. Without it, they don't feel fulfilled.

Several fears may impede your progress toward closeness.

•*The fear of not having a close relationship.* With this you jump into a relationship so quickly that you don't give it a chance to develop. Because of your sense of urgency, need, and fear, you turn it into a fantasy relationship. You ignore the real characteristics of the other person, make yourself insensitive to his/her shortcomings, select someone who is bound to hurt and betray you. You end up battered and bruised.

•*The overall fear of hurting the other person.* Because of this, you treat him/her like a fragile piece of china. You can't say what you really think, share certain important feelings. You create an emotional wall between you, thus turning what might have been a good relationship into a bad one.

•*The fear of responsibility.* Closeness means certain limits; for instance, you can't date every man or woman you meet. Also you have the responsibility of helping the other through difficult periods, of facing impending marriage. Some people can't take these on; they consider them burdens and restraints.

•*The fear of being exploited.* You willingly do things for the other person and then start to feel he/she will exploit you. You become hypervigilant and see manipulation and "being used" where none exists.

If you want to move toward closeness, be alert for three danger signals:

1. *When you latch on to a relationship that's going nowhere.* One woman went with a man for six years. She wanted to marry him. He very explicitly told her he didn't want marriage with her. She kept saying, "If I don't marry him, I'll be an old maid. I have to have him."

2. *When you inhibit yourself from saying things that are really important to you.* One woman was involved with a divorced man she rarely saw. She spent much of her time alone. Dissatisfied and knowing this lack of togetherness wasn't good for the relationship, she made one or two tentative attempts to talk about it. He brushed them aside. She gave up trying to discuss it with him. The relationship went on for a while but eventually ended, leaving hurt on both sides.

3. *When you find yourself doing things that make you lose your self-respect.* Roger was going with a girl

who worked near him. She insisted on meeting him every night after work and then going out. Previously, Roger had had the pattern of meeting friends or colleagues for a drink. When he talked to Joan about this, she answered, "If you really loved me, you'd be eager to see me at every opportunity." So Roger continued to meet her, in the process losing all self-respect. If a relationship entails losing your self-respect, it cannot develop into a good one.

When these or other danger signals become apparent to you, you must figure out the fears that underlie them and deliberately try to overcome them.

Emerson made two comments that seem to apply to the area of social fears:

• "He has not learned the lesson of life who does not every day surmount a fear."

• "We must be our own before we can be another's."

CHAPTER 7

GETTING CLOSER—
STAYING CLOSER

People seek closeness. They need to be close to someone else. Without closeness you feel incomplete, that something is missing from your life. Yet the pattern of fear, sometimes known to its victim and sometimes not, keeps far too many people from achieving this closeness so important to all of us.

WHAT CLOSENESS MEANS

By closeness we mean the sharing of being, the understanding of another person and being understood by him/her. In the ideal close relationship there is a sharing of feelings, not in the sense that you know what your partner feels but that you intuitively and directly experience what he/she feels as part of your own self. This experience of your partner's joy or sadness is the same as the experience of a heaviness in your own arm; it is not all of you but is a definite part of your own self. When you can achieve this partial merging with another, you transcend your own boundaries. Concomitantly, you experience a heightened fulfillment of yourself as an individual. You do not need to hide behind an emotional curtain. You can release your inhibitions and truly and fully show yourself and be yourself. You are more you than ever, and yet you are more than you.

THE DIFFERENT KINDS OF CLOSENESS

Many kinds of closeness exist.

Limited Closeness

The limits can be set for you by outside forces such as the situation itself or the time involved. Or, because of your internal needs, you can set your own limits.

1. *The situation-limited close relationship.* A shared experience can form a basis for the attainment of closeness. For example, when you travel in a group, you achieve closeness in the sharing of the trip adventures. The more intense the experience, the greater the closeness. Soldiers in combat experience great closeness with their "buddies." Even hijackers and hostages gain an empathic closeness—a fact well known to police hostage squads.

You also attain closeness with a co-worker where you share your feelings and thoughts to an intimate degree but where the person is only a peripheral part of your life. For example, an executive and his assistant tell each other things, share experiences, feelings, thoughts they would tell no one else. Often they do this after work over a drink or dinner. Sometimes the two people involved are of the opposite sex. Yet, contrary to popular impression, in a surprising proportion of such relationships, sex is not involved. Or, if it is, it is a by-product rather than the cause of the relationship.

2. *Time-limited closeness.* This frequently is the situation between lovers, particularly if one is married. Often it exists between friends. The time you spend together may be feelingful and rewarding, but then you go your own way. The relationship is not part of your major life thrust.

The patient-therapist relationship also serves as an

illustration of time-limited closeness. During the brief session, feelings may be intense and a deep empathy for each other may come about (when the patient experiences this empathy, it is called transference; when the therapist experiences it, it is called countertransference). Sadly, the patient and often the therapist as well may be incapable of experiencing such closeness in other life situations.

3. *The psychologically limited relationship.* Here you limit the situation to only part of yourself. Intellectual sharing typifies this. For example, as a graduate student I would talk psychology—fact, experiment, theory, speculation—with fellow students. There was no holding back, no fears of being thought foolish, stupid or ignorant. Instead there was complete openness and exposure of what we thought. From these discussions, we got a feeling of intellectual empathy, of warmth and closeness—but feeling was second because this sharing was limited primarily to the intellect.

4. *Pseudo-closeness.* There are people who recognize the need for closeness, but, because of fears and inhibitions, cannot achieve it. However, they fool themselves and convince themselves that they have this closeness. In actuality, little or none exists.

For example, one couple consulted me about their twenty-year-old son who was depressed and withdrawn and had become a college dropout. In discussion, they told me, "We were always a very close and happy family. Why, in all our years of marriage we haven't had a single fight—not even a cross word." As I talked more with them, I saw no closeness or any exchange of real and honest feelings, only words, platitudes, lies. They had trained their son to live that same way. However, he was stronger than they. Able to be more honest than they, he could not live the lie. So he became depressed. However, for him hope existed; for the parents, no hope.

The Closest Relationship

This does not involve these limitations of time or situation. It does involve the sharing of the trivialities of prosaic day-by-day living as well as more soul-sharing life experiences. It is not psychologically limited but has as a goal the complete sharing of every facet, every aspect of each other. Its aim is complete empathy and merging with each other. This kind of relationship rests on four basic feelings:

1. *Love.* This is first the feeling of loving and next the feeling of being loved. This is a background state, subtly changing but always there, even in moments of anger.

2. *Respect.* This is an essential acceptance of the individuality and dignity of your partner. It does not mean agreeing with or respecting everything the partner does, says, thinks or feels. It does mean giving the partner the right to faults and weaknesses as well as recognizing strengths and virtues. You encourage and facilitate your partner's growth as a person in his/her own right.

3. *Trust.* This is the mirror image of respect. Your partner may doubt you, disagree with you, dispute you. But you feel a basic trust that your partner accepts you as a person in your own right.

4. *Commitment.* With this, you accept the limitations the close relationship imposes upon you. You know that you are not always free to do what you want when you want. For the sake of increasing closeness, you willingly accept these limitations.

We all want this deep rich experience of the close relationship in which, through merging, the individuality of each partner becomes greater. The satisfaction comes in the striving to achieve it. And that's where tragedy enters in. In the course of living many of us learn things that make this striving even more difficult. Among these learnings are sets of fears that lead us in wrong directions and place obstacles in the paths of reaching out for whatever increasing closeness is possible.

HOW FEAR INTERFERES WITH THE DEVELOPMENT OF CLOSENESS

Because you form a unit in the close relationship, your fears can affect the entire style of your closeness.

•*Your fear can inhibit those four basic feelings on which closeness must rest: love, respect, trust and commitment.* For example, Ray M., a very bright man now in his early thirties, had been brought up in a highly disciplined, authoritarian home where his parents constantly repressed and restricted him. He grew up with a fear of accepting any limits imposed by others. Increasingly, Ray tended to avoid or rebel against any situation that imposed limits. In school, he was always behind in his studying, late with term papers. In his first jobs, he missed appointments or showed up late for them. Then Ray went into business for himself. Now, because no one on the outside set business limits for him, he became very successful. However, his personal life was not good. He would not get married because marriage meant limits. His fear of being restricted made any kind of commitment inconceivable.

•*You fear doing the things you have to do to attain these four basic feelings.* The fears can limit the experiences you share. More important, the fears can prevent the open communication of vital parts of your feelings and thoughts and so limit the attainment of closeness.

In the close relationship, far more than in social relationships, the interaction of uptightnesses and fears grows, spreads, ricochets back and forth. Your response to your own fears sets off fears and tensions in your partner. In turn, these strengthen your fears or trigger new sets of fears.

Often both of you, spurred on by different anxieties, play roles. Thus in the close relationship you:

•Say you feel things you don't feel.

•Pretend to be loving when you feel full of hostility.

•Counterfeit calm when you tremble with anxiety.

•Fight about the wrong things. You don't discuss, debate or fight about the real problems.

•Not only conceal yourself but take it for granted that your mate also conceals his/her inner feelings since you're so guilty yourself.

Thus you set up a joint spiral of increasing falseness, instead of a communion with another human being where feeling comes first, where you fulfill the other person's needs as if they were your own, still managing to satisfy your own needs and remain an individual.

RECOGNIZING YOUR FEARS

Many men and women don't recognize their fears as fears.

•*You believe you're talking about problems when the real problem is fear interplay.* For example, after a dinner party, Anne and John had a fight. She attacked, "You monopolized the conversation and said all the wrong things." She didn't realize that behind the verbal tirade lay her fear that people wouldn't like them, that John's excessive conversation might make friends cross them off their guest lists. Oversensitive, she magnified what John did. At the same time John had monopolized the conversation. His fear of being ignored made him come on too strong. However, both John and Anne thought they were fighting about manners rather than mutual fears.

•*You act like a lawyer building up a case.* With many examples, you prove that everything wrong is the other person's fault. Thus you keep from facing your fears. Conversely, you may always accept the entire blame for everything. You can't see what you truly fear because you say you're wrong about everything.

•*Because of your fear, you train your mate to act in the very way that upsets you*. For example, you become frightened and upset when your mate "rejects" you by withdrawing. Your mate soon learns that when he/she is angry and upset, the way to communicate it to you is by withdrawing—going into another room, even leaving the house. *You train your mate in how to hurt*. Your fears become worse. They begin to evoke fears on the part of your mate. When he sees how you become upset by anger or withdrawal this may stir up his fears of not being understood, of not having someone "strong" to count on. There you are on the marital seesaw.

•*You set up false goals*, determined by the need to minimize or avoid your fears. Instead of setting positive goals, you let fear control your actions. For example:

Complaint: "My husband reads science fiction all weekend."

Fear: Being exploited and taken advantage of.

False goal: Unreasonable fear led to tremendous pressure on the husband not to read sci-fi. (*Note:* She seems to have a real complaint, but unreal fear magnifies it.) The more pressure she exerted, the more unmovable the husband became. As soon as the woman changed her reaction, and, instead of pressuring him, ignored his sci-fi addiction, her mate became free to change.

Complaint: "She always talks trivia. All I hear about is the cost of cans at the supermarket."

Fear: Openness.

False goal: Because of his fear of openness, when Dan comes home he tells his wife nothing of what transpired during his business day. She has the entire conversational burden, so she talks about her housewifely chores. Dan does not lead the conversation into more interesting channels but just complains about "trivia talk." It's his fear of feeling communication that leads to this.

Complaint: "My husband is always at his mother's beck and call. He spends all his free time running errands for her or driving her to airports."

Fear: For the wife there are two: (1) she sets up a competitive situation with the mother-in-law and then fears losing the competition; (2) she fears her mate isn't strong enough for her, reasoning, "He's weak. If his mother can boss him around like this, I can do it, too, and I don't want to." For the husband there are two: (1) his fear of disobeying his mother; (2) his fear of obeying his wife and thus making his relationship with her similar to the one he has with his mother.

False goal: So much tension exists that neither husband nor wife can decide the legitimacy of the mother's demands. Because of this confusion and because the husband feels the need to fight his wife's pressure, he begins to do more things for mama. He has the need to say, "I'm an independent person. Don't push me too far." He wants to maintain independence in the face of unreasonable pressure rather than have an open discussion of how much responsibility to mother they, as a couple, should accept. Meanwhile the wife has set the false goal of reducing her insecurity about her husband's "weaknesses."

In all the above situations the people responded in terms of their own fears *or to the partner's uptightness* rather than to what the situation actually called for. Each had a false goal. Each false goal inhibited the development of the love, respect, trust and commitment so necessary for closeness.

FEAR STYLES

As a consequence of fear, men and women adopt styles. Do any of the following fit you?

1. *The placator.* Usually based on a fear of rejection, anger, not being liked by your mate. Trust cannot develop. Never considering your own needs, you go out of your way to do what you *think* your partner wants you to do. You avoid any expression of disapproval, dislike, anger. In the process you become dishonest with yourself, never admitting to yourself that you may be right and your partner wrong. The result: smouldering resentment, distance and the attitude "I do everything. I make all the decisions"; lack of contact ("I never know what he's thinking"). Sometimes you become a martyr.

2. *The empty lover.* Any expression of tender, warm feelings throws you. You can't say them or hear them. If your mate shows tenderness to you, you change the subject. The underlying fear: "If I let my tender feelings show, I will be vulnerable and get hurt." This has two consequences: (a) you become detached; (b) you stir up a feeling of doubt in your partner. He/she wonders, "Does he/she really love me?"

The converse may also be true. You cannot say tender things to your partner for fear that the partner will become vulnerable and get hurt by you. One man told me, "Of course, I can't tell her I love her when I do feel it. She will expect it to be forever and how do I know what I will feel five years from now? She'll be hurt when five years from now I don't love her." So he never said it and she was indeed hurt. This is a lack of respect. He did not respect his mate's ability to weather the potential hurt, her right to decide whether or not to risk the hurt for the sake of closeness. And so there was emptiness for both.

3. *The togetherness person who doesn't allow the partner to have independent areas of action.* Your fear: that the mate will meet someone else and split. You accomplish your goal of "doing everything together" either by discouragement ("You're always starting new things and never finishing them. Why bother to take another course?") or by taking over your partner's interests.

For example, Marilyn H. said to me, "I feel depressed, but I don't know why. I have a good marriage and a perfect husband." In reality, when Marilyn signed up for a course in Chinese cooking, Pete took the course with her. He did the same thing when she enrolled in a photography course at the local high school. When Marilyn determined to go back to work, Pete found her a job in his office building so they could lunch together every day. Marilyn felt her individuality slipping away. She had no breathing space in life.

When I interviewed Pete, he told me, "My wife is the most desirable woman in the world. I'm not worthy of her." Pete was certain that someday Marilyn would meet another man, fall in love and leave him. Without realizing what he was doing, he tried to minimize her opportunities for meeting men on her own.

4. *The drill sergeant.* Fear: being criticized. Only if things are perfect can you hope to avoid criticism. So you are constantly doing and *ordering your partner to do.* Cleaning the barracks for an inspection that never comes dominates over talking, being, loving each other. You become a victim of the "must syndrome." You say, "I don't have time to be with you now. I must clean out the attic." You may say, "We just can't spend Sunday being quietly together. We must have my sister over," or, "Never mind the sweet talk. You must . . . you must . . . you must . . ." Satisfying the nonexistent inspector takes precedence over closeness.

5. *The bookkeeper.* Fear: being exploited. You ignore or minimize everything your mate does ("You had a pretty easy day today"). Simultaneously, you build

up everything you do. When your mate suggests you perform some task, you become angry and procrastinate. In the marital situation, the bookkeeper is very oversensitive, constantly asking himself, "Am I being called on to do more than my share?" He keeps meticulous accounts of who did what.

6. *The adult child.* Fear: separation from or offending parents. This is one of the most common "outside" fears (affecting you as a couple but not between you as a couple) that interferes with the close relationship. It can show itself in many ways. Even though you've been married for years, mama and papa still know best. Dutifully you report to mother every night. You spend every vacation visiting "the family." The silver cord still binds.

7. *The penny-pincher.* Fear: spending money. In actuality, a host of different fears may underlie this pattern. You may fear poverty. You may fear being a spendthrift so you can't spend at all. Not uncommon is a woman's fear of spending money she hasn't earned. Not uncommon among men is the fear the wife will criticize the way the money was spent. This unreasonable fear may lead to unwanted tensions in the relationship and unwarranted demands on the partner.

The converse may also be true. The fear of poverty, of being a tightwad are just a few of the fears that may lead to spendthrift behavior. This, too, may lead to unwanted tension.

Whatever the behavior to which the fears lead, it results in a decrease of commitment and so weakens the chance for closeness. In the close relationship, one of the limits to be accepted is that decisions about the use of money is something to be shared. This will lead to discussion, frankness and negotiation of differences, and so closeness increases.

8. *The shut-in.* Fear: being trapped. You feel trapped in the relationship because of a variety of fears: fear of being on your own, lonely, managing as a single. All these lead to a feeling of not being able to

break up the relationship if you want to. Often when you manage to conquer this fear, a funny thing happens: Instead of leaving, you move closer to your mate.

THINK THROUGH YOUR FEARS

All fears can influence the close relationship. Your fear of cats, heights or flying can trigger tensions, angers, resentments that have a marked influence on what goes on between you and your partner. So can the social fears—of rejection, self-revelation, criticism. However, there are some fears that particularly shape the close relationship.

1. *The fear of loss or abandonment.* You feel your mate's possible desertion means the end of the world. You feel just as inadequate to cope with the complex and potentially hostile world as does the young child, abandoned by his parents. Usually you express this fear in the close relationship by constant placating, reasoning, "If I keep him happy, then he won't leave poor, defenseless me." But the fear produces more subtle expressions:

•It often underlies unreasonable jealousies and makes reasonable jealousies more painful.

•It keeps an impossible situation going. No chance exists of working out your relationship. Only hopeless misery lies ahead. The only rational solution is to end the relationship. But to you this means loss and abandonment, which you must avoid at all costs. Your fear is so great that you are willing to endure marital misery for the rest of your life.

•Conversely, the fear can lead to premature breakup of relationships. You are going through one of those tumultuous trouble situations that do come up in developing closeness. You are terrified of being abandoned, and there's a chance this will happen. So *you* leave. To you this is less frightening than being left. Says one thirty-two-year-old woman with a history of breakups, "I always leave. I'm always the rejector."

•You are so frightened of your partner's dying and your being left alone that you view any sign of sickness as an enormous danger.

CASE

Bill G. said to me, "I just don't feel well." He reported constant little pains, a general feeling of malaise, lack of energy. On some weekends he could barely get out of bed. His doctor had said, "Nothing is physically wrong." Bill was sure there was.

To help him, I had to understand his wife. Polly's mother had died when she was eight; this upset her so much that she had to stay out of school for a term. Polly got married right after college, and soon after her father died; this time she went into a depression. Now she was terrified that Bill would die. Her fears magnified any signs of sickness on Bill's part. If he came home tense or had a minor cold, she would send him to bed, serve him dinner on a tray, fetch for him. Bill loved the attention and looked forward to being put to bed and served, and experiencing Polly's tenderness. For seven years she had trained him to be sick and he had accepted it.

I did two things. For Polly I desensitized her to her core fear of loss. Using Systematic Desensitization in fantasy, we worked on teaching her to relax at such terrifying thoughts as "The doctor says Bill has to go to the hospital" . . . "He's in the hospital and there are tubes stuck all over him" . . . "I'm at his funeral; his body is being put into the hearse" . . . "He's dead— and I'm all alone at home. I have no one."

Along with this we set up a program of things (errands, etc.) for Bill to do each weekend *whether he felt like doing them or not*. One rule: He was never to talk about bad physical feelings with his wife unless his temperature rose over 101 degrees. *Exception to this rule:* Every evening for five minutes he was to give Polly a rundown of imaginary complaints. (He was not to talk of complaints he thought were real.) Polly had to listen to this and deliberately try to keep herself relaxed. If he started to talk about physical complaints at any other time, she was to ignore him.

This broke up Polly's fear and the habit to which she had trained Bill.

2. *The fear of change.* Some people fear introducing new things or new ways of doing things into their lives. This may involve staying in the same house for years even though your income merits a more comfortable house, taking the same vacation over and over, keeping the same social network and never making new friends. Instead of being married for ten years, you have been married for one year ten times. The closeness hasn't grown.

This fear assumes particular importance when it involves new feelings and new ways of relating. A close relationship must be alive, constantly changing, growing, reorganizing. You should be able to see your mate in new ways, view yourself in new ways, and do new things in a different way. If you fear change, you keep the relationship from maturing.

This fear can have particularly crucial consequences in the seventh and fifteenth years of marriage. Relationships seem to undergo major changes at those two times. If you're afraid of the new interactions that emerge, your distress and anxiety may direct the changes into destructive rather than constructive directions. This is why divorce courts are filled with people with the "seven-year itch" or "fifteen-year crisis."

3. *The fear of weakness* (your own). Because you consider your fears, doubts and anxieties as weaknesses, you're afraid to show them. You may be afraid to admit any error. In another extreme, you may be so afraid of not getting your own way (falsely believing that not getting your own way signifies your weakness) that you

permit no compromise. With this fear you place enormous demands on your mate.

CASE

Emily was raised with the attitude that it's "wrong" to be weak. Her New England family never discussed feelings or anxieties; they felt there was a wrong way and a right way to do things. If you did anything wrong, you were weak. After college Emily married Joe, a man who always presented a façade of calmness, never discussed his doubts. To Emily this represented strength. She didn't see Joe's problems in self-disclosure. After some years Joe felt he was "missing something" and over Emily's strong objections began psychotherapy. After a while the therapy began to work and Joe lost a good part of his detachment, began to experience and express more of his feelings of fear and conflicts. This threw Emily into a panic. She told Joe all sorts of stories about the disastrous effects of analysis, berated him for the time and money it took. She also developed an angry kind of depression and began to go to bed at 7:30 P.M. Her sexual drive disappeared. Her problems intensified to the point where she couldn't ignore them and she came to me.

I explained the problem to her in terms of her fear of weakness, and gave her fear exercises in three steps:

•Each evening she was to note three "weak" (anxious) feelings of doubt she had had during the day in her FCT workbook. For example, she had such qualms as "Did I buy the right brand of detergent?" and "Will I do the PTA talk right?" We did this for eight weeks, and at first she had tremendous difficulty coming up with any thoughts.

•She would write out a specific incident involving "weakness" and tape it to a wall so her husband could see it. He was to read it but make no comment. We spent three to four weeks on this task.

•She was to stop writing and tell these incidents to

her husband over dinner. At first Emily couldn't do this. She had to write out an incident and then read it to Joe. Gradually she became able to talk about them and free discussions developed. At this point she began to lose her fear of weakness and to get very interested in Joe's therapy. At our last session she told me she had decided to go into analysis herself.

4. *The fear of not "being completely understood."* To feel someone has complete empathy with you is a peak experience in the coming together of two people. You don't expect this feeling of complete rapport from acquaintances. You may achieve it occasionally with friends.

However, you fear you won't get it from your partner and feel you will remain forever apart and alone. You especially fear exposing yourself, to reveal the really intimate feelings. One depressed wife told me, "What if I really tell him all my innermost thoughts and he doesn't understand? I wouldn't be able to bear it." Without self-revelation you have little chance of achieving the understanding you crave.

Often you try to overcome the problem by testing. You send out messages in a code your partner cannot possibly understand. When he/she doesn't, your fear strengthens. For example, you say, "I have a headache." Your partner responds in a concerned tone, "Should I bring you an aspirin?" You feel depressed. He did not understand that you were talking about an argument with a neighbor (something you had barely mentioned). You weep inside, "He/she will never truly understand me."

5. *The special fear in remarriage.* Special situations may bring about their own sets of special fears, some realistic and some inappropriate. Unless these fears are recognized and shared, they may impede the developing closeness. There are many such special situations: interfaith and interracial marriages, extreme differences in

temperaments, styles and values. Perhaps the most common in our present society are the special problems brought about by remarriage.

In remarriage you can find all the fears you do in first marriage, but, beyond that, because of previous unfortunate experiences, you may magnify and distort these fears. Certain reality-based fears—nonexistent in a first marriage—complicate the situation. Your ex-husband may take a new wife and cut off child support, or he may simply disappear. Your ex-wife may harass you with constant "more" demands, brainwash the children, create havoc over visitation. Your combined his-and-hers household may mean war between two sets of kids. These complications may lead to increased tensions which further magnify the fears. These at least partially inappropriate fears may interfere with closeness.

Among these fears: the *fear of repeating a bad situation* so that you become oversensitive, perhaps hypervigilant, to certain things your partner may be doing; the *fear of being in second place* so that you are alert to signs that indicate your partner's present loyalty is to children (or even ex-spouse) and you might be sacrificed for their sake. The fears themselves are not the critical element. It is what you both do with them that is of prime importance. Depending on this, they may either: (a) decrease the four basic feelings necessary for closeness and this marriage too may fail, or (b) result in a sharing of experiences and feelings that lead to developing closeness.

In thinking about fear in the close relationship, it is extremely important to *pay attention to your own fears—not what your partner is doing*. Many people can't identify their fears because they don't know they have them. They just know something is wrong. The following account of an initial interview with a couple may help you to think through your fear.

CASE

Thirty-six-year-old Bob, an architect, and thirty-three-year-old Jane have been married for eight years and have a five-year-old son. Before becoming pregnant, Jane worked as a teacher. Over the past few years Bob has received several promotions and been given increasing responsibility. Here is an almost verbatim account of our conversation.

THERAPIST: Now tell me what the problem is.

JANE: He's the problem. He's like an old man. There's no fun in him. I can't go on living this way.

THERAPIST: You do sound frustrated. What would you like to have different? [*Note:* Therapist places emphasis on the changes desired rather than searching for historical material.]

JANE: I want him to be more alive. He never wants to do anything. I have to plan the vacations, decide when to have friends over, have to get him to take his own son to the park on weekends. Even getting an answer out of him is like pulling teeth. He's dead, dead, dead [*her voice rises to a shout*].

THERAPIST [*to Bob*]: Is that the way it is?

BOB: Yes, I guess so. I'm sitting at the dinner table and I can't think of what to say. There's something wrong with me. [*Note:* She puts all the blame on him and he accepts it.]

THERAPIST: Are you that way at work too?

BOB: No. At work it's great. I'm known as an idea man. They think I'm very creative.

THERAPIST: What keeps you from being that way at home?

BOB: I don't know. Maybe I'm neurotic. [*Note:* He is still accepting full responsibility.]

THERAPIST [*to Jane*]: How do you explain this?

JANE: It's obvious that he has a problem with his mother. He has some Oedipus complex. [*She goes off* into a series of stories about Bob and his mother. As she keeps talking, her anger mounts.]

Further probing shows that Jane has a history of automatic anger and yelling. However, she keeps blaming Bob for this. What emerges is that Jane has a fear of recognizing her own problems.

THERAPIST: Jane, look, all human beings have some kind of psychological problems. Tell me, do you have any such problems?

JANE: The big problem is whether I should stay married to Bob or not. How can anyone go on living with a man who is so dead, so weak?

THERAPIST: Aside from Bob, do you have any other problems?

JANE [*after a long silence*]: Well, I can't think of any right now.

THERAPIST: Jane, what do you think of people who have psychological problems? [Therapist is trying to explore just what the fear is and at the same time trying to make this fear obvious to Jane.]

JANE: Well, I guess I do think strong people don't have problems. If you have problems, it's a sign of weakness. Only weak people really have problems. [This is cognitive misunderstanding—an incorrect thought that seems to underlie part of the fear.]

THERAPIST: And you don't like weak people. It's a terrible thing to be weak, isn't it?

JANE: It must be terrible to be weak. If you are, everyone is so contemptuous of you. You know, maybe one of the reasons I'm so angry with Bob is that he has these problems and that makes me think he's weak and so I get angry and contemptuous of him.

THERAPIST: And so maybe if you admitted to having problems, like a problem with this automatic anger, then maybe that would mean you'd be weak and Bob and other people would be contemptuous of you.

At this point I began to examine Bob's behavior, and what emerged was his fear of being yelled at by a woman. He would do everything he could to avoid this situation. However, both Bob and Jane agreed that this automatic uptightness at anger hadn't really become a problem until Jane's pregnancy.

THERAPIST: What happened then?

BOB: When she was pregnant, she became more irritable and began to yell more than usual. Everytime I said something and she disagreed, she would yell. Everytime I did anything, she yelled.

THERAPIST: And so when Jane was pregnant and had this automatic anger reaction, you did whatever you could to keep her from getting angry and yelling at you. You just stopped doing things?

BOB: Yes. I remember thinking if I make a suggestion and she disagrees, she's going to yell, so I guess I just stopped making suggestions. And I just stopped doing things.

THERAPIST: But that didn't work either because now she just yells at you for not doing things. How do you avoid that kind of anger?

BOB: I'm in a trap. I can't avoid it.

JANE [*turning to Bob*]: Are you really that frightened when I get angry? I never knew it. My anger isn't really that bad.

BOB: I think it's worse than you think, Jane. I really do get upset and frightened by it, and I really do try to do things to avoid it. [*Turning to therapist.*] You know, I figured out another thing I try to do to keep her from getting angry. I think I try to make myself appear helpless. If I could convince her that even if I tried, I couldn't do anything about it, maybe she'll accept the situation and stop being so angry at me for not doing the things I really can't do. I think if I believe I can get her to accept that, maybe she'll stop yelling.

THERAPIST: We seem to be dealing with a couple of

interlocking fears and automatic reactions that feed into each other. You, Jane, have an automatic anger reaction. When certain things happen, you automatically respond with a flash of anger and begin to yell. We're going to have to break up this automatic reaction. What's probably kept you from doing this yourself is that you have another fear—you have a fear of letting yourself know you have problems. To you, having problems means you're weak, and if you're weak other people will be contemptuous of you. As a result, instead of your trying to change, you insist other people try to change, and, of course, no matter how much Bob changes you're still going to have that automatic anger.

With you, Bob, you're afraid of anger, of being yelled at by a woman. Because you feel you must avoid this, you end up by being inhibited, ingratiating, placating. This makes things worse because Jane sees this as a problem on your part, therefore a weakness, and if she sees a weakness in you, she gets upset and even angrier. Beyond that, your adopting this passive role tends to reinforce her avoidance of facing her own problems and so makes it more difficult for her to change. We have to get rid of this fear of women's anger. I think accomplishing this will also change your relationship with your mother. My guess is as soon as we begin to change the automatic and fear reactions, there's a good chance that the whole situation will straighten out.

SET YOUR
SPECIFIC CONSTRUCTIVE GOALS

•*Avoid sexual stereotypes*. In America we usually think of men and women as polar opposites. At one end of the pole is masculinity; at the other end is femininity. Neither sex is supposed to be much like the other. With this false concept, if a woman acquires such male-associated qualities as ambition, self-reliance, willingness to take risks, leadership abilities, she moves toward the masculinity end of the pole, in the process becoming less feminine. If a man acquires such female-associated qualities as compassion, gentleness, sensitivity to the needs of others, being affectionate, warmth, tenderness, he moves toward the femininity end of the pole, in the process becoming less masculine. The fear of breaking the stereotype may lead to a suppression of an important part of yourself.

Many couples carry this societal attitude into the marriage. The woman thinks, "I'm afraid to show him that I'm more competent about financial matters than he is. It will hurt his ego"—and so they pay too much on their tax return. The mate thinks, "I'm afraid to let her know how much I need warmth and affection. She'll think I'm weak"—and he buries his emotional needs. By maintaining sexual stereotypes, both fail to realize that if you show the qualities traditionally claimed by the opposite sex *you do not have to give up your masculinity or femininity in the process*.

Allow yourself to be *androgynous* (from *andro,* male, and *gyne,* female), meaning having the characteristics of both sexes and not being typed as either masculine or feminine. Realize that you can be both independent and tender, assertive and yielding, that there are neither masculine nor feminine but rather human traits. Thus you expand the range of behavior open to both of you and permit more freedom in the relationship.

•*Think through your goals in specific situations and how you can make what you want to have happen actually happen.* I repeat, the power of most fears to disrupt comes from the interactions they set off and the false goals to which they lead. To set up a program to overcome and change your fears, you must face them and move through them again and again until they lose their hold on you. If you do this, the fear will disappear. You accomplish this by action. You have to take specific situations—one at a time, whether a problem in communication or automatic anger—and decide on what you want to make happen, what specific things you have to do to bring this about.

Do not think about your marital interactions in the abstract. In selecting situations for change, take concrete and simple ones where you have the greatest chance of succeeding. The situations can be as simple as "dinner time tonight," "this coming weekend" or "planning our next vacation." For each situation ask the following questions:

- •What kind of feeling atmosphere do I want to bring about?
- •What kind of things do I want us to talk about?
- •How do I want my partner to act?
- •How would I like to see myself acting?
- •What can I do to get it moving in the right direction?
- •What can I do if I see it starting to go wrong?
- •How would I like it to end?

When fears and uptightness predominate in marriage, your goal becomes a defensive one: You think of what you don't want rather than of what you do. By keeping your eye on constructive goals, you reverse this process. Constructive goals usually involve freeing communication, increasing tenderness, learning to give and take marital criticism, negotiating problems and disagreements, thinking in terms of wants rather than musts, breaking up automatic reactions.

AN ACTION PROGRAM FOR MOVING THROUGH FEAR TO FREEDOM

Move Toward Closeness

At one time Simone de Beauvoir asked Jean-Paul Sartre if he loved her. She got a cryptic reply: "I'm here, am I not?" Many people have similar problems expressing feelings. This may stem from many fears such as rejection or looking foolish. A man may be afraid to break the "strong, silent male" stereotype.

In the close relationship men and women take a number of feeling holdback positions. Some people voice only what they *think*, not what they *feel*. Others can't say what they feel at the moment they feel it; they store it inside themselves. Some sad individuals can't articulate any emotions. In marriage this inability to express feelings places a tremendous burden on the partner; he/she must be a mind reader. Or perhaps your partner can express emotions freely and you become threatened. You say, "How can you feel that way? Where do you get such crazy ideas from?" Or you just ignore the partner.

Because you don't express your feelings you become insensitive to them. You become increasingly empty and anxious. Because you never reveal your true self, you are never really comfortable. You can't achieve the open sharing that marks the good close relationship. Here are three proven techniques to help you *learn* to communicate feelings. Practice them and eventually your expression of feelings will become a *spontaneous* expression of you.

1. *Feeling talk.* This is a phrase created by Andrew Salter, a leading New York psychologist. It means the continuous appropriate communication of your constantly changing state of emotional being.

EXERCISE IN FEELING TALK

Aim: To help you to say what you feel.

STEP ONE: Concentrate on saying what you *feel*, not what you *think*. Many times think talk is necessary but it is not an expression of feeling. Make a distinction between verbs of thinking and feeling.

Feeling verbs:

adore	delight in
cherish	care for
yearn for	want
hate	long for
detest	envy
despise	love

Thinking verbs:

infer	presume
suppose	conclude
believe	side with
consider	understand
imagine	interpret
guess	conceptualize

STEP TWO: Deliberately use the pronoun "I" as much as possible. Follow this with a feeling verb. For instance:

"I like this chicken marengo."

"I feel terrible about the way I left you on your own at that party."

"I don't care for the way you've gotten in the habit of stopping off for a drink with the boys every night."

"I resent the way your mother picks on me when she comes for dinner."

"I cried all day over the way you nagged at me last night for something that isn't my fault."

"I'm afraid of you when you get so angry."

"I want you to be like the man I married, not such a workaholic."

"I want you to be like the girl I married, not such a nag."

STEP THREE: If you have trouble using the pronoun "I," use these two devices:

1. Count the number of times you use "I" in the

course of a day. You might want to invest in a golf counter and click it each time you get the word out. Keep score in your FCT workbook.

2. Make a deliberate attempt to use the following three pairs of phrases as often as you can:

"I like what you said."   "I don't like what you said."

"I like what you did."   "I don't like what you did."

"I want you to_____."   "I don't want you to_____."

If you have trouble with any of these, start off with "I agree" . . . "I disagree."

STEP FOUR: During the feeling-talk training period, your partner must do his/her part: listen, respond with feeling. No wisecracks. This is a project for both of you.

CASE

Twenty-eight-year-old Rick P., a gaunt, inarticulate man who had grown up on a remote Oklahoma farm, and his wife, Kay, a big city girl, came to me for couple therapy. One of their major problems: Because he was afraid to talk in a feelingful way, Rick rarely communicated what was going on inside himself. Because she couldn't make contact with him, Kay felt desperate and lonely. Rick felt Kay didn't understand him and he yearned to be understood. He constantly felt irritated with her, and they spent 90 percent of their time in pointless fighting.

I gave Rick a series of assignments. Assignment one: to keep charts of how often he used the feeling-talk phrases. Assignment two: three times a week he and Kay should sit down with a tape recorder and Rick would tell what he felt about a particular topic. He was to choose the topic in advance. Kay's job: to listen to what he said, to put in her own words what she thought he was feeling, to ask questions when she wasn't sure what he was feeling. She was *not* to express her own ideas. At the end of each session Rick was to listen to the tape, count the number of feeling verbs he had used and enter them on a chart.

Following three weeks of feeling-talk therapy, one day they were sitting in my office. Turning to Kay, Rick said, "You have no idea of what it is to feel as conflicted as I do. When I'm on my way home from work, I feel I can't wait to get there, but at the same time I don't want to face all that tension and fighting. Caught up in my mixed feelings, I walk closer the street with my feet dragging."

From Rick this statement was like a six-year-old talking in calculus.

Shortly after this he made another meaningful statement. One of Kay's major complaints had been that when they made love, Rick never said anything tender. He had responded, "How can I? I don't feel it, and even if I did, I've never said things like that." But following the statement in my office two nights later, while making love, Rick said tenderly the greatest feeling-talk phrase of all, "Darling, I really do love you."

2. *Self-revelation.* No matter what your fears and pattern of conversational holdback, you can train yourself to communicate on a level of increasing closeness.

CASE

Because he feared self-revelation, Allan could communicate only one thing to his wife: anger. Because he really loved her, he wanted very much to change and give her the feeling interaction she craved so much. I asked Allan to prepare a story about some meaningful experience he had had between ages ten and twenty. His first draft went like this:

"Something important happened to me in high school. I tried out for the baseball team but only made substitute. In the middle of the season a couple of players got sick and I got my chance to play. My first time at bat I hit a home run. It was terribly exciting."

I pointed out to Allan that in telling this anecdote he had revealed little of his inner feelings and urged him to try again. After several trials his next version was much better:

"Ever since I was a little boy I wanted to play baseball. Part of this was inspired by my dad, who, when he was young, had played semipro ball. We used to play catch together, but I wasn't very well coordinated and felt frustrated that I couldn't be better. I tried hard, full of daydreams that I'd be great and yet knowing in my heart I wouldn't. When I made substitute on the high school team, I felt both excited and disappointed. When I got my big chance and hit that home run, it was like a dream come true. When I ran around the bases, I felt I was floating through the air. The back-pounding from my teammates was something I thought would never happen to me. [*In a very sad tone*] That was the only hit I got all season. In college I didn't even try out for the team."

Together, Allan and I worked out a number of stories like this. Gradually it became easier for him to bring in feeling aspects. He learned to relate stories to his wife about his first real love affair, his excitement at being elected president of his college fraternity, and his exhilaration at his first job interview. He progressed to stories about his emotions when he courted his wife and current experiences in the marriage.

When we started Allan possessed awareness only of his feelings of anger and resentment. Through the telling of these stories two things happened: (a) he became conscious of other things in his life, like pride in his daughter and anticipation of carrying out joint activities with his wife; (b) he became able to talk about these feelings.

EXERCISE IN EMOTIONAL EXPOSÉ

Aim: To help you communicate on a gut level.

STEP ONE: Take an important emotional experience (it can be funny, sad or even traumatic) that happened during your early adult years. It should be something that has real meaning to you (a relationship that failed or your first "crush"). Tell it aloud or into a tape recorder. Listen to how you sound. Think through how you can make the story more emotionally revealing.

STEP TWO: Tell it to your partner.

STEP THREE: The listening person should set aside his/her feelings and try to capture all the nuances of the story, to really try to get into your skin.

STEP FOUR: Ask your partner to tell a similarly revealing story. This time you try to get into your partner's skin.

3. *Change hurting to caring.* In the close relationship many people are afraid to express tenderness. They may fear giving: the closeness that might result from it, the possible feeling of being exploited. They may fear taking; this may make them feel dependent or weak. Some rationalize, "What if I get used to her caring for me and then she stops doing it?" As a result many couples get so caught up in the false goal of keeping bad things from happening that they do nothing to make good things happen. You become experts at hurting each other, but you lose sight of how to give pleasure to each other.

The caring-days technique, devised by Dr. Richard B. Stuart, now of the University of Utah, has a dual aim: (a) to make each partner aware of what *pleases* the other rather than what annoys him/her; (b) to form the habit of doing things just for the sake of pleasing, of learning to give and to take, thus making the relationship more rewarding for both.

CARING-DAYS EXERCISE

Aim: To learn to give and accept tenderness.

STEP ONE: Set dates for two caring days. These are best done on weekends. For instance, this Saturday you care for your mate; the next week your mate cares for you. Flip a coin to see who goes first.

STEP TWO: Let's say you go first. Make up a list of caring things to do. Many people find this hard. They get blocked by feelings like "What if I'm wrong? What if this shows I don't understand him/her?" You may be wrong but you don't have to be frightened. Look at this as an opportunity to "understand" more. It's by the making up of a creative list that you move through fear to understanding. *Caution:* In devising your list don't get caught up in the trap of a series of "*thing*" actions (like calling the sick relative of a mate) rather than *feeling* actions. These can be helpful in that they show you care, but it is much better to concentrate on small expressions of tenderness that say "I understand you." Some examples that patients have used:
   •Wife walking around the house without a brassiere because she knows it turns her mate on.
   •Husband wearing cologne his wife likes so much. She had bought it especially for the caring day.
   •Stacking partner's favorite records and playing them all day.
   •Building a fire and serving breakfast in front of it.

STEP THREE: Carry out your list. The caring partner should accept your pleasure in giving and not be overcritical or uncomfortable.

STEP FOUR: That night discuss your reactions. As with many of the suggestions and exercises in this book, Jean and I try them out on each other. It was Jean's turn first. She had her list typed on yellow paper and proceeded to carry out the agenda, which included giving me breakfast in bed, rearranging my clothes closet, cooking Sunday brunch, which I usually do, and going out to get the *New York Times*. She did all the things *she'd want under the same circumstances.* But I hate breakfast in bed, want to tend my own closet, like to get the *Times* and make brunch. Her caring day made me understand what *she* wanted. Jean began to learn to distinguish between what I really wanted and what she thought I wanted.

STEP FIVE: On his/her caring day your partner goes through the same process. Again, you accept. That night you discuss.

STEP SIX: After each of you has carried out one caring day, schedule another pair for the near future. Continue them as long as they give you pleasure.

Negotiate Problems and Disagreements with a Modern Marriage Contract

Partners have patterns. Often you and your mate avoid any discussion of troublesome matters because you fear talking about them will create marital discord. You live by the Munich syndrome: "Peace at any price." You say, "It doesn't really matter," when deep inside it matters very much. Or you both come on like rodeo cowboys, hoping strong talk will stifle possible controversy. Says one man, "When I oppose her, it's always disaster. She's never satisfied unless she makes every decision." Says one woman, "For fifteen years of marriage I've never had the right to oppose him. To get what I want, I have to cry."

In determining "Should I bring it up?" you have to

think through your marital rights ("Do I have the right to an equal share in determining our mutual life-style?" ... "Do I have the right to consider my own needs or must I consider only my mate's needs?") and then take action. More and more couples are discovering that modern marriage contracts that detail communication caveats, division of chores, and who gets what in case of divorce provide enormous help in overcoming problems over marital rights and decisions.

Many people fear bringing up difficulties because they have no idea of where to go from there. Once they utter the sentences "We have a problem. I'm upset about _____," they're helpless. Some people can't even get out the word *problem*. They just feel helpless. With specific solutions, you won't feel so helpless. By contracting for certain behaviors, you're forced to do what you're afraid of doing.

You can write a contract if you're a nearlywed, newlywed, unmarried and living together or are veterans of twenty years of matrimony. You can have a thirteen-page document, covering everything from rights, expectations and limitations to sexual, financial, household and parental responsibilities. Or you can have a verbal contract. One couple has both a chore contract and a communication contract. Posted on the back of the bedroom door, the latter contains items like "Please tell me right away when you're angry" and "Try to help me know when you're depressed about something."

By taking the trouble to write out a marriage contract you stabilize the relationship. Each of you knows where you stand. It's ambiguity that drives people to divorce. Even more important, a contract enables you to bring up things you have been afraid to say and to do so within a constructive context.

EXERCISE IN WRITING
YOUR OWN MARRIAGE CONTRACT

Aim: To overcome your fears through clarification and enforcement of marital rights and responsibilities.

STEP ONE: Think through the areas you want to cover. These might include:

1. Household responsibilities and division of labor. Some couples alternate division of household tasks on a monthly basis. Others do the chores each likes to do.

2. Provisions for whether or not to have a child, what church to attend, responsibility for social arrangements, birth control and who uses it. What happens if the wife gets a good job that requires a cross-country move? If remarried, does only the biological parent have the right to make decisions over his/her children —or can the stepparent play a part? Who gets use of what physical space in the house? One wife says, "We bought a four-room apartment. He has the den. We have a joint bedroom, but it is my space. I choose where the TV sits, what papers remain there. The space belongs to me."

3. Use of time. You might want to divide it into You time, Me time, Our time.

4. Financial arrangements over present property, earnings, savings, expenses. Some couples agree that all property "gained once the marriage is licensed shall be considered community property," thus insuring that a non–wage-earning partner will have an equal share in family income. Others pay expenses from pooled incomes and divide any surplus. Still others prorate expenses according to respective incomes.

STEP TWO: Each of you makes out your list separately and then you negotiate the final joint contract together.

STEP THREE: Whatever areas you itemize in your contract, be sure to set times to renew, reevaluate, amend and perhaps renegotiate. One Maryland couple found that their fourteen-point chore contract, drawn up two years ago, after they had been married ten years, wasn't working. Mary, a recent reentry woman with three children under eight, resented Dave's extensive traveling for "medical politics," so they drew up a travel contract that put limitations on his out-of-town expeditions. If he travels more than two weekends in a month, he must do all the chores during the next week. Says Dave, "The travel contract has been the most freeing thing in our marriage. By having my time defined, I know I'm free to plan my schedule in the way I want. I don't have to worry, 'Will we fight about this?'"

Learn to Handle Criticism in the Close Relationship

To achieve closeness, you must be able to give and take constructive criticism. Doing this clarifies problems and misunderstandings, paves the way for negotiation and resolution of difficulties. The very sharing of criticism can lead to increased closeness. You can learn from it. There may be something wrong with you; you may constantly interrupt people, have bad breath, talk too loudly. If your mate doesn't tell you, who will?

Many fears often clog critical interchange. Because you fear hurting your partner or counterattack, you may be unable to express criticism. You stay silent, but your resentments build up until you burst out with a critical attack at the wrong time, in the wrong place, about the wrong thing.

Often what seems to be unreasonable criticism may stem from your unwritten marriage contract. Couples enter marriage with both overt and unwritten expectations. A bride may assume that weekends will be fun-filled times and that her husband will share in the planning of them. He feels that his "contract" means providing a good living; to do this, he will have to work weekends. Neither communicates these beliefs. The result: she says, "Deadhead"; he says, "You don't understand the burdens I carry. Stop picking on me." Explore such criticisms to uncover the unspoken beliefs and expectations. If you don't, the unwritten marital contract may remain forever a hidden source of dissention between you.

A CLOSE RELATIONSHIP CRITICISM PROGRAM

1. *Recognize that you have trouble with criticism.* The following questions may help you to do this:

•Is the criticism in your relationship mostly one-sided? One of you does it all.

•Do you constantly find yourself filled with smouldering resentments but rarely express them?

•Does any criticism—from either of you—lead to a pointless fight or marital turmoil?

•Does criticism—from either of you—produce no reaction, lead to no new understandings?

•Does any criticism make you feel "I'm guilty"?

•Do you voice criticism at inappropriate times and in inappropriate ways?

•In your marriage do criticisms about trivia often assume major proportions?

Answer yes to the above questions, and you have some degree of fear about giving or taking criticism. Become goal-oriented. Move through your fear of criticism so that you can give it and take it constructively. Stop avoiding it, denying it ("I did not do that"), attacking ("You bitch" . . . "You bastard"), immediate agreement ("Of course, it's my fault").

2. *Learn to take criticism.* Your first response should be something that makes you feel less disturbed. Your

goal is not to change your mate but to make *you* feel more in command.

•Use feeling talk. Respond to criticism in the close relationship differently from the way you'd answer a casual acquaintance. Here your aim is to intensify communication. For instance, your wife criticizes the bad mood you were in that morning. You might respond, "I feel annoyed because that's the fifth time you've mentioned it and that's more than enough."

•Put it back on your mate. He says, "You spend too much time on the phone talking to your friends so we have no time to talk." You might answer, "You're coming on pretty strong, aren't you?"

•Use humor. One man responded to his wife's perpetual and usually unjustified criticism of his "dirty appearance" with various versions of a "Sexy, isn't it?" comment. Using this remark, he reduced his anxiety from 80 percent on the sud scale to 5. *Caution:* Be careful with the humorous approach. Overused, it may increase your problems.

•Use understanding. Don't always take your mate's criticism at face value. For example, you're married to a star salesman who has just returned from a disappointing trip to the West Coast. That night at dinner he criticizes your appearance, the food, the way the house looks. You must realize that your mate's upset is what matters, not the carelessly expressed words. This may be the time to ignore the words and say, "Boy you've had a tough week."

3. *Learn to give criticism.* If you have trouble criticizing, practice. It will get easier and less frightening. If you're the Caspar Milquetoast type and can't even get started, here are two things you can do.

•Write a script. Put in the criticism you want to voice and your partner's response. Start with low-level responses that won't trigger much anxiety in you. Then act out the script with your mate. Because you know what's coming, you won't feel too fearful. Don't change the script. No improvising. Here's a sample dialogue:

YOU: I don't like the fact that you invited your parents for dinner on Sunday. I want to do chores around the house.

WIFE [*low-level response*]: Maybe I should have asked you first. I'm sorry.

YOU: Whenever your parents are concerned, you forget all about my needs. I wish you would ask me in the future before you invite them.

WIFE [*picking up the pace*]: That isn't completely true. I often ask you. I do pay attention to your needs. I have the right to ask my parents over.

YOU: In the future please don't guess at my needs. Make a point of asking me.

WIFE: You're right. In the future I will ask.

Note: In the above dialogue the man makes it easy for himself by giving his wife nonthreatening responses. In future dialogues he will write responses for her that make it more difficult for him. Adopt the same practice in your scripts.

•Role-play. This technique offers a looser structure than a script. You start off with your criticism (this may be easier if you write it down beforehand) and then you both improvise. Limit your role-playing to two or three minutes. Use a kitchen timer. When the bell rings, you must stop.

In practicing giving criticisms in these relatively safe situations, you face the fear and desensitize yourself to it. This practice will make it easier for you in real-life situations.

Sometimes the way you criticize feeds into your partner's fear and makes the situation worse. *You may have to change the way you criticize.* Some tips if you constantly stoke your partner's fears:

•Don't give private criticism in public. A party is not the time for you to comment on either something your partner does right there and then ("What a stupid remark") or on something done in the privacy of your home ("He's so clumsy—you should see the trouble he has putting in the storm windows").

•Watch your timing. Do not say, "You should be more of a breadwinner" when your mate is in the middle of a tough job problem. Wait for calmer moments and then try, "What can we do to augment our income?"

•Keep away from comparison criticism based on the style of others: "My mother did it that way" . . . "My ex-wife used to _____" . . . "When I lived by myself, I used to _____."

•Do not attack your mate as a person: Cracks like "You're in love with your father, not me" get you nowhere except into a fight. Be specific. "Ellen, you spend half our time together talking about your father. It really upsets me, and I wish you wouldn't do it."

Stop Your Disruptive Automatic Reactions

No matter what the partner does, some people always react with guilt, anger, or withdrawal. These reactions can cause devastating hurt. Sometimes you don't react this way consciously. Over the years the pattern has become automatic.

Your partner does or says something—almost anything. You respond with your automatic feelings. This reaction leads to some kind of inappropriate behavior on your part: apologies ("It won't happen again"), shouting and yelling, retreat behind the newspaper. Your actions upset your partner. The situation gets worse.

If you have this automatic pattern, *you must get to know it*. Check yourself. You may not be aware of your withdrawal the very second you retreat behind the *Times,* but you sense it soon after. Check out your anger and guilt patterns. If these are automatic reactions, you can stop them through deliberate relaxation. Use the Instant Relaxation Exercise from chapter 4. I have used this technique successfully with many patients who had this problem. For instance, with Jane and Bob—whose initial interview dialogue I cited earlier in this chapter—I instructed Jane that every time she became aware of her automatic anger response and started to yell she was to think "Calm" as she exhaled, breathe in deeply, and then say what she had to say. If she forgot, Bob was to say, "Do your breathing exercise." It made a difference. By breaking up her automatic anger, both became freer to work on other marital problems.

This does not mean that you still won't feel angry, guilty or want to retire into your shell, but you will express and experience your feelings differently. Instead of a Robot Reaction, you will be able to communicate what you want to say in a way your partner can understand.

CASE

Grace, a woman in her early forties, told me she had two problems: a mild agoraphobia and a "bad marriage." According to her husband, she had a third: "a vile temper." Martin was terrified of Grace's temper outbursts, and whenever she got angry he would automatically retreat into a world of his own. He would flee to the den and hide behind a book. If she followed him, he'd go into the bathroom, lock the door and stay there for an hour. If they were in the car, and he couldn't physically withdraw, he'd stay silent. These withdrawals frightened her. As do many agoraphobics, Grace had a strong fear of separation and abandonment. When Martin would withdraw, she would become more frightened, express her fear with sharper anger which caused Martin automatically to withdraw even more.

Because Martin seemed the stronger, we began with him as the main fulcrum of change. As soon as he became aware of the feeling of withdrawal, he was to calm himself, then turn to Grace and say something—

anything—but preferably something angry. Martin had trouble expressing his anger, but he learned to change the subject or comment on what she was angry about. He stopped withdrawing. His ability to do this lessened her fears and was the first step in breaking up their marital anger-withdrawal Ping-Pong game.

Learn to Think in Terms of Wants, Not Musts

Your stereotype of what the "good wife" or the "good husband" is often plays an important role in the developing relationship. When this stereotype centers around the doing of things and is combined with the fear of criticism, it can become quite destructive. If you don't do what your stereotype says you should do, you will be criticized. To avoid the possibility of such criticism, you make the musts rather than the wants govern your marital life. For example, take the case of a young couple. Each has a full-time job and attends graduate school at night. The only time they have to be together is weekends, but they spend Saturday and Sunday in a frenzy of cleaning, polishing, scouring. They might make a better choice if they spent more time together and had a less perfect apartment.

By doing what you want when it's reasonable, you overcome the fear of not being the good mate.

EXERCISE IN
MINIMIZING THE MUSTS

Aim: To loosen you up to do what you want to do.

STEP ONE: List four personal constant musts. For example, "I must visit with my parents every weekend" . . . "I must have the house in perfect order all the time."

STEP TWO: Write down what you get from these musts. A feeling of being good? The avoidance of someone else's anger or criticism? What would happen if you didn't do your musts?

STEP THREE: What would you want to substitute? Would you rather make love to your spouse on a Saturday afternoon than visit your mother-in-law? Must you clean the attic when you want to take the kids for a ride?

With this must exercise Jean is my prize pupil. Many of her musts centered around serving me a gourmet meal every night. Her mother always had a marvelous dinner for her father. Her mother—dead for twenty-five years—would rise up from the grave unless she did too, she reasoned. Because of my hours, we don't eat until after 9:00 P.M. Monday through Thursday. However, Jean too works very hard during the day and the gourmet meal was a pressure. As a result, although the meal was excellent, Jean was often needlessly tense and over-tired at dinner. Once Jean got the concept of wants instead of musts, she took off like O.J. Simpson dashing for a touchdown. Now, on those days, she makes a point of doing something she wants to do in the late afternoon and we eat quick and easies. I'm relieved. I'd much rather eat hamburgers along with good conversation than have veal marengo with tension as a side dish. Jean says, "At first it was hard, but now—after doing this routine for a year—I feel completely without guilt. I'm me, not my mother."

ENDING THE RELATIONSHIP

Even when couples exist in complete disharmony, fears keep them from taking any breakup action. Besides the fear of abandonment, you may view a divorce as a confession of failure—if you have to break up the relationship, there is something wrong with you as a person. Even with the current high divorce rate, many middle-aged men and women still fear what "other people will say." Some fear disruption. Others fear new responsibilities: the burdens of earning more money and tending to practical matters of day-by-day existence. One man was afraid he wouldn't know how to shop for food.

The exaggerated fear of hurting the mate often serves to prolong connubial torment. You let the misery intensify, hoping "I wish he/she would be the one to make the break, to shoulder the guilt." Many couples come for marital counseling with the hope of getting the counselor to say, "You ought to break up."

Before coming to any decision about ending the relationship, you want to reassure yourself that you have tried in every way to make a go of it.

•In conjunction with your mate, make every possible effort to improve your marriage. No matter what your partner's faults, the degree of "terrible behavior," focus in on what *you* can do to save your marriage.

•If nothing works, try counseling. At the very least this will crystallize the actions you want to take.

You may find that all your fears of what will happen are realized, but, even so, you feel more at peace out of the relationship.

CASE

Marilyn, a chic advertising copywriter in her early thirties, had been living with Tom, head of a Manhattan research firm, for four years. Tom kept promising to get a legal separation from his wife, but didn't. As a result of therapy, Marilyn realized that: (1) in all probability he would not get a divorce; (2) she had no financial security. If Tom died, the wife would get everything. Marilyn had two options: to stay or reorganize her life without Tom. She decided on the latter course.

She says, "I had this terrible fear that I'd leave and then he'd get a divorce and go off with someone else. I kept thinking, 'Maybe I should wait another year.' I moved out, but couldn't give him up immediately. I kept on seeing him for three painful months. I had this other fear that I wouldn't meet anyone else. This has been realized. Tom's the best guy for me I've ever known. It has been a year and a half and I haven't met a man who interests me. I may never. But I couldn't go on living with him and respect myself."

You may find that the breakup solves problems for both of you.

CASE

Seth A., a personable, ambitious security analyst, wanted to be a partner in his brokerage firm, make money, have a warm family life, a country house, and a wife who shared these goals. When he married Norma, he made this very clear, saying, "I'll take care of the financial things; you take the social responsibility. My business requires lots of entertaining." But Seth didn't understand the depths of Norma's fears. A spoiled young woman, she feared doing anything that would express strength. She wanted to be taken care of completely. Norma couldn't take the responsibility of giving parties and entertaining business contacts. More and more they led a hermitlike existence. Norma refused all invitations because she might have to "pay back."

After seven years and two children, at Seth's insistence Norma began psychotherapy. Her therapist told Seth, "She's very narcissistic. There's a lot of passive dependency." Seth made the decision: "My life is slipping away. This marriage is not for me." He wanted out desperately, but a fear gnawed at his guts. "My father was an irresponsible playboy type who spent little time with my mother and me. If I walk out of this marriage, does that mean I'm like my father?"

Seth stayed in his marital rut until he was passed over for promotion, a situation he partially blamed on their not doing business entertaining. This mobilized him to come to me. Once we worked through the fact that his fear of acting like his father was groundless, Seth was able to ask for and get a divorce. Subsequently he met and married a woman who shared his goals. Continuing in analysis, Norma conquered her "dependency" and changed from an isolate to a woman with an active social life. Both Seth and Norma have new and happy lives.

True closeness with another human being at a depth level is an experience that those who have not experienced it find hard to understand. It is a mutual growth process. As Rainer Maria Rilke wrote: "For one human being to love another, that is perhaps the most difficult of our tasks, the ultimate, the last test and proof, the work for which all other work is but preparation."

CHAPTER 8 _____

SEXUAL FEARS

Ellen A., an attractive, intense woman in her thirties, felt her husband lacked "passion" during sex. When they came for therapy, we began a program to loosen him up sexually. Because John was an old-time movie buff, we set the assignment of having him play the roles of famous movie lovers. John started off as Rudolph Valentino. He felt his sexual play-acting deserved a four-star rating, but Ellen interrupted with "I can't stand this" and stopped the sexual act. The next night he attempted Charles Boyer, complete with French accent and continental charm. Again, Ellen pulled away.

In Ellen's premarital sex, she had never had a really fulfilling experience. Because of this, she possessed a strong fear that she wasn't "woman enough" to respond sexually. As long as her husband did nothing about his difficulties, she was able to put the blame on him, avoiding her own fears. When, through the fantasy play-acting, John started to come on strong in an exciting way, her fears soared to the point where she had to escape from the situation.

Ellen represents but one of the multitude of unhappy men and women who know only too well what Tolstoy wrote in the 1800s:"The true heartbreak is in the bedroom." Because of concealed fears, insecurities, angers, resentments, bitternesses, many of us turn the bedroom into an emotional burial ground or battlefield, instead of a place to share tenderness, excitement, love, with the goal of complete immersion in feeling and release of inhibitions.

Experts estimate that sexual problems of one kind or another affect more than half of all married couples in the United States today. Many stem from a single cause: fear.

SEXUAL DANGER SIGNALS

Begin to look for possible specific fears if you:

•*Deliberately avoid sex:* This does not mean the occasional time when you just don't feel like it but a general developing pattern of "not tonight." Check yourself particularly to see if you hold back from expressing affection lest this lead to sex.

•*Avoid sex without realizing it,* using as excuses fatigue, a "lack of time" because of too much work, chores, family obligations. Men and women who want sex make time for it.

•*Exist in a sexual rut:* You still enjoy sex but it has become an "always-the-same," unexciting routine.

•*Worry about certain aspects of your sexual life:* You may feel concern because you have fantasies during intercourse, because you have urges to do "weird things" or because you don't have these urges.

•*Have a sexual dysfunction or a "perversion":* Something—major or minor—may actually be wrong. You may be unable to maintain an erection, achieve a climax or have sex without performing some automatic, ritualized action.

SOME SEXUAL BASICS

In our society sex is a highly sensitive, emotionally charged area. When fear and anxiety develop, they often lead to sexual inhibitions and dissatisfactions. These become exaggerated because you think of sex as an isolated, encapsulated experience. You should know that:

•Because you use your body in sex, any physical disorder may influence your sex life. Unfortunately, too many people are too quick to attribute sexual problems to psychological causes rather than physical. That pain in your vagina during intercourse may be due to a developing ulcer. Your difficulty in getting an erection may stem from an endocrine imbalance. For *any* disorder, check your doctor before seeking therapy.

•Your brain, not your sex glands, primarily rules your sexuality. This means that all your past experiences, all the things you've learned in your life, and your present thoughts and attitudes influence your sexual activity.

•There is no such thing as the uninvolved partner. Your fears and anxieties, as well as your affection, tenderness and love, interact with those of your partner. They grow and multiply. If one has trouble, the other must be involved.

•In the close relationship, the goal of sex should be a physical and emotional sharing to the point where giving and taking become such a merging of body and mind that two individuals become one. You move to sexual fulfillment through feelings and simultaneously move to feeling fulfillment through sex. As Erich Fromm wrote: "Erotic love begins with separateness and ends in oneness."

Just as you can change other fears, you can change sexual fears, in the process turning bed into an area of heartthrob, not heartache. However, before you can get rid of your fears, you have to identify them.

THE FEARS THAT INFLUENCE SEX

Any fear can become magnified and create a host of sexual problems. Essentially, however, three kinds of sexual fears exist:

1. *The outside and tangential fears.* These represent fears, stemming from the tensions of everyday living or from fear-associated past experiences, that intrude into the intimacy of the bedroom even though they have nothing to do with sex or your relationship with your partner.

One man has such a fear of darkness that he can function only with a light on. A woman is so terrified of being seen having sex that she has to close the venetian blinds, pull down the shades and draw heavy draperies across the windows before she can relax. Another woman is phobic to thunder. If any chance exists of thunder or lightning, sex is out. This creates a problem since she lives in Tampa, Florida, the "lightning capital" of the U.S.A.

In one case, a thirty-two-year-old woman seemed to be easily aroused sexually, but during intercourse, could never quite come to climax. She had had severe childhood asthma. Now, as she approached orgasm, she became very sensitive to her changes in breathing and this rekindled all the childhood fears connected with asthma. She became very frightened and "had to get out of the situation." I had to desensitize her to the asthma-associated fear of dying as her breathing changed when approaching climax.

2. *The fears active in the relationship that also affect your sex life.* Such fears as rejection (if you don't look good enough, perform well enough, make too many demands, your partner will become angry, reject you, find a different lover), of being misunderstood, being exploited (or exploiting), expressing feelings, may lead to unsatisfactory sex.

Some couples carry the angers and resentments that stem from these fears under the sheets ("How can I make love when I'm so mad?"). Other couples exist in mutual disharmony; yet in the bedroom sex is great and keeps them together. Sometimes, anger can make sex better.

CASE

Gerry and Kathy, a couple in their early thirties, came to see me because he had turned into a wife-beater. They had a pattern of anger, followed by terrific sex. Gerry would get angry, begin yelling at Kathy and a big battle would ensue. Furious with each other they'd go to bed, and have magnificent sex. When they had sex at other times, it was pleasant but lifeless. Often Kathy would deliberately provoke Gerry's anger to get the exciting bed action. But lately his anger had gotten out of hand; he had beaten her so hard that he gave her a series of black eyes and huge bruises.

Exploration showed that Gerry feared his tender feelings. In his childhood Gerry's parents had been very sweet and nice to him to accomplish their own ends, manipulating him so that he'd do what he didn't want to do. As a result, he became frightened and distrustful of his own tender feelings. In the present, he really loved Kathy, but, feeling that he had to avoid tender feelings, he could express only angry ones. When angry, he could be spontaneous and alive. The rest of the time he sought refuge behind a wall of inhibition.

I treated Gerry by (a) correcting his irrational ideas about tenderness; (b) having him deliberately make tender remarks to Kathy. As his fear of feeling and expressing tenderness decreased; they no longer needed anger for good sex and the beatings stopped.

Just as you are afraid of disappointing your partner in other areas, you are also *afraid of disappointing him/her in sex*. Of all the relationship fears this can prove especially important. You often experience this as a pressure coming from the partner. You get so caught up in looking for signs of your mate's disappointment that you lose sight of your own satisfactions, thus making yourself the exploited. When you lose sight of your own feelings, you cannot share them and thus you leave a gap in the sexual interplay. This leads to complaints ("You're a good lover but too mechanical") and to the setting up of test situations ("Will my mate be disappointed the next time we have sex?"). Constant tension and loss of pleasure ensue. The more active your mate becomes, the more you fear disappointing. The use of contraceptives often signals sexual readiness and spurs the fears.

CASE

Ted and Marie came in with marital problems. He had a general fear of disappointing her, particularly in the sexual area. Use of any kind of contraceptive triggered his anxiety. When she inserted her diaphragm, this was a signal to him that she was expecting sexual satisfaction. Experiencing this as a pressure from her, he would get nervous and lose his erection. They had stopped using contraceptives completely, and had started to practice coitus interruptus. He would defer his ejaculation until after she had her climax and he had withdrawn from her. This produced more tension. She feared pregnancy. He felt cheated. I treated Ted with Systematic Desensitization in imagery, using such scenes as "You've just had sex and she looks disappointed" . . . "Marie tells you, 'Sex wasn't very good, was it?'" . . . "She bursts into tears and says, 'I'm just so frustrated.'" As Ted lost his irrational fear of disappointing Marie, he became more sensitive to her real needs, not just the ones he imagined.

Note: Fear of disappointment can lead to the so-called Madonna complex. When a man has feelings for his partner, he becomes concerned and frightened of disappointing her. This anxiety leads to sexual dysfunction. However, with a prostitute, he doesn't care how she feels, so no fear of disappointing exists. The result: He functions well only with a prostitute. The same may be true of the Don Juan who has a series of one-night stands in which no personal relationship exists and hence no fear of disappointing. With this fear, the man doesn't make a second date with the same woman.

3. *Specific sexual fears*. There are the fears directly related to sex and its outcome. The most common ones:

a. *The fear of inadequacy* (with the fear of disappointing, you generally find this fear in other patterns of the relationship; fear of inadequacy relates specifically to sex). By this time most reading Americans know all about performance anxiety. With this, you place emphasis on function rather than on pleasure and sharing. You mull and wonder, "Will I be able to have an erection?" . . . "What if I can't have a climax?" These fears create so much static that your natural sexual feelings can't get through and frustration results. This fear sets off secondary fears. For example:

•*The fear of your partner's contempt*. If your partner becomes aware of your difficulty, he/she will think less of you, actually become contemptuous of you. Because of this fear, you interpret the most well-intentioned comment as signifying derision. Both men and women often try to conceal their difficulties (such as by faking orgasms) from the partner as much as possible.

•*The fear of public humiliation*. Most common in men, this is the fear that other people will discover your difficulty and mock you for it. For example, Les had never been able to have a close relationship with a woman. Actually he had never even been able to date one who might know any of his friends. His fear: He'd attempt to have sex with her, be impotent (he had had a number of such experiences). She would become scornful and tell everyone he knew about it. These people would tell each other and soon the whole neighborhood would talk about him . . . his co-workers would find out about his potency problem . . . everyone would laugh at him behind his back or else regard him with pity. Les obsessed about this all the time until he came in for treatment.

•*The fear of your partner's inadequacy.* If your partner does have some kind of dysfunction, it only arouses your own fears of your own sexual inadequacy. You wonder, "If only I were man enough, she'd be able to have a climax" . . . "If only I were woman enough, he wouldn't be having this difficulty." This mobilization of your own fears leads to anger, frustration, avoidance and disappointment which in turn feeds back into your partner's fear of inadequacy. You may put all the blame on your partner for his/her dysfunction or take it all on yourself.

For example, in his first marriage, George had had the problem of impotency. He and his wife went to a sex therapist and resolved it. But because of other problems, they decided on divorce. After the divorce George had several sexual encounters with no problems. Then he remarried. His second wife couldn't experience orgasm during intercourse; she could get climax only by direct clitoral stimulation, either manual or oral. George became quite concerned about not being able to bring her to climax during intercourse. She kept telling him, "It's not your fault—I've always been like this" . . . "I enjoy intercourse even when there's no climax." George worried more and more about this until his own impotency started to return.

Sometimes even the anticipation that your partner may have difficulty leads to problems. For instance, recently a woman told me that she had lost all enjoyment of sex with her boy friend because of her own anxiety. Her fear: that he would have trouble getting an erection, would blame her and leave her. Until she got this idea, sex between them had been good. She had never discussed her feelings with him but her nervousness had communicated itself. For the first time he had the problem of impotency.

b. *The fear of being sexually abnormal.* Next to the fear of inadequacy, this is probably the most common disruptive fear. It consists of three separate fears.

•*The fear of the statistical norm.* What is normal for someone else may not be normal for you. Because of this ambiguity, people wonder about themselves. They hear stories from others (particularly the often distorted macho tales of men) and compare themselves. They read figures and reports (like Kinsey's) and compare. What is the normal frequency? Am I undersexed or oversexed? Is my climax full enough? Am I free enough or too free? The anxieties and tensions mount.

Among men, a frequent point of statistical comparison is penis size. "My penis is too small" is the frequent thought. Implied is the thought that it is too small to satisfy *any* woman, that he will be forever rejected and that there is not a thing he can do about it.

Among women it is more frequently the worry that they may have fantasies during intercourse (men may also have them but do not worry about them as much). "This is not normal," the women fear. Actual studies show that about two-thirds of women at some time during sex do fantasize and that the frequencies of such fantasies relate neither to sexual nor to marital adjustment.

•*The fear of being a pervert.* You get urges, desires, thoughts about doing what for you seem to be unusual acts. You may do them and get pleasure from the doing. Then you begin to worry about what these desires and actions may show about you as a person. You become frightened that you are a "pervert."

"Pervert" usually has one of two meanings. In the religious or ethical sense, it means that you are immoral, evil, bad, that you are a sinful person. In the scientific sense, it means that you are conflicted, immature, neurotic, have a distorted personality. In either frame of reference, the implication exists that there is something terribly wrong and grotesque about you as a person. You fear this is true.

In actuality, not even the experts agree completely

about what constitutes "normal" sex. Many professionals believe that it is "normal" if (i) it is between consenting adults (you do not impose it on someone); (ii) it is not compulsive (you can do it or not as you choose); and (iii) it is not exclusive (you can also find sexual satisfaction in other ways).

Of course, there are people whose behavior does depart from these standards of normalcy. There are the sexual variants like fetishists and transvestites. Here the fear of being perverted, with all its implications, mounts to great heights. They often think of themselves as "monsters" or "weirdos." Yet, in actuality, all they have is a problem behavioral pattern set off and/or maintained by a variety of specific fears. If you conquer these fears, you may be able to break up the entire behavioral pattern.

•*The fear of being inhibited.* Many people now take their standards of behavior from porno films, hardcore magazines and novels. Not only does anything go between consenting adults but you should do it all and like doing it all. If you don't, you're "uptight" and "inhibited," and this is just as bad as being "immoral" and "perverted." For example, with one couple, the wife thought she had sexual hang-ups because her husband enjoyed bondage and, while she wasn't frightened of it, she just didn't like it. They confused "not liking" with psychological problems and actually came in for treatment.

c. *Other sexual fears.* Many exist. You may *fear pregnancy*—childbirth itself, that you'll have a deformed child, the responsibility that childrearing brings, and actually having a child when you don't want children. You may *fear getting old*. With men it's a fear of loss of potency ("I'm not the man I used to be"). With women it's sexual attractiveness ("He won't want me when he notices those wrinkles on my neck. After all, I'm forty; he's forty-two; but he can get a twenty-five-year-old"). You may *fear getting physically hurt*. One woman had had a bad experience when she started to hemorrhage during intercourse; from then on she feared sex. Your fear may have a very subtle form of expression. One man, in an attempt to master his fear of physical injury, used to pick up male prostitutes and pay them to beat him.

All these fears lead to false sexual goals: to be the expert "technician," having a one-sided relationship (everything for you or everything for your partner), having orgasm the exclusive goal of sex, keeping sex stereotyped because you're afraid to try new things. You completely forget the real goal of sex: sharing both body and feelings so that two individuals become a single unit.

A PROGRAM FOR SEXUAL FREEDOM

All your sexual difficulties may be due to fears. It is your fears that keep you from changing. You may (1) know just what these fears are; (2) incorrectly think you know what the fears are; (3) just know something is wrong but not recognize which (if any) fear underlies it.

As in any fear area, the first step in change is to identify the specific fear behavior involved. You do this first by taking stock and then by taking action.

Take Your Sexual History

The following quiz should help you to identify and gain perspective on your sexual fears. Write the answers (this will take time) in your Fear Control Training workbook.

SEXUAL HISTORY QUESTIONNAIRE

1. As a child, were you ever punished for sexual behaviors (such as playing with yourself)?
2. Have you had any traumatic sexual experience?

3. Did you feel guilty when you first started to masturbate?

4. What were your fantasies when you first started to masturbate?

5. Remember your first sex play experience.
   —How old were you?
   —What happened?
   —What did you enjoy most?
   —What made you feel anxious or frightened?

6. Remember your first intercourse experience.
   —How old were you?
   —What happened?
   —What did you enjoy most?
   —What made you anxious or frightened?

7. Remember a really good sexual experience.
   —When, where and with whom did it take place?
   —What was so good about it?
   —How did it come about?

8. Remember a really bad sexual experience.
   —When, where and with whom did it take place?
   —What was so bad?
   —How did it come about?

9. Have you ever had a series of bad sexual experiences? What happened? What brought them about?

10. Consider your current sex life. Rate each of the following areas from 0 (terrible) to 100 (perfect) as you feel about them.

   Fantasies _____
   Masturbation _____
   Anticipation _____
   Physical affection _____
   Sex play _____
   New or different ways of sex _____
   Intercourse _____
   After sex _____

11. In your current sex life, list the things:
   You would like to be able to do but cannot.
   Your mate would like you to do but you won't or can't.

You would like your mate to do but your mate won't or can't.

12. In your current sex life, show the areas of greater difficulty. Each of the following statements offers a choice.

The physical aspects or the emotional exchange.
What you do or what your mate does.
What you do or what you feel.
Whether you take initiative or your mate takes initiative.
What you expect from mate or what mate expects from you.
Not enough sex or too many sexual demands.

13. List the specific things you would like to do more or do differently.

14. List the specific things you would like your mate to do more or do differently.

15. What kind of things can your mate do to help you change?

16. What kind of things can you do to help your mate to change?

17. List the specific fears, worries or anxieties that may inhibit your sexual freedom. With each one show how and where it may work to inhibit you.

Your answers should begin to throw light on things you may do to gain more sexual freedom. You should also go back to Uptight Inventory—I in chapter 2 to see if any of the fears listed there apply to you. Again, remember that such tangential fears as the fear of darkness may sometimes be active in the sexual areas.

Identify Your Fears Through Action

Although questionnaires may be extremely useful, they also have limitations because you may not really know what frightens you. By taking direct and constructive sexual action, you may not only bring about sexual change but may also uncover previously unknown fears. Here are two action programs that may be used for both purposes.

EXPLORATORY EXERCISE I—
GET TO KNOW YOUR OWN BODY

Many people are strangers to their own bodies. They fear their bodies and the strange, new feelings contact may produce. By getting to know your own body, you may find fears you didn't know you had, may lessen those fears and find new areas for exciting stimulation.

For women: Get acquainted with your body. Many women never have. Look at yourself nude in the mirror. What do you like? What don't you like? Practice using your pelvis. When you just lie there, it's devastating to your partner. Alone, practice using your hips. Bump and grind just like a burlesque queen. Take a hand mirror and lie down on the bed and look at your genitals. Carefully examine the clitoris, labia, vaginal opening and perineum (the area between the vagina and the rectum). How does this make you feel? Good? Or guilty, ashamed, anxious?

For men: Become narcissistic. Look at your body in the mirror. Flex your muscles like Charles Atlas. See how you look. Pay attention to how you feel in your arms, pectoral and abdominal muscles, buttocks, legs. Stroke different parts of your body: the sides of your neck, insides of elbows, nipples, abdomen, sides, thighs. Note what you particularly enjoy. Imagine being stroked by a woman or being kissed on those parts by a woman. Stroke your anus, testicles, penis. See what particular parts provide pleasure. If anything makes you feel anxious, keep touching that part repeatedly until you feel more pleasure than anxiety.

CASE

Martin R. came in with the complaint that—although he had no sexual dysfunction—he never really enjoyed sex. In foreplay he enjoyed stimulating his partner but would become extremely tense when she pleasured him. In intercourse, he would have an ejaculation but never a full, orgiastic feeling. He felt he was being cheated. I gave him the assignment of doing the above body exercise. At the next session, he came in all upset. When he played with his own nipples, he had started to get a feeling of pleasure!

Through some kind of distorted reasoning, Martin equated this feeling of pleasure with homosexuality. To him, experiencing a feeling of bodily pleasure anywhere except directly in his penis meant he was homosexual. This scared him. I explained to him that his ideas lacked validity and, to some extent, Martin managed to change his attitude. Because his thinking changed, he became able to play with his own body without panicking. For a month he kept on with the exercise, watching his anxiety decrease, his pleasure increase. This further reduced his anxiety. At that point he became far more responsive to all aspects of sex and stopped being afraid of his own sensuality.

EXPLORATORY EXERCISE II—
THE SEXUAL WEEKEND

This is a weekend for sex—and only for sex. Go to a hotel, motel or some new environment that has no association with the tensions of your workaday world. Remove anything that might interfere with sex—no alcohol or drugs, conversations with strangers, TV or card games. Take along a collection of erotic books and pictures. Look at them. Discuss them. Walk around nude most of the time. When you aren't nude, dress "sexy" by your partner's standards (get your partner to give you ideas). Don't bring problem areas (like Danny's orthodontia) into your conversation. You talk, think, act sex and love. Make suggestions to your partner for things he/she can do more of. Give feedback and make sure your partner gives it to you. Explore, innovate, share and magnify your feelings. At the end of the weekend, talk about the things you did—and schedule another sexual weekend.

CASE

Craig and Anne had sexual difficulties. Anne almost always found a way to avoid sex. So I assigned them the sexual weekend. On it, she kept saying, "Let's take a walk," and finding similar excuses for sexual avoidance. On Saturday afternoon they returned to their hotel room and carried out the "walk around nude" assignment. Anne began to cry, but she didn't know why she was so upset. However, later that night she was able to make love. In Anne's account to me of the weekend, I saw her core fear: She had a specific fear of seeing a penis (this fear of genitalia is very common).

We worked out a program.

•Craig was to buy a number of magazines showing nude men, some with limp penises, some with erect. Then he was to mount some thirty pictures on cardboard and give them to Anne.

•Anne was to arrange the collection in order from the least to most disturbing. At first this upset her. But soon she was able to take the least upsetting picture, look at it until she felt the first stirrings of uptightness, then close her eyes and relax. Over and over she did this until she could look at the picture without tension. She continued this procedure, every night looking at from one to three pictures, always beginning with the last picture she had mastered the night before. As she made progress in these photo-study sessions, she carried out an additional task. She took pictures of Craig nude, including close-ups of his penis, then she followed the same photo-study procedure. At that point she no longer avoided sex and could have sex with the lights on.

The sexual weekend had revealed the fear that was ruining her marriage.

Learn to Communicate

In a healthy sexual relationship, open and honest communication is vital. Sharing your feelings in words brings greater closeness and understanding. Exposing and discussing your dissatisfactions and problems leads to mutual attempts at solving them. The very act of discussion will lower your fear. Yet for many people the communication barrier looms like the Great Wall of China. Says one woman, "My current lover has delayed ejaculation. He takes a long time to come. But I can't get myself to say anything about it." If you do it positively, the average, healthy person will welcome criticism. It's not a question of "Should I speak up?"— but how? If you don't speak up about bed, you're likely to be disappointed in bed.

A COMMUNICATION PROGRAM

1. *Talk about sex.* If you have difficulty, *read.* Here the purpose of reading is *conversation about the books you read.* The reading serves as a good conversational beginning because many people find it less frightening to talk about books than sex. Many excellent books exist. To expand your sex life, read *Sexual Stimulation* by S. G. Tuffill, *Sex Talk* by Myron Brenton, *Woman's Orgasm* by Georgia Kline-Graber and Benjamin Graber, *The Joy of Sex* by Alex Comfort. For dysfunctions read *The New Sex Therapy* by Helen Singer Kaplan and *Human Sexual Inadequacy* by William H. Masters and Virginia E. Johnson.

In carrying out your sexual reading program, you should (a) both be in agreement that you want to expand your sexual openness; (b) each go through only one or two books—if you tote home an armful, chances are you won't read any or you'll get so busy reading you won't have time for talk; (c) if necessary, schedule a definite time for the talk. Don't expect immediate conversational freedom. You may find you can talk more easily than your mate. If that's the case, be patient.

2. *Advance from talk about books to talk about your own personal wants, needs, likes and feelings.* This may prove difficult. One way of getting started: the Sentence Completion Test. Psychologists use this technique to uncover patients' emotional attitudes and conflicts. Here, you use it as an aid to communication.

EXERCISE IN
SEXUAL SENTENCE COMPLETION

Aim: To provide a framework for increased sexual communication.

STEP ONE: Copy the following sentences in your FCT workbook (or on a piece of paper) and complete them.
- The time of sex I like best_____.
- The sexiest part of my body_____.
- The sexiest part of your body_____.
- I like best when I_____.
- I like best when you_____.
- My favorite sex fantasy is_____.
- During foreplay I wish_____.
- During intercourse I wish_____.
- I'm afraid to tell you_____.
- I wish you_____.

STEP TWO: Your partner does the same thing.

STEP THREE: Discuss the forms. In the discussion go only as far as you can go comfortably.

STEP FOUR: About a week later, fill out the Sexual Sentence Completion Test again and discuss. See if anything has changed during this time.

STEP FIVE: Switch. You will fill out the form the way you think your partner would fill it out about you. Your partner fills out the form the way he/she thinks you would answer. Swap and correct. This technique can clear up many misunderstandings.

3. *Use "dirty word" talk.* Sometimes sexual fears and anxieties are concretely expressed through inhibitions regarding the use of "dirty words." If you can release your inhibitions in this area, you may lower the entire network of your sexual fears. Using dirty words to make a request or as a description can excite. For example, saying "Suck my prick" or "Your cock feels so big in my cunt" may serve to add an extra dimension to your sex life.

CASE

Marlene yearned to feel "free and uninhibited." She also wanted to change her attitude toward sex; she was another one of the many women brought up to feel "sex is dirty." Her current problem: She could have climax only with direct clitoral stimulation but she never had climax during intercourse. Working together, this is what we did.

•We drew up a list of about fourteen "dirty" sexual words and arranged them in order of how upset she got with each word: breast . . . cunt . . . fuck . . . blow . . . suck . . . screw.

•She had homework. She had to work up a list of sentences, using these words, that her husband might say to her and then create a second list of sentences she might say to her husband.

Our plan was to first have her husband use the sentence to her and then she to him in the actual sexual situation. Marlene couldn't swing this. She *was* able to have her husband voice the sentence in the dining room after the evening meal. Over a matter of weeks they did this until she felt comfortable. Getting her to utter her sentences took a few weeks more. Finally, Marlene became able to say her "dirty words" sentences during sex itself. Not only did she start to experience climax during intercourse, but she suddenly became multiple orgasmic. Her husband—with whom I had had no contact—called to thank me.

Rehearse Success Not Fear

Under most circumstances, the pleasure and excitement of sex serves to counteract whatever fears may develop. Some people, however, train themselves to be frightened and so counter the sexual pleasure. Three techniques help: increasing your fantasies, carrying out sexual fear assignments, and direct desensitization of your sexual fear.

1. *Increase the excitement in your sexual fantasies and thus counter your sexual fears.*

SEXUAL FANTASY EXCITEMENT EXERCISE

Aim: To practice having more exciting fantasies.

STEP ONE: Make up a sexual fantasy. Note the amount of sexual excitement in it.

STEP TWO: Repeat the same fantasy and deliberately try to increase the excitement.

CASE

Alan X., a twenty-eight-year-old lawyer, brought up in a religious Catholic household where sex was considered "bad," came in for treatment, claiming, "I just don't seem to get turned on by women." I had him make up several fantasies and rate them on an excitement scale (0 to 100). In fantasizing about having sex with a girl he liked, Alan could only reach 15. I asked him to revise it to get it higher, so Alan added details like a water bed and managed to reach 35. For the next few weeks his assignment was five times a day to make up a sexual fantasy, rate the amount, then imagine the fantasy again and raise it by 10 points. After five weeks of this, Alan could achieve a level of 60 and felt increasing turn-ons with women in social encounters. Through fantasy, he had lessened his fears and permitted the sexual excitement to come through.

The fantasies you use may be as simple (the recall of a sexy kiss two nights ago) or as complex (you're the whip with thirty Neanderthal types at your feet) as you want to make them. If you have trouble creating sexual fantasies you might: (a) *recall fantasies* you had at other periods of your life and imagine them now. Initially you may not experience much excitement but this may help you get started; (b) *use props* like sexy pictures from magazines like *Playboy,* look at them and try to make up even a momentary fantasy; (c) *use other people* as a fantasy trigger—for instance, you're raping fifty gorgeous girls who resemble Farrah Fawcett-Majors . . . you're being raped by porno star Harry Reems.

2. *Set simple, sexual fear assignments for yourself.* Try to do the things you've been avoiding. Your responses to the Sexual History Questionnaire should furnish leads. Remember, sexual fears are like other fears. If you stop the avoidance that maintains the fear, eventually the fear itself will disappear. You follow the same rules you do for all fear assignments:

•Start with one that is easy for you.

•Pay attention to what you do, not to what you feel. Try not to let your anxieties interfere with your actions.

Of course, you will want to individualize your sexual fear assignments, but here are some suggestions: (a) Try a different *place*—the shower, outdoors, the kitchen table. (b) Have sex at a *different time*—in the middle of the night, a tender "quickie in the morning." (c) *Use props*. You can use different kinds of lubricants. The man puts hand lotion on his penis. The woman spreads Vaseline on her clitoris. Spray whipped cream on your partner's genitals and lick it off. You can also utilize dildos and vibrators. A woman can use a vibrator on her partner's penis; a man can stroke his partner's clitoris, nipples or other sensitive areas with it. Or masturbate her using a dildo. (d) *Practice different sexual acts you have avoided*. There must be some sexual positions you haven't tried: bottom . . . side . . . top . . . sitting . . . standing . . . dog fashion (the man enters from behind).

If you have difficulty getting started on your sexual fear assignments or if you experience too much anxiety in the doing of them, there are two steps you can take.

•*Find simpler, lower-anxiety assignments and do them*. No matter how much fear exists, you can always find some starting point. One way: Gently massage each other without touching any erotic areas. One couple started by simply lying together nude with their arms around each other. Another couple couldn't even do that. They had to start by lying together fully clothed, and, bit by bit, remove articles of clothing. The partner with the lesser fear has to be gentle, patient and understanding. In return, he/she will gain not just improved sex but greater warmth and love.

•*Create sexual scenarios*. The principle: to plan the sexual encounter in such a way as to maximize the pleasure, to fill it with the things you most like and, within this context, briefly to *bring in your fear assignment task*. The scenario serves as the base for your evening sexual plans. For those who fear doing new things in sex, game-planning often spurs heightened feelings. You may want to play the role of a famous screen lover (as did the man whose case I cited at the beginning of the chapter) or noted historical lovers like Anthony and Cleopatra, Heloise and Abelard, Romeo and Juliet (what would they have done if they lived?). You may elect to play games like Slave and Master (first you play Slave and your partner plays Master; then you reverse roles). Create whatever scenario appeals to you. One woman says, "I think of my life as a daytime serial. Every day I plan the exciting installment for that night."

Be sure your scenario contains your fear assignment. For example, one woman really wanted to perform oral sex on her husband but was inhibited by a fear of perversion. She could not take the smallest first step. They did work up a "favorite" scenario: She would be the simple farm girl and he the sophisticated city slicker (in reality he grew up on a farm but was not simple; she had grown up in Manhattan but was very unsophisticated). In the scenario the simple farm girl turned out to be far more knowledgeable than the city slicker. She would tease him repeatedly (something they found exciting) until he lost patience and "had his way" with her.

Within this teasing context she brought in the oral sex. At first she would barely brush her lips against his penis as part of her teasing game. Then she quickly would move to a more enjoyable teasing act such as giving his penis a quick squeeze and taking her hand away. He would play-act his frustration and plead for more. As they acted and reenacted this basic scenario with many variations, her penile lip brushings became longer and longer, turned into kisses, little bites, and finally into full oral sex. She had mastered her fear in this area and now could act out of choice.

3. *Use Systematic Desensitization.* Make a hierarchy of the things you have been avoiding or that provoke anxiety. Starting with the lowest, imagine or actually do each act and then relax until you can imagine it or actually do it without experiencing any disturbance. Then move on to the next item. If necessary, use the taped instructions in Appendix III.

Here, as a model, is a fantasy hierarchy I have found useful for men with fears of inadequacy. It is adapted from one used by Dr. Arnold A. Lazarus of Rutgers University for group desensitization.

- Kissing
- Caressing while fully clothed
- Undressing
- Sex play in the nude
- Getting into position for intercourse
- Intromission (entering)
- Intercourse
- Changing position during intercourse

With rather slight changes, the same hierarchy can be used for women who have sexual anxiety. Just remember that you must personalize your own hierarchy; you must make it fit your own fear triggers and tension levels.

Because two people are involved, you can make a reality desensitization very creative.

CASE

"He's uninterested in sex," complained Nancy when she and David came to see me. She pointed out that if she didn't actively—even aggressively—take the lead in initiating sex, they didn't have any. When she seemed to lose interest in the middle of sex, David made no attempt to continue. In actuality, it turned out that David had a great interest in sex but an even greater fear of rejection. He was afraid that if he wanted or started to do something and Nancy refused, he'd feel terribly crushed. This fear of being refused lay behind his lack of sexual initiative.

To break his avoidance habit, we worked out a reality desensitization in the form of a game. For the next few weeks, he was to ask Nancy to do a series of personal things: scratch his back, manicure his nails, give him a kiss. She was to refuse. He then had to convince her. If he was sufficiently persuasive and she felt like saying yes, she would do as he asked. We set up a point system. Each time David convinced Nancy, he got 5 points. Each day that passed without his making a personal request, he lost 5 points. The goal: 100 points. When he reached it, they were to go off on a fishing vacation.

At the end of the first week his score was −15. To encourage him, Nancy spread brochures of the fishing camp around the apartment. By the end of the second week David had scored +5. Suddenly he hit his stride. During the next week he scored 50 points. By the middle of the following week, they had made reservations for the trip. At the fishing camp the thought of Nancy's *no* never occurred to the delighted David.

Systematic Desensitization can be used for every kind of sexual fear—including that of perversion.

CASE

Lenore, a small, rather dainty woman, was married to Phil, a big, husky man. On her initial visit she confessed, "I'm afraid of sex but I don't know why." Her history showed that as a teen-ager, she used to have exciting bondage fantasies in which she was tied down, completely helpless while the man did all kinds of things to her. She still had these fantasies, and when Phil lay on top of her, or even embraced her, she started thinking of bondage, got the same delicious feelings that she had as a teen-ager, then reacted to these thoughts with terror: "I am a pervert." She became so frightened she had to push him away.

I treated Lenore with a combination of fantasy and reality desensitization. In imagery she would imagine such scenes as "You're at a party and a fellow guest speaks contemptuously of someone practicing bondage" . . . "You're tied to the bed and your husband says you're a real freak."

In the reality desensitization, Phil would hold her

tightly until she felt the first signs of discomfort. She would signal him to let go, relax, then have him hold her again. They did this for longer and longer periods of time until she could enjoy it without terror. Next step: Phil would lie on top of her, no sex but just holding her confined. Again at the first sign of disturbance, she would signal, he'd roll off and she'd relax. They did this for longer and longer periods. Her enjoyment increased and, at the same time, so did their sex life. Then they took the reality desensitization a step further. They actually went into bondage. Phil tied Lenore to the bed. She loved it, but he didn't! However, he realized her enjoyment, so on rare occasions—for her sake—they would practice bondage.

WHAT IF THE WORST DOES HAPPEN?

Sometimes the things that most frighten you do happen—or they have already happened. You may have a sexual dysfunction or you may have a variant behavior *that you don't want*. Many of these are either caused or maintained by your fears.

The Sexual Dysfunctions

Four major sexual dysfunctions exist. In men they are impotency and premature ejaculation. In women they are frigidity and vaginismus (when anxiety causes the vaginal muscles to tighten up so that intercourse becomes painful or impossible). Today most of these are relatively easy to treat. If you have been unsuccessful in treating your own problem, *seek professional help*. Two cautions:

•Be certain that it is primarily a sexual problem and not a problem stemming from the relationship itself or from a tangential fear.

•Choose your sex clinic with care. Many now exist. Some are superb. Some are incompetent. Select one that is connected with a reputable medical center or a university.

The Sexual Variant Behaviors

Development of a variant behavior is another "worst that can happen." Variant behaviors are out-of-control sexual acts that usually are accompanied by strong urges, high-pitched excitement and often the after-feeling of self-denigration.

•One type of variant thrusts himself on other people. This category would include men who publicly display their genitals (exhibitionists) or men who sexually molest children (pedophiles). These behaviors are completely unacceptable and must be stopped. They deal with victims, not partners.

•Other variant behavior takes place only between consenting adults. Here, it is the uncontrolled nature of the act that often brings about problems, at times leading to tension between you and your partner, bad feelings about yourself, and to a narrow range of sexual acts and feelings. If you can restore command over your variant behaviors so that you do them through choice rather than compulsivity, they become but one part of your sexual spectrum and lose their ability to harm the relationship or destroy you.

Many times fear sets off your variant behavior. Many times fear keeps you from getting rid of it.

•**When fear triggers the behavior.** In this instance, usually it is the nonsexual social fears (such as fear of rejection or criticism) that trigger the variant act. A situation comes up that triggers the fear. Your fears and anxieties mount to the point where you have to do something to gain relief. Somehow you have learned (perhaps even by accident) that the variant act will give you that relief. So, robotlike, you do it. Remove the fear trigger and you stop the act.

CASE

Sam S. had been arrested a number of times for being a Peeping Tom. A postman, he would go through apartment buildings, look through open peepholes, see what women were home alone, and hopefully find them in a state of *déshabillé*. While looking, he would become very excited and masturbate. These voyeuristic episodes were set off by fears of deprivation. Brought up in a poor family, all his life Sam had feared not having enough to eat or proper clothes. As a teen-ager, he had feared he'd never have a car. This led to stealing episodes and a six-month period in reform school. When working, he saved enough money to buy a car; the stealing stopped.

Now thirty-five, married for twelve years and the father of three, Sam felt deprived because he didn't feel free to have an extramarital affair. A very faithful husband, he didn't really want one, but he heard a lot of macho talk and the feeling of deprivation began and grew. The voyeuristic episodes generally followed the "locker room" type of discussions. Sam wanted to change. Using as a model the way the feeling of deprivation disappeared and the stealing stopped when he bought his own car, I decided to desensitize him to feeling deprived because he did not have extramarital affairs.

Using Systematic Desensitization in fantasy, I had Sam imagine scenes of men he knew talking about affairs . . . then going to a motel with a woman (not his wife). I knew that if he felt free to have an affair, the feeling of deprivation would go. In real life, he did have a very brief affair and then decided he wanted monogamy, and no extramarital lovemaking. The voyeurism disappeared.

•**When fear keeps you from getting rid of the behavior.** This condition usually involves sexual fears. The variant behavior distracts and limits you and so helps you to avoid the more feared aspects of sex.

CASE

Tim, a businessman in his thirties, used to get strong turn-ons with women who possessed shoulder-length hair. If he passed one on the street, he would experience such a strong sexual reaction that he would put his hand in his pocket and masturbate. He was living with a woman who had long blonde hair and his greatest thrill came from shampooing those thick blonde locks. Any contact with her hair set off a wild frenzy of erotic feelings to the point where his whole body would quiver. He wasn't turned on by other parts of her body. Underneath all his behavior lay the core fear that he would be sexually unresponsive. Tim not only felt "like a monster" but continually berated himself for his disinterest in anything but hair. He feared changing because "If I give up my fetish, I'll be completely asexual."

When Tim masturbated, his fantasies were always about hair. We used *orgasmic retraining* to get him to be turned on by other parts of Norma's body. This is what we did:

•During masturbation, when he reached the point of ejaculatory inevitability, he would deliberately switch his fantasy to imagining different parts of her body— breasts, thighs, genitals. In this way he began to associate sexual feelings with those images.

•We began introducing the different parts of her body into his fantasy at various stages, earlier in the masturbation process. First he would arouse himself with the hair fantasy. When he felt aroused, he would switch to thinking of other parts of her body until the feeling of sexual arousedness started to fade. Then he'd go back to the hair fantasy until the excitement built up again and then he'd switch to other parts of her body. Tim found he was able to hold these new images for longer and longer periods of time. Finally he was able to masturbate without any hair fantasy at all.

In life, Tim began to respond more and more to women in general—not just long hair. As he lost his fear of being unresponsive, he was able to give up the exclusive nature of his hair fetish. As he responded to women, he saw he was capable and no longer thought he'd be asexual. As he began to really thrill to other sexual acts, he no longer believed he was a monster. Incidentally, Norma never knew of Tim's hair fetish. She just knew he liked to shampoo her hair—which he still does.

CASE

Ever since adolescence, Bert A., a very successful married internist, had had a strong attachment to women's feet. At work he would notice a patient's feet, feel a strong turn-on, and immediately make up an elaborate fantasy in which he groveled on the floor, kissing her feet while she looked down at him disdainfully. Occasionally, he would go with a prostitute and pay her to act out that scene. These encounters did not end in intercourse. Bert would ejaculate while lying on the floor. In actuality, Bert was frightened of a woman's vagina. The foot fetish helped him avoid the vagina. He also associated dirt with a woman's vagina. The color of the pubic hair mattered. The darker the pubic hair, the more the association with dirt (he was married to a blonde).

We removed this fear by using slides. At a porno store he bought a series of slides of women displaying their genitals and brought the pictures in. We arranged the slides in order of hair color, starting with peroxide blonde and ending with jet black. In my office, Bert would sit in a chair with his eyes closed. When he was completely relaxed, he would look at a slide projected against the wall. At the first sign of disturbance, he would close his eyes and relax. He repeated this over and over until he could look at the slide for two minutes with no uptightness. Then we'd move to the next slide. Eventually we got to the woman with the jet-black pubic hair. At this point Bert noticed that he was sexually freer with his wife, but the fetish was still there. Then, on his own, Bert cut pictures of women's genitals from magazines and at home he practiced touching the pictures. Initially, he felt his fingers were dirty, but eventually he became able to touch them all without this feeling. At this point the fetish stopped.

Sometimes the fear of one partner can maintain the variant behavior of the other.

CASE

Molly and Jack came in because their marriage was in trouble. Jack insisted on dressing in women's clothes. He had a collection of jewelry, make-up, dresses, girdles and padded bras, and insisted on wearing these items when he made love to Molly. While making love, Jack was caught up in a series of masochistic fantasies so that Molly felt "great distance between us." As with most transvestites, Jack had no homosexual tendencies; he was just a man who dressed in women's clothes and derived intense sexual enjoyment from doing this.

In our discussion Jack said, "Nothing's wrong with me. It's her problem. Why does she get so uptight when I do this? Why don't you desensitize her to my wearing female clothes, and then everything will be all right." Jack wanted to stay married. If he believed giving up cross-dressing was necessary to save the marriage, he would do it. We all felt that as long as he had the idea that perhaps he could get his wife to accept him as a tv, he would *not* make the all-out effort to change. So we carried out Systematic Desensitization in fantasy *on Molly.*

First she imagined him walking in the house dressed

in women's clothes . . . then making love in the clothes to her. It took relatively few sessions to get Molly to accept Jack's transvestism. When I did a follow-up check by phone, I learned that the tension had disappeared from the marriage. However, I was disturbed by the case. I asked myself, "What did I do about her feelings for herself as a woman?" . . . "Did I perpetuate a pathological state?" These questions gnawed at me. A year later, writing up the case for a professional journal, on impulse I called and learned that Jack's transvestism was completely gone. For a while he had cross-dressed and read *Drag* magazine, but the joy had gone out of these activities and he got no turn-on. Many interpretations of this change are possible. All we know definitely is that when Molly ceased to react to his cross-dressing, Jack stopped doing it.

Again, I repeat, *you can change sexual fears.* This holds true whether you're a virgin with a fear of penetration or a fetishist. By overcoming the fear, you can change your sexual behavior and thus make your total life and personality happier. Why suffer, when you don't have to?

Sometimes by reducing a fear in the sexual area, you can influence another major life area.

CASE

George R., an ambitious, hard-working manager of a travel agency, came to me because he felt unhappy about his career goals. Several times he had had opportunities to form his own agency. He couldn't take the risk. George felt, "I'm not man enough to carry it off." George traced his insecurity to a lifetime history of believing his penis was too small. This had started during adolescence. Now, rationally, he had convinced himself his penis was average, but the feeling persisted. In recent years it had become exaggerated because he believed he wasn't a good sexual partner. During several premarital affairs he had felt the women were "making believe" they thought him a good lover. Now, he reasoned, "How good can I be if I can't satisfy my wife? She really knows me."

An interview with him and his wife brought out the fact that Louise was fairly happy sexually. She had no complaints, enjoyed the sexual experience and was astounded to hear George had these feelings. She had two sexual problems: (1) a mild difficulty letting herself go; (2) trouble talking about sex. This second problem had increased because any time she tried to communicate any feeling, George would change the subject.

First, we trained Louise to become more verbally expressive. She had to put her feelings into words: "I really enjoyed your tenderness" . . . "You're really a good lover" . . . "I like it when you stay in me for so long." If George brushed her remarks aside, she was to keep right on: "Don't you see how good a lover you are . . . how happy you've made me?" During this part of the training George was to make himself accept her complimentary remarks and encourage her to continue to say them.

Then, using a series of scenes about his penis being too small, I desensitized George to that insecurity: "You're in the shower at summer camp and all the other boys have bigger penises" . . . "During sex at college, the woman asks you, 'Are you inside?' " . . . "You've just finished having sex with your wife and she seems dissatisfied." I also used a second desensitization hierarchy: He had to imagine his wife giving him sexual compliments in various situations.

Over a course of three months both George and Louise found their sex life had become more satisfying. Besides that, he began to feel more confident in many nonsexual situations. A year later George and a friend formed a partnership and opened their own travel agency. By conquering his sexual fear, he expanded both his emotional and professional life.

CHAPTER 9

THE OBSESSIVE-COMPULSIVE

On a recent weekday afternoon, I had just begun a session with a patient when my office doorbell rang very loudly. I called down the stairs, "Who's there?" A woman's voice answered, "It's Mary from Sarge's Delicatessen. Your wife called from Connecticut. She says go turn off the stove right away. Your house is about to burn down!"

I raced to the kitchen, saw various pots on the stove but no lit jets. Nonplussed, I returned to my patient. That night I got the story from Jean.

In her usual state of doing several things simultaneously, that morning she had cooked dinner, worked on a forthcoming book, and left on an 11:00 A.M. train for Westport to give a speech. As the express roared past Rye, Jean suddenly thought, "I left the eggs boiling! The house will burn down. The insurance won't cover it. We'll never be able to pay back what we owe." *By the time she got to her destination, she was in a panic*, and rushed to a pay phone to call me. My line was out of order. She tried the landlord. He wasn't home. She called two friends. They didn't answer. So Jean called our neighborhood delicatessen, identified herself, explained the situation and begged, "Can you walk over, buzz Dr. Fensterheim's doorbell and tell him to turn off the stove. You've got to speak to him personally. Don't leave a note. He won't know it's there." The woman who answered reassured, "I'll do it myself."

Jean managed to deliver her talk (all the time seeing gusts of flame instead of the audience), call back Sarge's and learn that the message had been given to me. She came back home in a state of collapse, paralyzed by imagined possibilities.

This kind of behavior typifies the obsessive-compulsive. Unlike phobics, obsessives do not have a direct fear of a given object or situation. They fear the *imaginary potential consequences stemming from their thoughts about the situation or object.* Often they feel that by carrying out protective rituals they can prevent these disastrous consequences.

People with an obsessive personality tend to be perfectionistic, rigid, dependable, punctual, precise. They like things to be done "right now" and "in the right way" and cannot tolerate any form of ambiguity. Often they are accumulators, have a passion for list-making and concern themselves to an inordinate degree with health and dirt. The majority are introverted, intelligent, and come from middle- or upper-class homes.

Obsessive-compulsives fall into two categories:

1. *The obsessive-compulsive-obsessive.* Here the obtrusive thoughts dominate, haunt, cling to the cortex like adhesive. You can't banish them from your brain. Instead of attempting to control the thoughts, you develop a passivity about them and let them push you around. These upsetting thoughts can take three forms:

•*Indecisiveness.* With obsessional doubts you become a debater about trivialities: "Should I leave a fifty- or seventy-five-cent tip?" . . . "Should I take my umbrella or not?" Offering pros and cons for each side, you become immobilized while your tension grows. Every bedtime one woman takes twenty minutes deciding whether to turn out the light. Each weekday another victim spends so much time deciding whether to drive to the city by bridge or tunnel that he constantly arrives late for work. When you must make a more important decision, you become more obsessive, going for days, weeks, months weighing alternatives. The time for action passes. The event itself may have forced you to go one way or the other, but you didn't make the decision. Sadly, you wonder why "life doesn't go the way I want."

•*Horrific temptation.* Suddenly, a terrifying thought, usually involving aggression, sex, or something you don't want to happen, darts into your mind, spurring sharp anxiety. The aggressive thoughts often concern people close to you (you imagine your spouse has cancer, your mother dying) or important objects in your life (your new house catches fire). Or *you* can be doing something hostile; you mutilate a friend, stab your child. The thought becomes so real and strong that you physically avoid the sight of any sharp object. With sexual thoughts, you imagine doing things you don't want to do with people you don't want to do them with. Most common: homosexual thoughts in heterosexual people. You think of performing a homosexual act, become anxious, worry that you are homosexual, and thus become more anxious.

•*Rumination.* In this most common form of obsessional thinking, you continually ponder about past and future fears and frustrations. You think "I will fail" . . . "I have failed" . . . "If only I had ———" . . . "He doesn't like me" . . . "Why did my boss give me that funny look when I passed his door?" For example, a news editor on a major daily dwells for days on how he should have handled a certain story. He makes up imaginary memos in which he answers possible complaints from the managing editor. In actuality, in fifteen years the managing editor has never complained.

Obsessives tend to rationalize and justify these thoughts. For example, if you think constantly about how "terribly" the boss treats you, you convince yourself you're "thinking through the problem." Or you have an insurance attitude: "If I worry about it (getting fired, being stood up) enough, it won't happen." Most of the things people worry about do not happen. Thus, when no disaster occurs, you get reinforced, and say to yourself, "This kind of thinking works. I didn't get fired today."

2. *The obsessive-compulsive-compulsive.* Here ritual activities dominate your life. By performing a certain act, you relieve your anxious feelings or avoid them completely. For example, you touch something "covered with germs" and "contaminate" your hands. You become increasingly nervous about spreading the contamination, so you carefully wash your hands over and over and the anxiety disappears—until you become contaminated again.

•*The rituals:* Although compulsive handwashing is probably the most common ritual, many others exist. Some are so pervasive that they completely debilitate you; others are mild eccentricities that have little impact on your life. Whatever the ritual, you work out every detail and perform it over and over.

•One woman is obsessed by the thought of germs on her kitchen counter ("They'll make the whole family sick"). She scrubs the counter with plastic wool and Ivory soap, first with a circular motion, then up and down, finally side to side. Then, using the same series of motions, she rinses it off with a clean cloth, then a second and third cloth. Believing she might have missed something, she repeats the same process again and again. It takes her three hours to clean the counter after each meal. During this period she agonizes, "If I don't do it in just this way my husband and children will get a disease."

•One man has a mild compulsion in the shower. For the area between navel and knees, he uses one cake of soap and washcloth; for every other area he uses another piece of soap and cloth. If he doesn't do this, he feels dirty and has to take another shower immediately, this time "washing myself properly."

Anything can become a ritual. One student has to take all required reading to her adult education class;

each week she carries ten books in a special satchel she had made for that purpose. A house husband has to have every can with the labels facing outward; he uses a string to make sure they're in an even line. You may have a compulsion to count (you can't enter a room without counting all the legs on the furniture) or to keep things in order (you have to arrange the blankets on your bed in a certain way or you can't go to sleep).

•*Checking:* Compulsives triple and quadruple check. Often you doubt you've performed a task that you just completed minutes before. You go back four times to see if you locked the car, left a cigarette burning, the gas on. One man worries constantly, "Did I sign my name to that check?"; he always calls up the recipient to verify. A jeweler returns to his office an average of five times nightly to make sure he locked his safe. Once he went from Westchester to Manhattan on a weekend to check.

If you're an obsessive-compulsive, you should:

a.   Realize that usually the pattern of thoughts and rituals increases when you're tense, overfatigued or feel physically unwell.

b.   Learn to recognize the difference between constructive and nonconstructive thoughts. A constructive thought leads to action or learning. A nonconstructive thought leads to depression and anxiety. The thought content may be the same. You think, "I'm in a rut. I do the same things over and over." If you add the thought, "What can I do to get out of the rut?" that's constructive. If you obsess, "My life is terrible—everything is just so boring," that's nonconstructive. You have to learn to recognize the thoughts over which you want to get control.

c.   Understand the difference between conscientiousness and compulsiveness. Conscientiousness represents goal-oriented behavior with the purpose of getting something done. With compulsiveness, you have the goal of controlling your anxiety. You carry out your rituals and/or checks, thinking, "If I get every little detail right, I won't feel so anxious." Often this kind of thinking results in a failure to organize your life in terms of priorities. You can't see that some things are important, some moderately important, some trivial. The result: You put too much energy into the trivial. If something trivial goes wrong, you care just as much as if it were a major event.

For instance, it takes one woman an entire week to do her family laundry. She goes over every garment belonging to her three sons, husband and self, examining each for possible tears, loose buttons, etc. After she finishes, she does it again, thinking, "Maybe I missed something." She does the same before she sends clothes to the cleaner and when they come back. Margie is so busy with the laundry that she has little time for anything else—like pleasure.

The way these obsessive thoughts and compulsions affect your life varies widely. Sometimes victims require hospitalization as did one young mother who compulsively picked her two-year-old son's scabs until he bled. *If your condition is severe you must seek professional help.* Fortunately, most cases are not that severe. Fortunately, too, the methods, developed for the very obsessive by such clinical researchers as Drs. Isaac M. Marks of Bethlehem Royal and Maudsley Hospitals, London, and Leslie Solyom of McGill University's Allan Memorial Institute, Montreal, work even better with mild garden-variety forms of this condition.

A PROGRAM FOR MILD OBSESSIVE COMPULSIONS

Break Up the Obsessive Process by Controlling Your Compulsions

Helpful technique: *Response Prevention.* This is the way it works. You have the habit of both thinking certain thoughts and becoming anxious or frightened about them. By performing the ritual, you get relief from the anxiety. Thus your ritual serves as a form of escape; by executing it, you remove yourself from the upsetting situation. However, as with other automatic fear reactions, escape prolongs and strengthens the fear response. You don't give yourself the chance to learn that *what you fear will not happen*.

To keep yourself from escaping, you must prevent yourself from performing the ritual. If you prevent the ritual response and, instead, practice going through the obsessive anxiety calmly, the obsessive thoughts will eventually stop. It's analogous to agoraphobia, in which the cure is not escape from the frightening situation, like a crowded department store, but staying there and calmly going through your panic. The difference is that here the thoughts in your head serve as the frightening situation.

In carrying out response prevention your predilection for list-making and counting can prove an aid.

CASE

The compulsive cleanliness of Irma M., a twenty-nine-year-old housewife, was driving her husband mad. Unable to distinguish between important and trivial tasks, as her husband entered the house, Irma would immediately grasp the vacuum cleaner to sweep the floor after him. During dinner she would repeatedly jump up to empty the ashtray, raise a picture an inch, adjust a curtain. Because she was so involved with these tidying tasks, she often burned the dinner. Irma refused any weekend expeditions ("I have too much to do in the house"). They had to stop entertaining because for four days before a party Irma cleaned like Craig's wife. Pete couldn't take it.

I had Irma make up a list of fifteen daily chores and rate each on a scale of 1 to 3. One represented the most important—bedmaking, dishwashing, etc. Two stood for moderately important, those it would be nice if she completed. Three signified the trivial tasks. She came up with four of the latter: silver-polishing, mirror-washing, dusting every piece of furniture, sweeping up after her husband's entrance.

Her first assignment was *not* to do any of these four chores for one week. This proved too hard for Irma; by the third day, she gave in to her feelings of tension and did them all. We created an easier assignment: For one week she had to refrain from polishing the silver. She accomplished this. Then she had to refrain for another week. This time it proved easier. Every two weeks we eliminated another task. Within three to four months, the home atmosphere had changed from strife to relative tranquility. One night Pete came home, noticed dust on an end table, and called this to Irma's attention. She shrugged it away saying, "I didn't think it was important."

Preventing yourself from yielding to the compulsive urge may prove too difficult for you to accomplish by sheer willpower. You may need help from another person. Effective method: Set up a contract in which, by refraining from your ritual, you can earn something you want very much from the other person.

THE COMPULSIVE'S CONTRACT

Aim: To prevent your ritual response.

STEP ONE: Clearly specify the response you want to prevent—checking to make sure all doors are locked, compulsive handwashing, etc.

STEP TWO: Describe the reward you want to receive from your partner—social (a night on the town), a special gift, sexual favors.

STEP THREE: Specify what you must do to earn the reward. For example, you begin by establishing that you earn the reward if you refrain from the ritual for a day. After earning the reward at one level, you raise the ante—to three days, a week, a month. In earning it, you must keep a record on a calendar. Check off the days you *do* stop the ritual, not those you don't.

CASE

Fred A. had constant obsessive thoughts about other people dying: "My mother will get a heart attack" . . . "If John flies to California, he'll crash" . . . "What will I do if my wife dies of cancer?" To get relief from these thoughts, Fred had developed a series of rituals. He used to brush his teeth about forty times a day (carrying tube and brush in his pocket), wash his hands compulsively, step on cracks in the sidewalk, and constantly straighten all the clothes in his closet by taking all jackets and shirts off the hangers and putting them back. We worked on all the rituals successfully until only the closet compulsion remained. To overcome that, Fred drew up a contract with his wife. The premise: He would give up his closet checking in return for more home entertaining, something he enjoyed and his wife disliked doing.

FRED'S CLOSET CONTRACT

CLAUSE ONE: Fred had to refrain from closet checking for seven days (these did not have to be consecutive). Then he could claim his reward.

CLAUSE TWO: At this point his wife would immediately invite another couple for dinner. Until Fred earned his reward, no company at all.

CLAUSE THREE: After earning his reward twice, Fred had to go fourteen ritual-free days to earn the next reward for another dinner.

CLAUSE FOUR: If at any point Fred managed twenty-one consecutive ritual-free days, they would have either a cocktail party or dinner for twelve. The choice was his.

Fred found the first few weeks of carrying out the contract very hard. At the end of the second ritual-free week, the tension from his thoughts became so strong (on one occasion his wife went shopping and he thought she had died en route) that he almost reverted. However, he yearned for that cocktail party, so he kept at it. As he mastered his obsessive thoughts and closet ritual, many feelings emerged. All the worries about dying somehow had masked a lot of the anger he felt toward his wife and had been unable to express. Now he could voice the anger, not hide it in checking. As the tension from the obsessiveness became reduced, his wife got her real reward. Fred became a more tender lover—and he stopped talking about people dying.

You can also set up a self-contract.

CASE

Connie M., a thirty-year-old high school teacher, had three loves in life: baseball (she went every weekend in season), basketball (as often as she could) and binge eating. When she came to me, Connie was 120 pounds overweight. The craving for food would start in midmorning and increase as the day went on. At work, she could control it. As soon as she left school, the bingeing would start. Weekends turned into orgies. She would eat a loaf of bread in one evening and eleven bagels for breakfast the next morning. I explained to Connie that she had to go through the binge feelings and not give in to them. She got the concept but couldn't carry it out. I had her set up a self-contract. It was spring. Each weekend she had to refrain from a certain amount of bingeing in order to go to the ball game on Sunday.

First we tried a contract of no bingeing before 5:30 P.M. This didn't work. Next, to get to that baseball game, Connie had to have one binge-free day during the week. Connie picked Friday and scheduled dates with friends for that night; with her friends she felt too ashamed to binge. She was able to control herself when she got home. Next, we drew up a contract with two binge-free days, then three, etc. Sometimes Connie earned the right to attend the game; sometimes she lost. But *she stuck with the contract.* By January (the middle of the basketball season) she had gone through seven binge-free weeks, and the compulsive "I must eat" feeling was diminishing. She had also lost twenty-five pounds. It was a beginning.

In using Response Prevention, never discuss your obsessive thoughts with other people and don't write them down. Doing that will only make them stronger. By calling attention to the thoughts, you increase them.

Break the Habit of Uncontrolled Thinking

1. *Learn to relax.* The more tense you feel, the more fear-provoking thoughts you have. It's logical to assume that by learning to relax, you can indirectly control your thoughts. The problem: Many obsessive people experience difficulty relaxing. Their disturbing thoughts of future or past disasters keep intruding. Often I hear the sentence, "My body's relaxed, but my mind isn't." The following exercise is especially designed for those who are prisoners of their thoughts. Its purpose: to help you gain deliberate control over your thought processes so you can reduce your anxiety. You will do this by evoking a series of images.

EXERCISE IN THOUGHT RELAXATION

Aim: To relax your mind.

STEP ONE: Put the exercise on tape so that you can use it when tension is building up and you want to relax. You might have a friend with a soothing voice record it for you. Another alternative: Have a friend read it to you. However, the latter technique is not as effective because he/she may not be around when you need the anxiety reduction.

STEP TWO: Allow five minutes for the exercise.

STEP THREE: Allow a seven-to-ten-second gap of silence between each question.

STEP FOUR: As you do the exercise, lie down or sit back in a comfortable position. Find a quiet place where you will not be disturbed. Keep your eyes closed throughout.

STEP FIVE: Now begin. I am going to ask you some questions. You answer inside yourself, not aloud. Your answer can be "yes," "no," "maybe," "sometimes" or even no answer at all. Your response to the question is your answer.

Can you let your eyelids feel heavier and heavier?

Can you let your right arm feel more relaxed than your left arm?

Can you imagine looking at an object in the far distance?

Can you imagine watching a beautiful sunset over a body of water?

Can you imagine what a painting of a sunset might look like if it were done by a modern abstract painter?

Can you remember the smell of fresh strawberries?

Can you remember as a child the good taste of ice cream on a summer day?

Can you imagine a country lake in the summertime?

Can you imagine a country lake in the winter?

Or in the fall when the leaves are turning?

Have you ever smelled fresh bread or cake baking?

Can you count the colors in a rainbow?

Can you imagine looking at a campfire on a pleasant summer night?

Can you let yourself feel the warmth radiating from that campfire?

Can you let your legs and thighs feel pleasantly heavier?

Can you imagine looking at a beautiful flower right in front of you?

Can you imagine smelling that flower?

Can you listen to the sound of your own breathing?

Can you breathe easily and comfortably the way you do in a deep sleep?

Can you imagine a pleasant scene or think of the word *calm?*

Can you allow your whole body to feel calm and relaxed?

Calm and relaxed?

Calm and relaxed?

(Additional ten-second pause)

Now you may open your eyes but stay relaxed. The exercise is over.

STEP SIX: Practice this exercise often enough so that you remember the questions and can go through the routine without a tape. You can even do it riding on a bus on your way to a tension-making appointment.

2. *Use Thought Stoppage.* This is the technique I outlined in chapter 4 where *as soon as* and *every time* you have an obsessive thought you want to control, you say STOP! to yourself, then "Calm," and relax your muscles. The Thought Stoppage method takes

time. You must also possess the motivation to stick with it. It is particularly useful for hypochondriacs who want to change. Unfortunately, many don't for two reasons: (a) to them, their imaginary diseases are real; they really do have all those aches and pains; (b) through their fancied health problems they get other people to pay attention to them or they feel free to pamper themselves.

CASE

Ken J., an accountant in his late thirties, felt sure he would die of some disease like pneumonia, appendicitis, ulcers, arthritis or a heart attack. He walked around with a thermometer in his pocket and constantly took his pulse. Several times a week he checked in with his internist, cardiologist and ear, nose and throat specialist. Ken had little concern about his hypochondria; to him the symptoms were very real. However, his perpetual stops on city streets to take his pulse caused friction with his girlfriend. At her urging he came to me.

We used the Thought Stoppage method. Ken found that STOP! by itself wasn't strong enough, but the technique worked if, as he said STOP!, he stamped his foot. If a co-worker remarked on this new habit, Ken explained it with "My foot keeps falling asleep." It took seven weeks to control his constant thoughts about illness. Then Ken developed a new worry: "What if I really get sick? Will I ignore it?"

Tip: As a useful alternate try the Hashmark Technique. For example, recently an analyst came to me with the problem of inability to concentrate. As a patient would free associate on the couch, Dr. Smith's mind would wander. This interfered with his work. He knew he was missing clinical information and he also had trouble reading professional papers. I gave him a simple exercise derived from Thought Stoppage: *As soon as* and *every time* he became aware of his lack of attention, he should make a hashmark on a sheet of paper and deliberately concentrate on either paper or patient. On the initial day he had two pages covered with hashmarks. However, from then on, they decreased until eventually he got through the day with no hashmarks.

3. *Use the "blow-up technique"* (a phrase I am borrowing from Dr. Arnold A. Lazarus of Rutgers University). In this you combat your obsessional thoughts by exaggerating them. You may have tried to gain control of your thoughts by stopping them and failed. If you venture the reverse technique and blow up the thoughts, you may be able to see how ludicrous they are. For instance, one secretary constantly worried that she would get fired because her work was too slow. I had her carry her thoughts to mental hyperbole: "I'll make some little error which will destroy the company . . . I'll be put on a blacklist. No one will employ me. I'll starve . . . I'll have to go on relief . . . The blacklist will also include members of my family. My nephew and niece won't be able to get jobs either. We'll all die of starvation . . ." By deliberately doing this, she eventually was able to control her thoughts.

CASE

Nan and Joe, both in their late twenties, were living together. Obsessively jealous and certain he was having an affair, Nan would start off each evening with a barrage of questions: "What did you do during lunch hour?" . . . "Whom did you talk to during the day?" . . . "Why did you come home so late from work?" . . . "Was that letter from some girlfriend?" For some months Joe, who was completely innocent of any playing around, answered the questions factually, but finally exploded. They made an appointment for a session with me.

We tried Thought Stoppage and Response Prevention. Nan couldn't do either. So we experimented with the blow-up technique. I told Nan that, instead of asking questions, she was to exaggerate what was on her mind. When Joe answered, he was to build up ridiculous details. For instance, Nan would say, "I'm sure that you met a girlfriend and went right off to a hotel and spent your lunch hour making passionate love." In his response, Joe would voice something like, "You're right. She was waiting for me in front of the building the way she does every day. But she wasn't alone. She brought a friend. We didn't go to a hotel. I know a restaurant with a private dining room. The three of us made love and for kicks the waitress joined in too."

Both found this fun. When she was alone, Nan used it on herself. Every time she did, she began to laugh and soon the obsession lost its hold. *Note:* When I first began to use this method, I was a little afraid that it might strengthen the obsessiveness. There have been times it has not worked, but it has never made the thoughts worse.

Substitute Learned Competency for Learned Helplessness

Because the fear situation exists inside your head, you cannot get away from it. Your rituals provide only temporary relief. Any release from the terrible thoughts seem to happen accidentally, not because of anything you do to control them. This kind of situation leads to a much-studied condition called learned helplessness, which many theorists feel serves as the greatest inducer of depression. This is probably one of the main reasons depression so often acts as a concomitant of obsessions. In addition, because the obsessive mainly seeks relief from anxiety, he often loses sight of more rewarding goals in life. Combined with the passivity about the thoughts, this deepens the depression.

The following exercises, which I developed in the course of treating many obsessive-compulsives, should provide a feeling of learned competency, enable you to substitute an active orientation for a passive one, and help restore a search for positive life goals.

COUNTERING LEARNED HELPLESSNESS—I

Aim: To defeat learned helplessness by gaining control of pleasurable reinforcers.

STEP ONE: Your assignment: Each day *deliberately* do something—preferably something trivial—that will afford you a momentary feeling of pleasure. As soon as you have done it, write down the action in your Fear Control Training workbook. If you experienced the slightest feeling of pleasure, put a check mark after it. The key word here is *deliberately.* You have to think in advance, "I will do such and such to see if it gives me pleasure." Do not fall in the trap of thinking, "An hour ago I did such and such and it made me feel good, so I'll count that as part of the exercise." The "trivial" aspect also matters. Most people tend to ignore the trivial pleasures they can give themselves in the course of twenty-four hours. You stand your best chance of success by this deliberate doing of trivial pleasures.

Tailor your actions to the things that give *you* pleasure. On a beautiful day one man took a walk after lunch instead of going right back to his office. Another used body powder after a shower. Another bought a record for the pleasure of listening. You can start to read a new best seller, spend time in the library, luxuriate in the tub for an hour, just take a big stretch.

STEP TWO: For the first week do one pleasurable thing a day. Then for the next three weeks do two a day. For the purpose of this exercise you cannot repeat the same action. If you do, it does not count as part of the exercise. You will find the exercise gets more difficult as you go along.

COUNTERING LEARNED HELPLESSNESS—II

Aim: To defeat learned helplessness by increasing your self-respect.

STEP ONE: Each day deliberately do something trivial that will increase your self-respect. Follow the same procedure as in the above exercise. After you've performed your self-assignment, write it down in your FCT workbook and put a check next to it if you answer yes to the question, "Did this answer increase my self-respect?" This exercise differs from the first because sometimes the things you have to do to increase your self-respect may not be pleasurable.

STEP TWO: Do one action a day for the first week; then for the next three weeks perform two actions a day.

CASE

Larry M. came in with a moderate depression which he had had for several years. He got no joy out of his marriage, his job, his life. A sales manager for a manufacturing concern, he felt upset because his constant depression had started to affect his relationships with customers. Larry had a pattern of continual self-put-downs. After a conversation, he told himself, "You didn't handle that right." Before a pending business appointment, he would think, "You're not good enough to handle it properly." He felt he wasn't good enough for his wife ("Look at the way I spoke to her at breakfast!"). Because of his depression, his sex drive had suffered. He couldn't tell me one good thing about himself.

I explained to Larry that if he had someone who walked alongside him all day long, constantly putting him down, through sheer repetition he would come to believe it. This is what he had done to himself. We used a combination of Thought Stoppage and the helplessness exercises. To increase his sense of pleasure in life Larry treated himself to ice cream for dessert, started using aftershave lotion, joined a theater club. His first "self-respect" action was to buy his wife a bouquet of sweetheart roses. Because he felt he had been inconsiderate of her, this gesture of affection made him respect himself. He also started doing exercises every morning. He hated them but felt better about himself for doing them.

As Larry began to achieve a feeling of being in control of his pleasures, he also gained control of his put-down thoughts. Because he gained awareness of his own need for self-respect, he became a more assertive personality. From her heart his wife paid him an accolade: "It isn't just that you're calmer and more fun to be with. You seem stronger. You've acquired dignity."

CHAPTER 10 ————————————

OVERCOMING YOUR FEAR OF FLYING: A LEARNING PLAN

During World War II, Daniel M., a young bombardier, was shot down over the Hump in the Pacific. From then on he refused to fly. Recently Dan, now in his fifties and father of two children in college, lost the job of magazine space salesman that he had had for many years. After eight months of unemployment he landed the post of New York sales representative for a Texas-based organization. Two days after Dan started work, the Texas boss called and commanded, "Fly here tonight. I need you for a meeting first thing tomorrow." Dan agreed. Ten minutes later, Dan called the boss back, saying hesitatingly and fearfully, "I can't. I just can't get on a plane."

The next day Dan got fired. Panicked at the thought of job-hunting again, he couldn't eat or sleep. His tension grew. Five days later Dan dropped dead of a heart attack. In actuality, his fear of flying had triggered the coronary that killed him.

Fear of flying can abort or ruin business careers, end vacations before they begin, put marriages in peril, cause endless anguish and self-flagellation. Many people feel they are alone in their fears. They say, "I'm different. No one could be as terrified as I am." Nothing could be further from the truth. Industry spokesmen estimate that twenty million people in the United States alone suffer from aviaphobia.

Often the flying phobic, who is able to board a plane, follows a pattern, experiencing fear prior to, during and after the flight.

For example, Terry R., a twenty-six-year-old literary agent, says, "If I knew about a business flight a month in advance, I'd dream about it. I'd read the papers looking for news of crashes. Two weeks before the trip, I'd get gut-wrenching panic. I didn't think about anything else but the trip. I knew I'd have a stroke or heart attack on the plane. A week before I'd call up my relatives and tell them where to find my bankbooks and jewelry. The night before the flight I couldn't sleep. At the airport I'd check in, have three Bloody Marys and think, 'What am I doing here?' I kept telling myself, 'You can leave.' By the time I got on the plane I was a wreck. The pressure was so intense I thought my head would burst. My stomach was in knots and my heart jumping out of my chest. All my attention was on the sound of the engine. By the time we landed I was a zombie. I couldn't unpack and my legs didn't seem to work."

Terry's pattern typifies that of many aviaphobes, but it differs in one respect. She conquered her fear of flying. She accomplished this by taking the Fear Control Training methods we have outlined so far in this book and applying them to aviaphobia.

Studies show that unless you want to *you no longer have to suffer from fear of flying.* In 75 percent of the cases, the Fear Control Training method works.

In other words, the odds are three to one in your favor that you can gain command of your fear. This does not mean that you'll no longer be afraid to buy a plane ticket, to hear the plane door close or the sound of the engine change. *You may still possess the fear but you can control it.* Again the FCT premise: Fears are learned behaviors. If you can learn to change your behavior, you can reduce your fear.

The following eight-point program is specifically designed to help you overcome your fear of flying. Any

FCT program must be custom-tailored to your individual needs. Select from this what will help *you* the most.

AN EIGHT-POINT PROGRAM TO OVERCOME YOUR FEAR OF FLYING

You Must Have the Willingness At Least to Attempt to Change

Don't expect magic. As with all unlearning, relearning, new learning, you have to be prepared to expend time and energy. Part of your willingness to change stems from your current motivation (one woman felt she "must take action" when, during a flight home from Rome, her three-year-old daughter asked, "Why are you sitting with a blanket over your head and crying?"). Ask yourself two questions: (1) "Am I willing to put in the necessary work?" and (2) "Do I want to get rid of the fear *now?*"

Check to See Whether Your Fear of Flying Produces Rewards You Actively Desire

Two types of rewards exist.

1. The fear of flying *adds* something to your life, something important to you that otherwise would not be there. It may be attention, power over others, decision-making privileges.

2. The fear of flying may *subtract* something from your life, in general removing the need to do something that you don't want to do. For example, the inconvenience of traveling, the obligation to visit certain people.

You may be fully conscious of the reward. For instance, Craig M., a banking executive, came to see me under pressure from his superiors who wanted to promote him to a job that would require much flying. Craig told me, "If I could fly, they'd send me all over the country and I'd rather be with my family than get a promotion." Craig was fully cognizant of his reward. He was also aware of the price he paid for his phobia: no promotion, no salary increase, some loss of self-esteem. However, he was willing to pay this price and told me, "Thank you, but I'd rather not overcome my fear of flying." He made a deliberate decision to keep his fear.

You may be completely unaware of the reward you gain from your fear of flying. In another instance, Carol C., a very passive wife and mother, had great difficulty in saying no. The problem was at its very worst in relation to her demanding parents, who lived three thousand miles away on the West Coast and constantly commanded her to "visit us." Carol would have been going to Los Angeles many times a year except that her terror of flying kept her from boarding a plane. No matter how she tried to give in to her parents' demands for a visit, she was unable to do so. She couldn't go by train because that would require staying away from her three young children too long. In this case, Carol's fear of flying kept her from doing what she didn't want to do anyway. However, she was completely unaware of the reward she gained by her fear.

Ask yourself, "Is there any way in which my fear of flying benefits me?"

Evaluate What Frightens You

You don't have to rid yourself of the fear but learn to be in command of the symptoms.

•*You must think through what really frightens you. It is not sufficient to say you are afraid of flying.*

All people who fear flying are not frightened by the same thing. Many fear crashes and being crippled or killed. Others fear storms, the confinement, the height, loss of self-control, not being in control (a common core fear of achiever-perfectionist types), human error, mechanical error, hijacking—to name a few of the most common.

It is most important to know specifically what the *core* of your fear is—what it is that really frightens you. Different core phobias make you responsive to different cues in the environment. Even with the same core phobia, people have learned to fear different things.

EXAMPLE ONE: Ms. X, Ms. Y and Ms. Z fear crashing. But Ms. X experiences terror at takeoff, Ms. Y during the middle part of the trip when she anxiously scans the skies for signs of lightning, and Ms. Z goes through agony during the landing.

EXAMPLE TWO: Mr. A, Mr. B and Mr. C also fear crashes. Mr. A can get into a Piper Cub which flies relatively close to the ground but feels terror in a 747. Mr. B is the reverse. In a large plane, he feels relatively comfortable but would no more get into a small plane than he would enter a cage with a hungry tiger. Mr. C can't make himself get into any plane.

After you identify the core phobia, you have to learn the specific cues that relate to it: the specific sights, sounds, thoughts, and occurrences that set off and heighten your own fear reaction.

•*Take your own flying history*. The fear of flying is like all other fears: Although all people with the fear of flying have certain things in common, the specific fear is yours and represents the product of your life experience. The following quiz should help you to analyze your fear symptoms, the cues that set off your fear and what you can do to face that fear. Fill in the answers in your Fear Control Training workbook. This will take time, thought and honesty.

FEAR OF FLYING QUIZ

Aim: To help you pinpoint your fears and the cues to which you respond.

1. Have you ever flown? Yes_____ No_____
2. Have you flown with relative comfort? Yes_____ No_____
3. What was the longest flight you have ever taken?
4. Did either or both of your parents have a fear of flying?
5. When did you first become aware of your fear of flying?
6. About how many flights have you taken since then?
   None_____ 1–5_____ 6–20_____ More_____
7. Has the fear been getting: Better_____ Worse_____ Staying about the same_____
8. When do you experience the fear? In answering this, use the scale of 0 to 100. 0 = no disturbance at all. 100 = panic and sheer terror. Put the extent of disturbance next to each of the following items:

Item	Rating
Talking of taking a plane trip	_____
Getting ticket	_____
Packing for trip	_____
Night before trip	_____
On way to airport	_____
At airport	_____
Boarding plane	_____
Fastening seat belt	_____
Taxiing to runway	_____
Climbing after takeoff	_____
Early part of flight	_____
Midflight	_____
Near end of flight	_____

Item	Rating
Losing altitude for landing	_____
Coming into landing	_____
Landing—touchdown	_____
Leaving plane	_____
Others	_____

9. Generally how do you experience the fear? Check those that apply.

Tension_____		Shaking_____	
Feeling faint_____		Feeling nauseated_____	
Palpitations_____		Others_____	
Feeling hysterical_____			

10. What were the worst feelings you ever experienced?

11. Are you afraid of feelings you *might* experience? If so, what are they?

12. Do you get thoughts along with the fears?
      Yes_____ No_____
    —Do you mull them over and over with gradually increasing fear?
    —Do they suddenly pop into your mind bringing on high levels of fear all at once?
    —Are the thoughts generally of the same thing or do they keep changing? What are the usual contents of the thoughts?

13. Do you have other phobias that may be connected with fear of flying?

Small places_____
Being trapped_____
Heights_____
Physical injury_____
Death_____
Losing control of your feelings_____
Not being in control of the situation_____

Going crazy_____
Looking foolish_____

14. What cues set off your fear reactions?
Rate each cue, using the following scale:

0 = not important at all   2 = quite important
1 = slightly important   3 = extremely important

Size of plane_____
Length of flight_____
Time of day_____
Time of year_____
Closing of door prior to takeoff_____
How crowded_____
Position of seat (aisle, window, etc.)_____
Who's in next seat_____
Changes in engine sound_____
Changes in plane vibrations_____
Unusual sounds_____
Unusual movements of plane_____
Height at which flying_____
Looking out window_____
Weather_____
Turbulence_____
Signs of possible malfunction_____
The flashing of "fasten seat belt"_____
Pilot's voice on intercom_____
Pilot's voice sounds blurred over intercom_____
Sounds from other passengers_____
Physical sensations of flight (for example,
pressure changes in ears)_____
Being afraid_____
Having to sit passively in chair while pilot
controls your life_____
Others_____

15. What kinds of things have you done—or can
you do—to help control, even partially, the fear?

Relax_____
Read_____
Listen to music _____
Work_____
Converse_____
Travel with someone you know_____
Travel alone_____
Watch a movie_____
Eat_____
Drink_____
Walk around plane_____
Do a puzzle_____
Play a game like chess, solitaire_____
Others_____

16. What did your original fear of flying have as a core fear? *Note:* It may have been different from what it is now. Your original fear may have changed.
　　—How did you learn this original fear?
17. What is your core fear now?
18. What is the worst thing that can happen to you?
19. Do you gain any rewards from your fears?
　　—What does your fear of flying add to your life (like attention that you wouldn't ordinarily have)?
　　—What does it subtract from your life that you really do not want in your life (like visiting your mother-in-law)?
　　—How important are these rewards to you? Can you get them in some other way?
20. What things do you do to make your fear worse?

Your answers to this quiz should help you to plan your retraining program. From them, you should establish your main fear and the cues that set it off, the things you already do to try to manage the fear as well as the things you do to intensify the fear. Look for possible payoffs for being frightened; you may have to do something about these before you can master the fear itself. Pay special attention to cues that set up only a slight amount of fear (like the size of plane or time of flight). These may serve as good takeoff points for your program.

Get Information about Flying

Experts say that chances of a recurrence of the terrifying "freak" two-plane collision at Tenerife airport are reassuringly slim. Flying by commercial jet in the U.S. is now at least fifteen times as safe per passenger-mile as driving a car. The passenger who shows his ticket to the smiling stewardess and buckles himself into his seat has a 99.999 percent chance of arriving at his destination safe and sound. In 1976 the U.S. airlines had the fewest accidents in twenty years. Another fact: There are ten times as many flights operating safely today as there were fifteen to twenty years ago—and they're operating under weather conditions that fifteen or twenty years ago might have grounded them.

Reading books like Robert Serling's *Loud and Clear* and the various aviation magazines (check your local library) may help you to get over that paralyzing dream of falling . . . falling . . . falling through space. By reading you'll learn that it takes as long for a pilot to qualify for command of an aircraft as it does for a doctor to qualify for practice. Seven years is the average time a copilot serves before he wears the coveted stripes of a captain. And a pilot's training never stops. His flying ability and his capacity for command are tested twice a year by special check flights and by comprehensive examination. You'll also learn that every jetliner is equipped with a device that stridently warns a pilot who is unknowingly flying toward a mountainside, a tower, or on the ground.

The airlines are increasingly aware of the need to help people get over their fear of flying and will be pleased to answer your questions or refer you to someone who can. Get in touch with the publicity or promotion director of the major airlines in your city (if you live in a small town you may have to contact airline officials in the nearest major city).

Control Your Tensions

Your tensions do two things to you: (1) they build up your anxieties before you board the plane—and may even keep you from getting on it; (2) during the trip you become more and more tense so that your trip functions as fright training. That's why aviaphobes who do fly *do not get better*. With each flight the fear may get worse. In one experiment, conducted by Dr. Leslie Solyom, Allan Memorial Institute, McGill University, Montreal, Fear Control Training for fear of flying obtained relatively poor results with participants who had done a lot of flying just prior to the FCT project. Their continuing reinforcement training in being frightened was such effective training that it proved difficult for them to unlearn.

If you practice countering your tensions, you will pull down your preflight fears and give the in-flight fears a chance to dissipate.

1. *Use the relaxation exercises.*

EXERCISE IN
FLIGHT RELAXATION TRAINING

Aim: To calm down.

STEP ONE: Practice both the Full and Intermediate Relaxation Exercises in Appendix I until you feel fairly adept with them.

STEP TWO: Take an armchair at home and practice these two exercises as if you were sitting in an airplane seat. If you would feel embarrassed by other people noticing your outward signs of tension (such as my instructions to grimace when you tighten your facial muscles), practice tightening these muscles with a minimum of outward signs.

STEP THREE: In the days prior to the flight, do either the Full or Intermediate exercises at least once a day. If you feel quite tense, do it more frequently. Your purpose: to keep down your general level of tension.

STEP FOUR: On the night (or nights) just before the flight, do the exercise just before you go to sleep. This should: (1) help you to sleep and (2) lead to a deeper, more refreshing sleep than you would ordinarily get.

STEP FIVE: On the way to the plane, do Instant Relaxation. Take a deep breath; hold it; let it out slowly, picture a pleasant scene, say "Calm," and relax.

STEP SIX: Bring your relaxation tapes and a cassette player aboard the plane with you. The airlines permit this. Most players have an earplug attachment so that you can listen to the relaxation tapes with privacy. Do your exercises on the plane: that is what you have been training yourself to do. Start doing them as soon as you settle yourself in your seat and use the Full or Intermediate exercises throughout the flight as needed.

CASE

Forty-year-old Daisy M. hadn't flown for twenty-five years. This refusal to fly had become a source of tension between her and her husband because it limited their vacations and family visits. He had started vacationing alone. This bothered Daisy and she came to me. I gave her relaxation training and when she saw she *could relax herself* she decided to accompany her husband on a brief trip to Pittsburgh which he had to make for business. She took her cassette player and relaxation tapes in a tote bag. Also, per my instruction, she told the stewardess about her flying phobia (this was good because many people fear the stewardess seeing their anxiety; it affords some relief if you explain in advance). On the plane Daisy started her relaxation exercises before the plane began taxiing to the runway. Soon after the plane took off, the stewardess came by, took one look at Daisy and commented to the husband, "First flight in twenty-five years! Why she is the most relaxed person on the plane."

2. *In addition to performing the relaxation exercises, think through other things you can do to minimize your tensions.*

•*Avoid certain stresses.* For example, at work try not to get involved in a major project that will require an important decision just prior to a flight. If you are nervous about entertaining, do not give a party the day before you leave. Put off the big confrontation with your neighbor about the broken fence until you get back. Although you may want one or two close friends to accompany you to the airport as a support, don't have a mob of well-wishers see you off. Just one person saying, "You look so pale. Are you sure you will be all right?" may panic you more. Above all, pace yourself so that you don't get overfatigued.

•*Counter your tension.* From your answers to the Fear of Flying Quiz, you have already noted that some things frighten you less than others, that there are certain things you can do to control your panic. Take steps to utilize this knowledge. Here are some things you may be able to control if they are important to you:

Size of plane. Are you more comfortable in a jumbo aircraft or a smaller one? The 747 provides a feeling of spaciousness and reduces the feeling of claustrophobia which affects so many fearful flyers. On the other hand, some flyers become overwhelmed by its vastness and start wondering how it can stay up in the air. Decide what kind of plane to take on the basis of your personal choice.

Where you sit. People with a fear of heights usually feel more comfortable in an aisle seat. This has two advantages: You can get up easily and you don't have to look out of the window. Others opt to sit next to the window because they "can see what's going on."

When you travel. Initially try to arrange your flight so that you don't travel during peak periods. The hustle and bustle and the chance of getting bumped because the airline has overbooked will only add to your anxiety. On summer weekends leave before 2:00 P.M. on Fridays, if possible. Don't travel on the day before Christmas. Also, remember that runways covered by snow and ice can create sticky takeoff and landing conditions.

Use of lures. One woman gets herself to fly from Cleveland to New York because she promises herself an all-day shopping binge as a reward. Another makes exciting plans for "the minute I arrive." She says, "I'm terrified in planes but I love to travel. I manage to fly to London for a vacation because I arrange in advance to have breakfast with a close friend right after the plane lands."

Use of distractions that will make you more comfortable on the flight. If your quiz response suggests that chess would accomplish this, bring a chess set on board. If it's reading, take along several different books. If you can't get a good read from one, you may get it from another.

CASE

John A., a well-known philosophy professor, received an invitation to deliver the keynote address at a meeting of a learned society in Mexico City. Because of his busy schedule, he would have to fly both ways. This terrified him. At the last minute, John came to me in a state of panic. I tried teaching him relaxation, but he was too tense. It would take too much time to train him and he had only a few days before the departure flight. Instead we deliberately planned three actions that would counter his tension:

•He would take his wife along. He hadn't planned this but decided that her company would make him more comfortable.

•Because he feared the length of the trip, we set it up so that at no point would he be in the air for more than one and a half hours. To achieve this he had to go to Mexico City in a very roundabout way, making four stops!

•He would carry out a series of diverting tasks while aloft. John came up with three: (a) to organize the bibliography for his new book. He already had the names on index cards; he would check these against a copy of the manuscript; (b) he enjoyed doing cross-word puzzles. He went out and bought a book of them; (c) he and his wife frequently played gin rummy, so he brought along a deck of cards.

With these aids, John got to Mexico and back. Since then, he can fly anywhere as long as he doesn't have to stay in the air for more than an hour or so and has work to do or games to play.

Stop Your Fear Instructions

Besides working themselves up into a tense state, prior to a flight, many people prepare themselves to feel terrorized on a plane by giving themselves detailed instructions. Their minds whirl with commands like "There will be turbulence—I'll panic and start to scream" . . . "Something is sure to go wrong with the plane. We'll crash." Two FCT techniques should help you to gain control over these thoughts.

1. *Use Thought Stoppage.* This method proves highly effective for people with the ruminating "I'll die" kind of thoughts. As soon as you become aware of a fearful thought about flying, tell yourself STOP!,

breathe in and out, think "Calm" and relax. Do this *every time you become aware of a panicky thought about flying no matter how innocuous it seems or even if this particular thought seems to produce very little anxiety.* In this way you keep your fearful thoughts from building up. When in doubt, say STOP!

2. *Use Thought Switching. Note:* With this method, which I outlined in chapter 4, you will need at least three weeks for practice before your flight.

•Identify your fear instructions and replace them with nonfear instructions. For example:

Fear instructions	*New self-instructions*
"I will be very upset when boarding the plane and may even panic"	"I may be tense while boarding the plane but I will be able to relax most of it away and will remain in command of myself"
"I will pay special attention to the sounds of the engine during the flight and will get upset at any change in these sounds"	"During the flight I will distract my attention from the sound of the engine by reading, listening to music or conversing. If I find I am getting upset, I will be able to relax it out and to keep relatively calm"

•Again, put each statement on a card. Each time you perform some frequently done behavior (drinking coffee, combing your hair), read one of the statements to yourself and then repeat it to yourself. In this way you change your self-instructions from those leading to fear reactions to those leading to increased command behaviors.

CASE

Ralph C., a thirty-six-year-old stockbroker, feared flying. His anticipatory thoughts all revolved around the fear of being trapped once he got on the plane. He constantly rehearsed how he would feel suffocated and kept instructing himself to feel increasing anxiety as the plane door closed behind him.

I helped him work out a series of opposite thoughts: "If I get that suffocated feeling, I will be able to take a deep breath and get rid of it" . . . "If I begin to feel anxious, I will be able to relax and keep the anxiety under control" . . . "If I feel trapped and confined in my seat, there are a number of things I can do to get command of this feeling—like getting up to walk around the plane."

For his Wall Street job, Ralph had to make many phone calls in the course of a day. He put his statements on a set of cards and kept the pack on his desk. Before each business call he would read one of the cards and then dial. In two months Ralph had a business flight coming up. For sixty days he performed his thought-switching routine and his anxiety decreased enormously. He was able to make the trip with no problems.

Stop Sensitizing Yourself to Your Fear.
Instead Desensitize Yourself

The Systematic Desensitization technique in which you progressively desensitize yourself to graded fear situations, *always* relaxing and successfully countering the fear before you go on to the next situation, has proved just as powerful a treatment method for aviaphobics as it has for people who fear birds, bugs and elevators. Again, you can do this in fantasy, in reality, or by combining the two techniques. Remember to:

• Identify the cues that set off your fear of flying.

Doing this will enable you to custom tailor your desensitization of your own fears.

•Rank them in a hierarchy in ascending order. Be sure to use your Fear Thermometer to rate the amounts of fear. Again, in constructing your hierarchy, you can make use of *time* (you stay at the airport observation booth for two minutes . . . ten minutes . . . a half hour), *distance* (you are a block from the airport . . . ten feet away . . . inside the airport . . . at the ticket counter), *size* (you are in a Piper Cub . . . a piston-propelled plane . . . a jet).

In using reality desensitization two problems exist: (1) it's expensive; you have to be prepared to spend money on actual flights to overcome your flying phobia; (2) you can't leave a plane in mid-air in order to relax. Here is an example of a reality hierarchy used by one patient. In all situations, he did the assignment, relaxed, and repeated it until he felt completely in command of it.

1. Walk around shopping and ticket areas at Kennedy airport with wife. Keep away from flight and observation areas.

2. Do the same thing alone.

3. Repeat the process at La Guardia with wife (this is a smaller airport; people feel closer to the planes and hence experience more anxiety).

4. Do the same thing alone.

5. Go to the observation deck at Kennedy. Stay there for increasing amounts of time until he can do it for one hour comfortably.

6. Repeat the above at La Guardia observation deck.

7. Take the shuttle flight to Boston (about forty-five minutes) with wife, have dinner there, and take return flight with wife.

8. Fly to Boston with wife. Return immediately alone. Wife takes next flight.

9. Fly to Boston on a Saturday afternoon and return by self.

10. Take an evening flight to Boston alone and return (flying in darkness was one of his special difficulties).

11. Fly to Puerto Rico with wife (he had to go there on business). Fly home alone several days later.

In using fantasy desensitization, you have more freedom. Be sure to include the items that generate your specific anxieties and which enable you to call forth vivid images. Here is an example of an imagery hierarchy which I have found useful for many people who fear crashing.

Scene	Fear Thermometer Rating
1. You read newspaper headline: "Plane crash. Two dead."	10
2. On television, you see films of the plane wreckage.	20
3. In the airline office, picking up your ticket.	25
4. Near the end of an uneventful flight.	30
5. Midflight. There is a funny sound to the engines.	45
6. Starting to come in for a landing after an uneventful flight.	45
7. Midflight. "Fasten seat belts" sign goes on.	50
8. Midflight. Some turbulence.	60
9. Same. Cabin attendants look a little worried.	70
10. You've just boarded the plane and are walking toward your seat.	75
11. Midflight. Turbulence. Plane has funny vibrations.	85

Scene	Fear Thermometer Rating
12. Plane rushing down runway for takeoff.	90
13. Pilot over intercom: "There's some engine trouble. We have to make an emergency landing."	95
14. Plane wobbling and out of control. Someone screams.	100

Remember, you can combine fantasy and reality desensitization.

CASE

Hal S., a young, unmarried lawyer, had learned from his mother to fear planes. The result: In his twenty-seven years he had taken just one flight and that had unnerved him to such an extent that he couldn't sleep for a week. His fear was so intense that even talking about a plane or looking at a picture of a jet would trigger tension. We worked in stages.

1. Buy aviation magazines. His task: to go through the publications, looking at the pictures. When he felt any twinge of uptightness, he was to close his eyes and relax until the uptightness was gone. It took about three weeks until he could read the magazines without tension. This new feeling generalized. When friends spoke about planes or when he saw flying commercials on TV, he no longer experienced the anxiety twinges.

2. Go to airports. First assignment: to go to the shopping section at Kennedy, find a comfortable seat and stay there for increasing periods of time until he could swing a two-hour stint. Doing this on weekends, the process took Hal about two months. Then he repeated it at La Guardia, where the sounds of planes are much louder. This took only a few exposures. Sec-

ond assignment: to go to the observation deck, listen to the planes; watch them take off and land. At the first feeling of discomfort, he was to close his eyes, relax himself, go back to the shopping for ten minutes, come back and watch the planes again. He did this first at Kennedy, then at La Guardia. This routine also took about two months until he could watch the planes without any feeling of discomfort. At this point Hal started to believe that eventually he could get himself up in the air.

3. We commenced imagery desensitization. Here are some sample scenes (because he had been on a plane only once, Hal had trouble coming up with anxiety-provoking scenes).

•Hearing about a plane crash on the radio.

•Boarding plane.

•Being seated in a plane. Flight smooth and calm.

•Being seated in a plane. Lots of turbulence. Plane bounces around.

•Pilot says, "Hold on. We're going to crash."

This went so well that Hal planned a plane trip. However, we ran into a snag. He couldn't get himself to go to the airline ticket office to buy his ticket.

4. We used more fantasy desensitization: leaving ticket office with ticket in pocket . . . smiling ticket agent writing out ticket . . . he's next on line . . . telling ticket agent, "I want a round-trip ticket to_____"
. . . giving ticket agent his name and address (with this, he felt committed). *Note:* As Hal became involved in definite action, he could use scenes that were real and specific.

5. Then another reality assignment. He went to another airline ticket office to make inquiries about his scheduled flight. The point: to relax out his tension. He repeated this process with several different airlines and then went and picked up his ticket.

On the actual trip Hal was lucky. The flight was smooth and he experienced relatively little anxiety. Soon afterward, his girlfriend suggested a holiday weekend. Hal agreed. Because this was an impulse flight, there was no time for anticipatory anxiety to build up. He had another good flight and this gave him the confidence to make a third trip on his own several weeks later.

Sometimes you can desensitize yourself not just to the plane fear but to some other fear that makes flying difficult. For example, in the case of one young executive, his fear of flying was part of a whole claustrophobic condition. He followed my "closet program" and stayed in rooms of increasingly smaller size with the door closed for increasingly longer periods of time. When he succeeded in mastering the broom closet for thirty minutes, he found that his lifetime pattern of claustrophobia had broken up. Even though we had never treated flying directly, Lou was able to make a reservation and fly to Chicago. However, for his first flight he carefully chose a huge 747.

Join an Existing Fear of Flying Group or Form Your Own

Under various titles, fear of flying groups are mushrooming throughout North America. For example, in cooperation with Air Canada, Drs. Gerald Kroetsch and Gerald Pulvermacher operate Fear Relief Centres of Canada in Toronto, Montreal and Ottawa for aviaphobes. The seven-session course (last session is the graduation flight) costs $190 and has an 85–95 percent success rate. In the United States for the past three years Pan American World Airways has sponsored a "Fearful Flyers" training program. It also consists of seven sessions, costs $100, and so far has been conducted by Captain "Slim" Cummings in Miami, Atlanta, Houston, Chicago, Philadelphia, Westchester County (New York), Detroit, New York City, Washington, D.C., Dallas, and Boston.

Both programs feature training in relaxation, sharing

of experiences, lectures by stewardesses, maintenance men and pilots, tours of air traffic control and the radar room at the airport, a mock takeoff experience, and the final flight. Captain Cummings tells the story of the chairman of the board of a major corporation who drove 1200 miles round trip to attend each class of the "Fearful Flyers" sessions in Atlanta. The program worked. Now he flies all the time.

Check your local airline to see if any fear of flying programs exist in your city or in an adjoining city.

If not, you might try to organize your own program. Use initiative.

•Get together a group of friends or acquaintances who fear flying. Ideally, you should have a minimum of fifteen. If you cannot get a large enough group from your immediate circle, announce to the membership of your clubs or associations that you are forming a group specifically to combat flying fears. You might also put an announcement in your local newspaper. *Warning:* Be sure to state that the group is just for fear of flying; if not, you might get participants who are looking for "encounters" and Esalen-type therapy.

•Obtain the services of a psychologist or psychiatrist who has had experience in this area. It is extremely important that the group be led by a competent professional. If you don't know one, you might write the Association for the Advancement of Behavior Therapy, 420 Lexington Avenue, New York, New York 10017, for a list of members in your area. Or write for a list of the Clinical Fellows of the Behavior Therapy and Research Society, c/o Eastern Pennsylvania Psychiatric Institute, 3300 Henry Avenue, Philadelphia, Pennsylvania 19129.

•Approach a major airline in your area to request its aid. Usually the airlines will cooperate with groups of people who want to overcome fear of flying.

Here is a suggested seven-session program, adapted from those sponsored by the Fear Relief Centres of Canada and Pan Am. Each session should last approximately two hours. You might want to speed up the process and have two sessions a week. You also have to work out on your own the fees involved. Be sure to finish with a graduation flight to a nearby city.

First session: Psychologist lectures on unlearning of learned fears. Group discusses their core phobias and pinpoints the various cues that trigger aviaphobia. Give out copies of the Fear of Flying Quiz. Homework: do quiz.

Second session: Beginning of relaxation training. Psychologist demonstrates for group. Make sure each participant has a relaxation tape. This can be the Full and Intermediate Relaxation Exercises from this book or the psychologist may have his/her own tape. A special feature of this session should be a lecture by a pilot, followed by questions and answers. Homework: practice relaxation.

Third session: More relaxation training. Talk by a stewardess or flight attendant followed by questions and answers. Explanation by psychologists of Systematic Desensitization in imagery and in reality. Homework: (1) practice relaxation, and (2) preparation of your own desensitization in imagery.

Fourth session: Continuation of relaxation training. Lecture by jet propulsion engineer or maintenance expert. Psychologist gives more examples of Systematic Desensitization. Homework: (1) continue relaxation practice; (2) work on your own imagery hierarchy; (3) give yourself a reality assignment—like going through a book with pictures of planes.

Fifth session: More relaxation training and imagery desensitization. Showing of a film about air travel (this can be rented or supplied by an airline; make sure it has sounds of takeoff and landing). Homework: (1) practice relaxation; (2) work on your imagery desensitization scenes; and (3) give yourself another reality assignment like staying in an airline ticket office for longer and longer periods of time.

Sixth session: Go to the airport (you will have

worked this session out with airline officials). Go through the shopping areas; listen to announcements of flights; go to the observation deck. If possible, visit the radar room and control tower. With airline cooperation, you may actually be able to sit in a grounded plane.

Seventh session: Graduation flight to somewhere nearby.

Overcoming your fear of flying will have direct and indirect consequences that benefit both your life and sense of self.

Says one thirty-five-year-old career woman, "I've been on a high for months. Not only did I get a promotion, but now I can deal with other things I'm not crazy about. For the first time I realize I can change my behavior."

Says a young mother, "It's had an effect on my marriage. I feel better about myself and more in control. Because I'm happier I can relate more to my husband."

Says a noted forty-six-year-old lawyer who feared flying since he crashed at the age of eighteen while in the air force, "All these years I flew for business because I had to, but I always got sick. In the first thirty minutes of the flight, I always threw up. I tried drink, Dramamine, heavy meals, light meals. Nothing worked. I hated not being in control of myself. I decided to discipline myself by taking flying lessons. It was weeks before I went up. I spent the time learning data about planes. Finally I got up and eventually got my license. At first I flew only on good days. Then slowly but deliberately I escalated the tension: I flew in snow, rain, clouds, alone in a single engine plane. For my forty-sixth birthday present I gave myself a share in a plane.

"It's been a tremendous ego trip. I feel I can control my own destiny. Conquering my fear of flying got me through a horrendous divorce which should have put me in the noodlehouse. I told myself, 'You came through a thunderstorm, you can do this.'"

One woman ruefully admits to just one disadvantage in getting over flying fears. She says, "Whenever I used to fly, everyone would gather around afterward and ask 'How are you?' . . . 'How was it?' Now no one asks. I've joined the ranks of 'So you flew.' "

It can be done. It has been done. You can do it.

CHAPTER 11 _____

_____

CONQUERING
FEAR ON THE JOB

"I cover every angle so that I don't get criticized. Other employees go home at five. I stay on for hours."

"My anxieties about speaking in public have kept me from the success I would like. In my job I should be on panels and addressing groups. I can't. I know I'd break down in the middle."

"Every day I'm sure I'm going to get fired. I know it's crazy, because I have a three-year contract. To reassure myself, I take it out and look at it every night."

"I'm deathly afraid of people on the job finding out how frightened I am inside. I want my image to be calm, strong. I feel people would look down on me if they knew I spent every day in terror."

Your job situation serves as your most direct and prolonged confrontation with reality. Your job fears affect far more than your paycheck, influencing your elbow room in life, personal relations off the job, your future and very self-esteem. One unmarried thirty-two-year-old writer with a history of frequent job changes says, "I'll be able to stand it if I'm a fifty-five-year-old spinster, but not if I'm a clerk-typist."

JOB FEARS

1. *The realistic job fears.* Some companies, usually with an autocrat as boss, intentionally use fear to keep

employees in line and get the most out of them. Because of their own psychological needs, some supervisors have a style that provokes fear. Circumstances arise when—for reasons having nothing to do with you —a strong chance exists that you will be assigned an undesirable project, be demoted or get fired. You may not be able to change these realities. You can change your disturbed reactions to them.

2. *The fears you bring into the job situation that do not bear directly on the work itself.* If you fear flying, you refuse the post that requires constant traveling. If you fear heights, you cannot take that good job on the forty-fifth floor. Discussing office conferences, one claustrophobic executive says, "Before a meeting I go to the bathroom a thousand times. I have to wear clothes that make me comfortable. I chain-smoke. I must be in the seat near the door; I go early and put my pad and pencil there. All during the meeting I want to scream, 'Hurry up and get finished.' I feel so alone, so different. No one knows how trapped I feel."

3. *The fears directly connected with your work.* Your irrational fear of making mistakes or criticism may bring on tension and actually cause you to make mistakes or to pay so much attention to inconsequential trivialities that you neglect more important work aspects, even lose your creativity. Because of fear, you may avoid the specific work task and procrastinate, turn in your work late, fail to complete assignments.

Fear of public speaking exemplifies a common specific job fear. Your fear of foreign languages, science or numbers can also handicap your growth. Two people can handle the same fear very differently.

EXAMPLE ONE: An ambitious cosmetics executive had always felt apprehensive about any form of math, but she wanted vertical mobility. She recalls, "I was vice-president for product development at an advertising agency before I learned how to prepare a budget. I sat down with an accountant and *learned* how."

EXAMPLE TWO: A twenty-three-year-old man quit his job as a high school teacher ("no future") and began work as a shipping coordinator for an import-export firm. Because he thought he'd eventually get the chance to travel, he took his low-level job, entailing keeping track of what ships were at ports. Soon he got a promotion, requiring the figuring out of tonnages— how many tons to pick up where, how much fuel a ship would need to travel thousands of miles. However, every time David looked at the numbers, he'd panic. He couldn't bring himself to learn the simple arithmetic processes needed for this job. Regretfully, he returned to teaching.

4. *General fears of the job:* the fear of success, failure, learning new methods, new responsibilities, asking for a raise, risks, changing jobs, quitting. One woman was terrified of leaving her publishing job even though management had indicated clearly that it would like her to go. She got another post and even with this security was afraid to go. She agonized, "I want to stay. I'm afraid of something new."

•*The different level job fears:* Some of the most typical:

Stage One: at the beginning level: No matter how confident, most young people when they start out in the job market are uneasy. Suddenly the rules are different; it's not a case of "getting there" by studying harder. First you have the monetary fear: "Can I get a job?" You worry about proving yourself: "Will I measure up?" . . . "Will I know what I need to know?" After landing a job, you're afraid to ask when you don't know something. You may fear you took the wrong job ("I went with IBM, but I had those other offers from AT&T and Process Data. Maybe I should have accepted one of them").

Stage Two: at the intermediate level: After several years you've proved yourself and even received several promotions, either at the same company or via job shifts. Then another level of fear emerges: *the fear that you're not getting as far as your peers.* Suddenly, a peer acquires a significant job. This creates anxiety, and you begin to wonder about your own progress.

You may *fear being caught in a rut.* To yourself, you say, "I've been here five years and I feel I'm stagnating. I've got to get different experience. I don't want to get stuck in the same job too long," and you start to job-hunt. You may fear *the institution.* You like your work with a stimulating company, but one morning the thought stabs, "What an organization man/woman I've become." You don't like the contrast between the commercial you and you, the former college idealist.

Stage Three: advanced level fears: If you're in a good post, from the age of thirty-five on, you have the *fear that comes with visibility.* You recognize that you're functioning in a managerial sense and that makes you vulnerable. You begin to realize that the organization won't protect you, that your fortunes are tied to someone else's coat-tails (your boss, a top-level contact). You may have an identity crisis, feeling "Life has passed me by. What am I doing with this corporation?" This fear is most acute for those at the top.

•*There are fears of age, job security and being vested in the company pension plan.* Retirement fear occurs at three points:

Around vesting time: Usually an employee gets vested (having the legal right to a certain amount of pension) after ten years with the firm. Around year eight, you start to worry, "I'm close but not vested yet."

In your fifties: You worry that it's too late to make a move, that you'll be eased out because of age, that the company will force early retirement, thus reducing your pension benefits.

The over-sixties fear: "What will I do when I retire?"

•*The interpersonal fears that influence your relations with superiors, peers, subordinates:* In securing the work situation you want, these fears are often more important than your competency.

EXAMPLE ONE: Through the Peter Principle, David, a likable, not-too-bright man with a talent for mending political professional fences, had risen to a middle-management job in a company where the president was a personal friend. Aware that he lacked a high IQ, David was frightened of being challenged by anyone. With care, he was just about able to handle the new job. He got a bright subordinate who caught his errors, but the assistant's challenges upset David so much that he couldn't sleep. He managed to get the bright assistant transferred and replaced him with a new subordinate who did not challenge. Eventually David made a disastrous decision and all his pull at the top didn't help. He lost the job.

EXAMPLE TWO: Sally, a file clerk, had a core fear that people would get angry with her. She was so alert to this that she tended to attack first and constantly sent out anger signals. Reacting to this, her co-workers would counterattack. For example, a fellow worker would comment, "You look pretty good today," and Sally would respond sullenly and with an angry look on her face, "Do you think I look rotten the rest of the time?" In almost every work situation she stirred up unpleasantness. As a result she constantly lost jobs. She couldn't understand this and would say, "But my work is so good."

EXAMPLE THREE: Peter feared authority. Everytime his supervisor called him, his stomach coiled into knots. He coped with his fear by being very compliant. When his boss asked his opinion, Peter would give the answer he thought his boss wanted. This worked fine with his supervisor who wanted a yes man. Then Peter got a new supervisor who really depended on staff judgments. Because of his fear of authority and inability to change his pattern under the new regime, Peter lost his job.

5. *The special fears of women.* Despite progress, to get ahead many women—particularly the talented— feel they have to be superwomen. The fear lurks that they won't be as good as a man, the system will get in their way, they won't be treated fairly or can't manage a job and family. Unmarried women who hold mediocre jobs feel fear about the future. Some women in their forties and fifties fear younger women. New horizons have opened. Today's graduates get tapped because they have a better education. The older woman may lose her job because she lacks that Harvard M.B.A.

Essentially on the job all fears break down to three basic ones: *nonreality fears,* because of your insecurity you see danger ("If I lose this job, I'll never get another one"); *reality fears* ("The company shows a big profit, but I haven't gotten a raise in three years. That signals me that something is wrong"); *reality fears to which you add nonreality fears* ("Business is bad. There will be firings. I'll be next and I'll never get another job").

A FEAR CONTROL TRAINING PROGRAM FOR SURVIVAL SUCCESS AND GROWTH ON THE JOB

Set the Correct Job Goals

Your fears and misconceptions of the realities of the working world lead you to inappropriate goals. In turn, these false goals strengthen your fears and bring about new ones. Sometimes you can break the destructive spiral by setting new, more appropriate goals.

1. *Recognize your neurotic job goals:* Some common ones:

a. *The goal of being liked, even loved:* Everyone

wants to be liked, but sometimes this need gets out of control and you become a victim of the praise-rather-than-a-raise syndrome. You possess such a strong need for approval that you fear if you say no to a request (no matter how unreasonable), stand up for yourself, succeed in a difficult project, other people will not like you. In order to be liked, you do things that get you into trouble on the job.

For instance, Bill and Joe were competing for the same promotion—one that involved a transfer to another city. Bill started to be increasingly concerned that Joe and other friends would dislike him if he won out. To avoid his anxiety, he began building up a case for "not wanting to move my family." As soon as he voiced this to the supervisor, Joe got the job.

In another instance, in his eagerness to be liked, Joshua was always helping out co-workers. If they didn't ask for assistance, he would volunteer it. To keep up with his own work, he had to stay late every night and take work home on weekends.

This false goal may be based on a misunderstanding of the difference between the job situation and a close personal situation. In the close relationship you want to get even closer. On the job your aim is to get the job done and achieve your career objectives. The boss is not your mother, father, brother, sister, spouse. He/she doesn't have to love you. Many people—women particularly—act as if the job were a close relationship, concerning themselves with feeling aspects rather than goals. Conversely many men react to the close relationship as if it were a job; they want to be logical, reasonable, to compete and win.

On the job being respected is far more important than being liked. Compare the following statements about two men under consideration for an important project.

STATEMENT ONE: "He's a nice guy but he can't handle responsibility."

STATEMENT TWO: "He's a bit tough to get along with but he sure gets the job done."

To whom would you give the assignment?

    b. *The goal of omniscience:* You must know everything, be able to handle everything. You can't reveal any "weakness" such as doubts or any lack of knowledge. You don't ask people for help, advice or information. This not only places unfair burdens on you and sometimes leads to wrong decisions but it also keeps you from learning. Usually this false goal stems from a fear of being inadequate and is related to the social fear of being "found out." If others see you don't know something you should, they will learn how inadequate you are and dismiss you from business considerations. They will also hold you in contempt as a person.

CASE

Roger A., a high-salaried executive in a prestigious public relations firm, spent his working life in a constant state of terror lest his peers find out he didn't know what he should know. His work was good and he had received numerous awards for projects and annual reports.

    However, on the job Roger's core fear brought about a number of problems. (i) He constantly denigrated his own work. His job required working with various experts. Roger could see only the contrast between their knowledge and his. By concentrating on what he didn't know, he completely failed to recognize the expertise he had. (ii) Because he feared asking questions, he lacked the ability to learn. Over the years he stayed at the same level of knowledge. (iii) His job necessitated holding press conferences. He was so afraid of being asked something he didn't know that he held them only when the firm's president pressured him. When new management came in, Roger got fired.

c. *The goal of mastering impossible situations:* If you can't, you rationalize there must be something wrong with you. One woman was fired. She reacted, "I am the only one who would have failed at this." She didn't take into account the Jove-like boss who required perfection from employees, the fact that she had lasted for two years when all her predecessors had lasted a bare six months. Six months after she was fired, the entire staff was let go. She was so upset by the idea of being vulnerable to being fired that she vowed always to be her own boss. She scraped up money and opened a boutique—a business career for which she had no liking but which protected her from being fired.

d. *The need to be indispensable:* You feel that nobody can replace you, do your work as well as you, that the company will collapse if you leave. Behind this thinking lie such fears as those of being fired, rejected, found inadequate. A common fear: that you're unimportant. Rather than doing something important, you combat your fear with the false assumption that you're highly influential in a trivial job.

e. *The goal of winning approval from friends and relatives:* Other people love to tell you how to run your life, particularly how to solve your job problems. They'll say, "Don't take that crap from your boss. Tell him off." They'll inform you when to ask for a raise, special promotion, quit. Usually they don't know enough about your special situation to proffer good advice. However, if your goal is to win their approval, you might just do what they say. Often this works against your own best interests.

This false goal becomes especially destructive when it comes to setting career goals or choosing specific jobs. You want job security so you head for civil service, but friends and relatives counsel, "You need more challenge." You change goals. Or you may enjoy the idea of making a lot of money, but your well-meaning cronies advise, "Do something with more security," so you switch goals. In both cases your false goal prevents you from doing what you want to do and have a right to do. Behind this goal lie fears of being criticized, disappointing people, making mistakes. Such fears can influence the entire course of your professional life.

2. *Select your reality goals:* To some extent these depend on ability and training. Obviously, you can't be a commercial artist if your drawing of a flower resembles a tree. However, your goals should represent your own inclinations. Take your pick: security, making a special contribution to the world by helping the underprivileged or joining the foreign service, rising up the executive ladder, constant challenges, to have the job simply a place where you earn a living. With the latter, there is nothing wrong with working at a nonchallenging job from nine to five and rushing off to keep a nightly tennis date. It becomes wrong when you feel guilty about your own chosen goal.

In choosing a reality goal, remember two things:

•Every once in a while, ask yourself, "Will this current job take me where I want to be five, ten, twenty years from now?"

•Goals can change.

CASE

Robert A., a personable widower of forty-seven, had two grown, self-supporting children and a highly desirable $70,000 job with an advertising agency. Recently, he got offered a far more challenging job where he would be right up there in the corporate management with lots of clout in the power hierarchy, something he had always wanted. There was only one hitch: The job paid $5000 a year less. Robert considered this a demotion. His sister said to him, "Bob, you're still acting as if you have a wife to support, kids in college and a mortgage. You want the job. They're offering you a five-year contract. You'll make up the money, but at this point the money doesn't matter. See yourself for what you are now—not with the goals you used to have." He took the job.

A Program for Job-hunting Fears

Before you concern yourself with fears on the job, you first have to get one. Unfortunately, many people have fears that keep them from job-hunting. Here is a program to get you started.

1. *Overcome the small fears that immobilize you.* Job-hunting consists of doing many tasks: writing a résumé, thinking through your strengths and weaknesses, setting up appointments, answering want ads, researching possible opportunities. You may fear several of these. As a result, you dwell on the fears or concentrate on avoiding the job-seeking acts that spur the fears. In this way you maintain the fear, build up lethargy and depression, and your job hunt becomes increasingly difficult. What happens to most people is that a crisis arises (like unemployment insurance running out) and they are forced to mobilize themselves and find a job.

You don't have to wait for a crisis. Reverse the process. Focus on what you have to do rather than on what scares you.

Analyze the situation. Think through a list of various jobs you're willing to take with the aim of eventually getting the right job. Many people fear not getting the ideal job immediately. With every turndown you're convinced you've done something wrong that proves you're no good. One way to control fear: Change your long-range goal for a more immediate one. For instance, you're a reentry woman, with long-ago experience as an assistant buyer in women's dresses. You want to be a buyer. Possible jobs for now might include salesperson in a boutique or department store, executive trainee at a store, clerical worker in a merchandising school, secretary, assistant, or showroom receptionist for an apparel manufacturing firm. Any of these could eventually lead to your long-term buyer goal.

a. *Make a schedule for tomorrow.* List the things you want to accomplish. Keep this list well within the bounds of achievement. For example:

•*Make a series of phone calls:* Write out the number you intend to make (ten is a good average). These can be to your own business contacts, friends who might know people, former college professors, complete strangers who work in the area you want.

•*Write letters* (three a day) to people you don't know but would like to know. Say just that. Do not contact the personnel office of a big company. The point of your letter (or your call) is to get you in to see the person with the authority to hire you. Try the vice-president of the specific area to which you think you can contribute something. In your letter tell what you can do and use some version of the sentence, "I'd like to talk to you about future employment." He can't say, "We're never going to have any future openings." What you want to do is get that appointment.

•*See friends*—for lunch, in their office if possible, for a drink at the end of the day. You never know from where your next job lead will come. An in-person chat can prove more effective than a telephone talk. Try sentences like, "Can you give me any advice?" . . . "Do you know any people I can call?" . . . "Have you heard of any openings lately?" Trigger your friends to act on your behalf.

•*Use the library:* Some, like the New York City Public Library, have special services for job-seekers. Read books about your chosen work field: how the jobs within it are sorted out, who does what, what areas of knowledge are involved, what current and future problems confront leaders in the field. Also read more specific literature from professional organizations, trade magazines (for instance, if you want advertising, read *Advertising Age*). Professional organizations often have excellent libraries. Check them out.

b. *List each item on your schedule separately on a page in your FCT workbook.* At the end of the day put a check next to each task you accomplished. Some people devise scoring systems—for instance, marking a percentage of the tasks they carried out that day. Others reward themselves for accomplishing the entire list (for instance, you have earned the right to watch TV all evening or have a champagne cocktail). You can also make a contract with your spouse or close friend for a reward (he/she treats you to a concert).

By focusing on what must be done and doing it, you minimize the small fears.

c. *Learn the skills of handling company question-naires and interviews.* Because you fear certain questions will come up that you won't know the answer to, you become so frightened that you may completely avoid the job-seeking situation. If you know how to handle these questions, you won't feel so scared.

•*In advance, prepare your answers to possible questions on an employment form that might cause you difficulty.* For example:

QUESTION ONE: "Why did you leave your last job?"

The truth: You were fired for just cause.

Answer: "It was really a dead-end job. My work was stagnating."

QUESTION TWO: "When did you last work?"

The truth: You've been unemployed almost a year.

Answer: "I took a year off to investigate career possibilities and come to some life decisions. I know now just where I want to go."

QUESTION THREE: "Have you ever had a mental illness?"

The truth: You've just come out of the hospital for a depression.

Answer: "I've had a rough time, but it made me face and work through some problems most people tend to ignore."

Try your answers out on friends and get their opinions. If necessary revise your answers. Use each application you fill out as an experiment; see how the employment agency representative or prospective employer reacts. One good principle: on any application form avoid filling in a blank that may he held against you. You're better off explaining face-to-face in an interview.

•*Learn to conduct yourself well at the interview:* Because you're afraid you don't know how to act at one, you may have been avoiding interviews.

Role-play possible problem situations with a friend acting as the interviewer. This will lessen your fear. Cover possible problems that might come up. For example:

QUESTION ONE: "What will you do if your husband transfers?"

Answer: "We've made the decision that if I get this job, Bill will get another job in this area."

QUESTION TWO: "Why have you had three jobs in four years?"

Answer: "To get experience during my formative professional years. I got it. Now I want to settle down with one company."

QUESTION THREE: "Who will take care of your children?"

Answer: "The housekeeper."

At the interview itself you must be prepared for questions you haven't rehearsed. In answering, never be negative. For instance, the interviewer asks, "What is your greatest weakness?" Do not tell him/her you have a tendency to procrastinate. Say something like, "I have a tendency to get so involved with my work that I have trouble leaving the office at night." Or if the interviewer asks—and they always do—"Do you have further questions about working here?" venture, "It sounds so challenging. I guess my most important question is 'When can I begin?'"

A word about salary. Don't let fear make you sell yourself short. Your previous research should enable you to know going rates for the job you're after, but always wait at least ten seconds before responding to any salary offer made to you. The interviewer may say, "Oh, well, we knew we couldn't get you for that" and offer higher. Also remember you have a right to ask questions.

2. *Sometimes your fear may preclude your going directly after the job you want. In that case use direct fear reduction techniques:*

EXAMPLE ONE: Because John feared rejection, he couldn't get himself to apply for jobs he wanted. Failure to get the job signified "I am a worthless person." He overcame that fear by deliberately applying for jobs that were a level or two beyond his qualifications. Because he knew in advance that he wasn't equal to these jobs, he was able to see the turndown for the "You're not qualified" viewpoint that it really was, not a rejection of him as a human being. In actuality, he became so skilled at handling these interviews that he got one of these jobs on a probationary basis.

EXAMPLE TWO: In any interview situation one woman got coward's cramps. The very thought of someone "judging" her made her shake with nerves. To solve this, she applied for a series of jobs she would not have taken under any circumstances, even at a huge salary. She could do this because, under these circumstances, the interviewer's judgment of her mattered less and hence her fear was less. After a number of such try-out interviews, her fear had decreased to the level at which she could apply for jobs she wanted.

A Program for
Relieving Tensions on the Job

Your job tensions may be realistic (the need to meet a deadline), partially realistic ("If I don't meet the deadline, the boss will fire me") or completely unrealistic (because of fears you set up situations where the slightest critical comment throws you into agony). Whatever the cause, you suffer the consequences: fatigue, irritability, difficulties in concentration, tension headaches or sleep difficulties. Even when the tensions actually exist, you can reduce some of the consequences with a systematic program of relaxation.

1. *Relax out your general tensions.*
    a. *Use the Instant Relaxation Exercise (chapter 4) every hour on the hour.* Do it during working hours wherever you are and whatever you're doing. You'll find people around you don't notice.

I have used this quick relaxation technique on myself. For example, one night I was scheduled for a brief interview on local television to be followed by phone questions from listeners. That night a rainstorm washed out the telephone wires and calls couldn't get through. The host was unprepared for the longer interview he now had to do on live camera. As he began questioning, I could feel his anxiety. This made me tense. While he talked, I made myself sit back in the chair, half listening, and imagine a pleasant scene and then relax. Then I answered. Not only did I keep myself from becoming a tension victim but, at the program's conclusion, the host said, "You were so relaxed that it made me more comfortable."

    b. *Try the Give-Yourself-a-Breather Exercise.*
Sit comfortably in a chair, close your eyes and breathe in and out. Each time you exhale, say or think to yourself, "Calm." The exercise should last anywhere from one to five minutes. In initial training perform it

five to six times a day. As you become proficient, start doing it with your eyes open.

The next time you're in a pressureful situation, take two or three deep breaths and, as you exhale, say "Calm" just the way you do in the exercise.

c. *Do away with tension headaches.* Tension, whether general or part of a phobic response, is not equally distributed through the body. It tends to settle in specific muscles. The result: specific tension headaches stem from a tightness in the muscles of the forehead and the muscles that control the eye movements, or you may get them when the muscles at the back of your neck and shoulders tighten up. Learning to relax these specific muscle groups may enable you to control your headaches.

EYE MUSCLE RELAXATION EXERCISE

- Roll your eyes to look out of the extreme left corner of your eyes.
- Hold this for about seven seconds, calling that degree of tension 100 percent.
- Count down: 90—80—70, gradually relaxing your eyes as you do until, at the count of 0, your eyes are closed and relaxed.
- Repeat the process.
- Do the same thing, looking out of the right corner of your eyes. Repeat.
- Squeeze your eyes tightly closed (this is 100), hold this seven seconds, count down in the same way. At zero your eyes should be closed and relaxed. Repeat the squeezing.

At the first sign of a headache, do this exercise. If your headache comes from eye muscle tension, this will afford relief.

NECK AND SHOULDER EXERCISE

You can carry out this exercise either sitting or standing. Pull your shoulders back so that they almost touch. At the same time arch your neck, pointing your chin toward the ceiling. Let the tensions build up, but don't strain your muscles. Hold this for about seven seconds, then explosively relax.

    d. *Cure your insomnia.* Most insomnia results from tension. Because your muscles are tight, you experience trouble falling asleep. As you toss and turn, tension increases and sleep proves more difficult. After several nights of this, you may actually develop a fear of getting into bed because you know you won't sleep. This spurs more tension. The next day you feel so tired you can't work. This increases your tension.

A PROGRAM FOR INSOMNIACS

•*Check your habits.*   Do you do anything that stimulates you just before going to bed (like watching a TV program on violence)? Pay particular attention to what you eat and drink. One man who came to me for insomnia treatment told me he drank about twenty-five cups of coffee a day. He certainly knew of the stimulating effect of coffee, but never thought to connect it with his sleep problem. You should also check out your medications. You may not realize they have a stimulating effect. For example, one insomniac also had sinus trouble and used to spray his nose at bedtime with Neo-Synephrine. It was this drug that kept him awake. When he stopped the nighttime spraying, he became able to sleep. Even if a medication doesn't have a stimulating effect, you may react atypically. Check it out.
•*Use the Full and Intermediate Relaxation Exercises in Appendix I to relax your muscles.* Make just one

change. Instead of ending them with instructions to be wide awake and alert, substitute "Now calmly reach over and turn off the machine. Keep imagining the pleasant scene or the word *calm* and drift into sleep." Play the tape and do what it says. Play it two or three times; you're up anyway. Also keep a record of how long it takes you to fall asleep each night. If this training method works, you should note a fairly steady decrease in this time over a period of weeks.

•*Try the metronome method.* Buy a spring-driven metronome (the kind you have to wind) rather than an electrical one. The former eventually runs down and won't keep going all night. Set the metronome to the beat of 60 a minute and lie in bed listening to it. Minimize the sound to where it barely intrudes on your consciousness. If it lacks volume control (and it usually does), stifle it with pillows until the sound is just right. Some people find this relaxing. Try it as an experiment to see if it helps you.

•*Carry out a stimulus control program.* This method, adapted from the work of Dr. Richard R. Bootzin of Northwestern University, is based on the fact that you have learned to associate bed with not sleeping rather than with sleeping.

Set an appropriate time to go to sleep. If you are sleepy at that time, get into bed. If not, wait until you feel signs of sleepiness.

If, after twenty minutes, you have not fallen asleep, *get out of bed*. Do things: Read a nonexciting book, listen to music, write a letter, think pleasant thoughts. Do not return to bed until you feel sleepy. At no time stay in bed more than twenty minutes without falling asleep.

In bed, you do not read, eat, watch TV, listen to the radio. Just try to sleep.

Regardless of the time you fall asleep, you must get up at your usual time in the morning.

No naps during the day or early evening. Sleep only in bed at bedtime.

2. *Work out methods for handling specific tension-producing situations.* On the job upsetting situations exist which you cannot change and with which you must learn to live—such as the common one of the insensitive, rude, angry boss. Standing up to him just makes things worse. Anytime he says something to you in his own abusive manner, your tension level shoots up too high for relaxation to counter it. Introduction of a task-oriented approach serves as one method of handling this.

CASE

Mark J. worked for a nasty curmudgeon who constantly criticized and accused him unjustly. This upset Mark to the point where he couldn't sleep and fought with his wife. His co-workers didn't like the boss either, but they managed the attitude "That's the way it is." Mark and I set up a program with the goal of taking the boss's temper less personally.

We concentrated on task orientation by turning the situation into a game. When the boss came on strong, Mark was to imagine himself in various roles: (a) as a playwright looking for dialogue; (b) as an anthropologist studying ritualistic patterns of the head of the tribe; (c) as a clinical psychologist observing life situations. It worked. Because he felt slightly removed from the situation, Mark took the boss's outbursts less personally. He still didn't like it, but he became able to live with it. Then he realized that he couldn't change his boss but he could change his job. Because he was no longer in a state of uptightness, he didn't take the first offer that came his way but stuck it out until he found just the job he wanted.

Learn to Cope on the Job

Being calm is not enough. The purpose of calmness is to allow you to use your coping skills. This also works in reverse. Often, if you know what to do and do it, your actions will curtail your anxiety. Remember, coping is a learnable skill.

1. *Learn to ask for a raise.* Although many organizations possess effective systems of review and insurance of pay equity, some do not. If you want a raise, you must ask for it. To many people the idea of doing this is so frightening that they get an attack of mental St. Vitus's dance. If you have a few techniques at your disposal, you may be able to at least try.

•Plot a careful strategy. *Before you talk to the boss,* get information about what friends earn in comparable jobs. You also want data about why you merit an increase. Statement to avoid: the bald announcement "I want a raise."

•You might start your discussion with an innocent "I'm wondering if our pay scale is right." Get the dialogue going. Then go on a nonthreatening discussion of ranges, when the company reviews pay scales. The boss may respond, "We don't have ranges. We try to keep competitive and we review regularly." That's your cue to try, "I got a raise six months ago, so I presume I get one at least once a year. That's the policy at my friend's firm." In this way you've established a framework. Remember this conversation. In a few months you may want to recall it to your boss.

•You may have to ask for a raise directly. Do not threaten "either-or." Give yourself room to maneuver. Every case is individual, but you might try something like, "I've got a serious problem. Social Security is up $300. The cost of living has risen. Other people in my same job make more. I really like this company. I don't want to leave. What do you suggest I do?"

The boss may answer, "Nothing can be done. You're better off out." You respond, "I won't leave you in the lurch"—and start looking.

One young woman worked as a reporter for a major wire service. She had been there for two years with no raise. One day she gathered her courage, drank two martinis for lunch, and spoke up to her boss. To her amazement, he said, "We thought you'd never ask. We were beginning to think you too timid for the job." She got both a raise and a promotion.

2. *Learn about money.*   The late Bernard Baruch, I am told, said that each person needs two skills: the skill of the craft by which he earns his living and the skill of making money from his craft. Too many of us excel at the first and neglect the second. This inability to cope with money can create many fears, operating in your present and affecting your future. Here are some tips from David McLaughlin, principal, McKinsey & Company, and author of *The Executive Money Map.*

•If you're worrying about hanging in there to get your pension, think through its actual worth. Remaining five more years may be worth $5000. Go through the math. You can't collect until you're fifty-five. For that relatively minor amount, you may stay on and ruin your working life. Why not get another job at $2000 a year more?

•If you can, don't have your job serve as your only source of income. Start saving. Take the attitude: "My finances are my responsibility." Set up programs that build up your personal net worth; for example, buy a house or co-op.

•Realize that the key to pay progress is rapid promotion. Don't change jobs (even in the same company) without a proper pay boost. After five years an executive should make at least $1000 for every year of his/her life ($27,000 annually if twenty-seven, $30,000 if thirty) if he/she is going to be in the upper half of the executive population.

•You should know the amount of your life insurance coverage, how much salary continuance there would be in case of long-term disability, after sick pay runs out, and what the maximum is under group major medical plan.

•Realize that salary is just the tip of the iceberg in the managerial level. In the executive ranks salary accounts for only 40 to 50 percent of total pay. When you move, negotiate a total pay package, including a leveraged bonus, some forms of stock equity, if possible, and if the risks are high, an employment contract.

3. *Know when to quit.* Quitting a job means taking a risk. Even if you have a good new job lined up, you still have the realistic fear of "Will it work out?" the adjustment to new situations, routines and people. If you aren't certain of whether or not to leave your present job, you constantly weigh pros and cons, heightening your fear and impairing your judgment. Approach it in a businesslike manner. Ask yourself these questions:

•Do you feel your job is monotonous?

•Do you feel your job is a dead end as far as work career is concerned?

•Do you hate your boss?

•Are others with your same talent ahead of you professionally?

•Do you feel that putting in extra effort into your present job is just looking for trouble?

If you answer yes to all or most of these, maybe it's time to quit. Keep your present job while you look for another.

4. *If you want to rise up the executive ladder, use the coping skills that have worked for others.* Some do's:

•Learn something in depth, but don't overinvest in a speciality. Always remember you move up in a company on the basis of contribution. You must keep current and avoid "technical obsolescence"; somebody may come from behind who's twice as good.

•Aim for increased exposure and visibility. To get ahead, you want to apply your efforts to consequential tasks, working in the area where the greatest chance of recognition exists, not on minor but necessary matters in a back room. Look for special projects. Create them or go to the boss of another department and say, "I'm really turned on by _____ project and I'd like to be considered for something similar."

•Find a powerful advocate. This is known as the get-yourself-a-rabbi technique. You don't have to pick the very top boss but someone ahead of you in the power hierarchy who's impressed by you and who's good at moving people along. By allying yourself with a person in power, you may not only move up in the company, but often may move along with him/her when he takes a more challenging job.

•Know some basics on promotions. According to columnist Sylvia Porter: (a) The great majority of promotions in top executive spots are made from within the firm. (b) The average age of newly promoted presidents and chief executive officers is now in the early to mid-forties. (c) The top four rungs of the corporate ladder from which executives are being promoted today are: operations-division management; finance; marketing; administration. (d) The least likely corporate specialities from which business people are being promoted to top jobs are: public relations; manufacturing; international; research and development.

•Set definite targets for two years hence. What kind of knowledge will you have to have to do that job you want? What kind of experience? What kind of people must you know to reach that goal? See the gaps in your knowledge and set out to remedy them. Analyze the fears that may keep you from reaching your goal. Are you too sensitive to criticism? Do you fear not being in control and want to do everything yourself? Are you afraid to take opportunities when they come at an inconvenient time?

5. *Set yourself coping tasks.* In your head you know just what you want to do, but because of fear you just mark time. Whatever it is, break the act into specific tasks and use them as fear assignments.

CASE

Donald J., forty-five, had been with the same company for twenty-five years, during which he had risen from mailroom clerk to controller. Management changed, and Donald was sloughed off to a lesser job. He knew he had to get out or he'd be put out. Dismissing the facts of his many contacts, excellent reputation, and professional expertise, Donald sat there like a frozen duck. He feared two things: (a) He wouldn't get another job because of his age; (b) This was the only firm he had ever known; how could he manage at another organization. Desperate, he consulted me.

For treatment we worked out a series of fear assignments. Donald was to:

- Contact a headhunter
- Role-play mock interviews with friends
- Set up interviews
- Talk to colleagues who knew the job market

Conscientiously, Donald carried out the tasks. As he did, his fears went down. He got results—three job offers, all for more money than he had been making. Now he has a new and challenging job—plus the considerable pension he'll eventually get from the previous one.

Act Assertively on the Job

Many job fears stem from misunderstanding of assertion on the job. At work, the goal of your behavior has to be movement. This depends on your short-term and long-term goals.

CASE

After much frustration, a reentry woman who had taken courses in commercial art landed a job with a boss who fired people rather quickly. On her third day the boss said, "There's a rush deadline. Keep on at what you're doing until you finish, even if it means having a sandwich at your desk." With much resentment Gloria followed orders. Later she said to me, "I wanted my lunch hour off for shopping. What should my assertive response have been?"

I told her, "Your assertive response is, 'Yes, I'd be glad to do it.'" At that point her goal of keeping the job was far more important than lunching out on a specific day.

Job fears may develop in five areas of assertive difficulty.

1. *The ability to say no.* There's a basic rule: In saying no on the job, you cannot offer a vague answer like, "No, I don't feel like it" as you might to a friend who suggests you go to the movies together. You must tell the reason why and offer an alternative ("No, I'm sorry but I can't stay late. I have an appointment for the evening and there's no way of getting in touch with the person. Shall I come in early tomorrow?").

It is equally important to learn to say yes when presented with the opportunity to get where you want to go. One ambitious bank executive had the chance to meet the powerful company president, but turned it down saying, "I have to be at the suburban branch that day and I've already broken two appointments." She missed a golden opportunity.

2. *The ability to make requests and ask favors.* If you don't ask for what you want, nobody knows you want it. However, remember in the work situation the criteria for appropriateness varies, depending on whether you make your request to superior, peer or subordinate.

3. *The appropriate expression of positive and negative feelings.* If you're a superior, give feedback to your employees. If you want to express anger, choose your

battleground carefully. Don't fight over something relatively unimportant.

4. *Ability to start, maintain and end conversations.* The social aspects of the job often determine the success of your interpersonal relationships at work.

5. *The ability to handle criticism—justified and unjustified.* Inadequacy in these areas can produce many fears. If lack of assertiveness is your problem, your approach should be through Assertiveness Training rather than Fear Control Training. You might read our detailed book *Don't Say Yes When You Want to Say No,* and Jean's *How to Be an Assertive (Not Aggressive) Woman in Life, in Love, and on the Job.*

Reduce Your Specific Job Fears

Sometimes specific job fears are so strong that you can't progress professionally until you lower them. Naturally, your first step is to identify the fear, to know exactly what frightens you. The Uptight Inventories from chapter 2 should help. Do you fear being criticized? Presenting a report? Giving people orders? Making mistakes? Keep notes on when and where you experience discomfort. Also note exactly what kind of incident triggers your nervousness—for example, the boss entering your office or an annoyed look from a co-worker.

1. *Sometimes you possess the capability to perform differently but you don't do it.* If you know what the unwanted behavior is, it may be within your power to change it.

CASE

All his working life Tom L. had had some fear of authorities. At present the fear was particularly severe because Tom had a brusque boss who always seemed irritated with him. Tom didn't know why. One day he approached the boss, who immediately said, "What are you going to complain about today?" Suddenly, Tom realized that he only spoke to the boss when he had something to complain about. Then he saw that through his chronic complaining he was bringing about just the situation that terrified him—he was annoying the boss and making him angry. Thereafter, every day Tom deliberately went up to the boss and exchanged some pleasantry. Within three weeks, his superior had stopped being difficult.

2. *Sometimes you discover that your fear is a consequence of a more general fear that you must first resolve.* For example, you have claustrophobia. You can't shine at meetings because instead of thinking about work you sit there feeling trapped. Reduce the claustrophobia and you'll do better at meetings.

•Outside of the job stay in increasingly smaller rooms for longer and longer periods of time.

•Make each meeting a practice treatment rather than a test situation. Don't ask yourself, "Am I going to get anxious?" Instead, ask, "How long can I stay in the meeting before I have any signs of anxiety?" Keep a record of the time you spend before you start getting the panicky reaction.

•Counter your anxiety. For example, if you start to feel anxious, begin to make up fantasies. Imagine everyone in the room wearing just underwear or the chairman hawking frozen yogurt on the street.

3. *Sometimes you must confront the actual job fear.* For this, the Systematic Desensitization methods often prove helpful. Here are examples with two common job fears.

CASE

Problem: fear of anger from subordinates
Treatment: reality desensitization

Martin G., a commercial artist, was promoted to art

department head of a home sewing company. In his
new post, he ran into trouble. Two subordinates tended
to procrastinate in their work. When Martin chastised
them about this, they responded sharply. Martin was so
afraid of their anger and not being liked that he stopped
criticizing. As a result of this pattern, he had been fired
from two previous jobs. He didn't want it to happen a
third time.

In my office we took a series of attacking sentences
employees might say and created answers that would
make Martin feel good if he could utter them.

Criticism: "You are a real slave driver."

Answer: "This is due by 4:00 P.M. today" or, "This
is not the kind of work we can show the agency."

Criticism: "You're too fussy. This work is good
enough."

Answer: "You're wrong. Please redo it along the
lines we've discussed and have it on my desk after
lunch."

I would say these and similar sentences to Martin
until he was able to relax and come up with a calm,
task-oriented reply. Eventually he was able to make
the same replies in the life situation.

CASE

Problem: fear of public speaking
Treatment: fantasy desensitization

Stan M. worked for a major insurance company. He
was being considered for an executive position that
would entail traveling around the country explaining
the firm's policies to various groups of salespeople and
also occasionally addressing large formal conferences.
This was beyond him. He had no trouble talking on a
one-to-one basis but experienced difficulty even speaking up at small staff meetings in his home office. As we
discussed his phobia, it became evident that three public speaking situations set off his fear: (a) the number
of people involved; (b) how well he knew members of

the audience; (c) the formality of the occasion. Stan then made up an imagery hierarchy which used the three variables.

•He gives a brief talk to eight people in the home office. He knows them all well.

•Same situation but with twelve people. Again, he knows them all well.

•Same situation with twelve people. He doesn't know four of them.

•Same situation. He doesn't know seven of them.

•He's visiting a branch office. Talks to four people. Knows two.

•Same situation. Talks to eight people. Knows two.

•Same situation. Talks to eight people. Knows none.

•He's standing in front of twelve people in a small auditorium. Knows none.

•He's standing in front of twenty people. Knows none.

•He's standing in front of fifty people. Knows none.

•He's on a platform addressing an audience of fifty high-level insurance executives. Knows none.

As he carried out the desensitization, Stan began to notice that he was speaking up more at staff meetings. Eventually he requested his superior to allow him to give a brief talk at one of the branch offices (starting life desensitization). While giving the talk, he felt tense but also experienced a sense of accomplishment and satisfaction. At the end of sixteen treatment sessions he was going around giving talks at branch offices, feeling completely confident. When he was scheduled to give a talk at a formal meeting seven months later, he came back for a booster session. A year and a half later, he called to tell me he had just been made a vice-president.

If your fear of public speaking keeps you from job advancement, use the above case as a model. Make up a list of the things that frighten you most about public speaking in ascending order. Is it the topic? Your knowledge of the topic? The number in the audience?

Length of the talk (usually it is easier to say just a few words than deliver an address). Time of day? Being the kickoff speaker? After you prepare your hierarchy, start imagining the scenes, relaxing after each one. Do *not* go on to the next scene until you can imagine the one you're working on with no disturbance.

You can use this technique (either the life or imagery method) to reduce many of your fears that interfere with job performance—for example, with the specific fear of getting fired or the general fears of success or failure. In utilizing it with general fears, you must come up with the specific situations that would evoke fear in you—for instance, agreeing to take on an assignment that is just a bit beyond you. If you follow the general rules for Systematic Desensitization outlined in chapters 4 and 5, you have a good chance of lessening your fears.

By reducing your fears you may change a whole professional style.

CASE

When we married, my wife, Jean, was going nowhere in her career. As public relations director for *Seventeen* magazine, she had spent many years doing the same thing, earned the salary of a middle-league executive secretary and was grateful "for having such a good job." Passively, she accepted the situation. She certainly wasn't happy about it.

Part of her problems stemmed from lack of assertiveness. She didn't know how to set short-term and long-range goals and had enormous difficulty saying no (once she canceled a long-planned European vacation to write a speech for a co-worker who pleaded, "Please help—you know I can't write my own speeches"). Assertiveness Training helped her to begin a new career as a full-time free-lance writer.

Long after the Assertiveness Training some fears persisted—particularly the fear of asking for money and the fear of female authorities. We began Fear Control Training because these problems lay within her and did not involve relationships with others. Clinging to her old habits, Jean was extremely reluctant. She hated all the desensitization procedures, but she did them. Faithfully, she made up and carried through the various hierarchies involving asking for money. Nothing changed. She was still giving speeches for nothing and agreeing to write books for minuscule advances.

Suddenly everything came together. One day I heard Jean responding to a call from the president of a professional organization who asked her to be key speaker at a luncheon. Jean said, "Look, I haven't got time to do it for nothing and I know that's your policy. Better get someone else."

"What is your fee?" asked the woman.

Without a second's hesitation, Jean named it.

The woman said, "You're right. You should get paid. The fee is OK."

Jean also managed to swing a lucrative book contract. She gave herself a series of fear assignments (checking out advances of other nonfiction writers, memorizing the Author's League contract, which spells out desirable terms for writers), then she asked for what she wanted—and got every single item.

Until recently, Jean had little consciousness of the effect of these new actions on her career or sense of self. Some weeks ago her editor called to tell her that the jacket of her new book was ready. Jean brought it home and said to me, "From a professional point of view, it's a bad jacket, and my name is in too small type. I don't like it." She asked for no advice so I gave none. The next night, she said to me, "Oh, I wrote Laura a letter and said how I felt. She called up today and said they're changing the cover. My name is going to be in big type."

For the first time in Jean's career she had not turned the authority figure into a mother who must love her. I asked, "How did you swing it?"

She said simply, "I guess I just stopped running scared. I did what I had to do."

On the job situation do what you have to do to achieve your own individual goals. Stop running scared!

CHAPTER 12

CONCLUSION

Not every case has been a success.

Sometimes I fail. For example, twenty years ago, when I was practicing psychoanalytically oriented therapy, I treated Len R., a successful, recently married businessman who said to me, "Everything in life is going well for me. Why aren't I happy?" Len had a tremendous fear of spending money on himself. He couldn't do it; the guilt was too great. For two years I saw him three times a week. In our analytic sessions we explored how his mother had constantly blamed him for everything and trained him to feel he was a "worthless person" who deserved nothing. We uncovered his childhood fantasies (where simultaneously he was the all-powerful king, dominating his parents, and the infant in the crib, being treated with affection and love by his mother). The treatment brought about no change. Len stopped.

About ten years ago, soon after I switched to Behavior Therapy, Len came back to see me. I was sure I could treat him behaviorally, thinking if I could put him in a position where he could spend money on himself without the feelings of guilt and anxiety, this would free him to appreciate the good things about himself and his life. I used Systematic Desensitization plus exercises in spending money on himself, starting with very trivial expenditures. Initially, he responded well and for three weeks felt free from depression. Then the whole pattern returned. Nothing we did thereafter helped. Len stopped treatment again. I didn't blame him.

Today I would not begin treatment by directly treating Len's inability to spend money. Instead, I would focus on the fact that the core of his depression is the learned helplessness he acquired by never being able to please his mother, and that today, as an adult, he maintains this state by doing to himself just what his mother used to do—constantly finding fault and telling himself he's worthless. I would realize that until we reduced this learned helplessness and the behaviors that maintain it, we would not be able to make real dents in his fear of spending money on himself and his inability to allow himself any pleasures.

The point: Behavior Therapy is a constantly changing field. The new clinical treatments for learned helplessness are only a few years old. I wish Len would come back. This time treatment would work, I am sure.

Sometimes the patient fails. For example, Warren came to see me because he led a "miserable, isolated life." In my office we used Systematic Desensitization in fantasy and seemed to be getting good results. However, we had the problem of transferring them into life. To do this, I gave Warren a series of exercises through which he could begin to face his social fears. But whatever the exercise and no matter how simple, Warren couldn't bring himself to do it. For instance, he was supposed to do one task which involved getting coffee and cake at the church social after the service. No people were involved, just getting the food, but he would not push himself to take this initial first step. Not only did Warren fail to carry out the assignment, but he stopped attending church and dropped out of treatment.

At some point you have to take a stand and face your fear. Some people won't. To make Fear Control

Training work, you must be willing to do things that initially will make you feel uncomfortable or a little frightened.

Treatment records show that in the vast majority of cases Fear Control Training will work. When it works, you can begin to run your life out of choice, not from fear.

CASE

When Dick L. consulted me four years ago, he came in with two presenting problems: (1) the fear that he was homosexual when he wanted to be heterosexual (he had this fear because he had homosexual fantasies and a very limited social life); (2) a chronic low-grade depression. Reared in a devout Catholic household, Dick had always wanted to become a priest, but, because of his fears, he felt to become a priest meant running away. If he joined the priesthood, it would not be out of conviction but as a way of avoiding those aspects of life which frightened him. Instead he began to do graduate work in economics.

He came for treatment because he had begun to experience severe anxiety attacks, relating to his fears of being homosexual. I treated him in several ways: (1) Fear assignment tasks to build up his social life and help him work through his dating behaviors; (2) Thought Stoppage for his fantasies; and (3) Systematic Desensitization in fantasy for his fears of being homosexual. After a year Dick thought he had things under control.

I saw Dick periodically as problems came up (for example, when he got a promotion on his current government job which called for supervising people, he found he had problems in being an authority). When I saw him a year ago, he said, "Life is fine but I still feel depressed." I formulated this for him in terms that he still hadn't found a main thrust in life. I felt certain that he was on the right track and that, in the course of living, Dick would find this feeling of real commitment.

Recently, Dick came back. I was amazed at the change in him. The depression was gone. He had an air of confidence and quiet maturity. He told me he had decided to become a priest, saying, "Now, I know I'm not doing this because I want to avoid lay life or because I'm afraid of life. I've made the choice based on the feeling that this is the right thing for me to do." He is now undergoing rigorous training for the priesthood and loving it.

As you begin and go through the Fear Control Training process, remember:

•It isn't the fears themselves that are so destructive but the fear of being afraid that paralyzes you. Take off those fear-tinted glasses. Do the work you have to do to find out your fears and take the actions you have to take in order to learn not to be afraid. All the words in this book—or any book—won't help you unless you get out into the arena and do something about your fear.

•Controlling and reducing your fears builds up a momentum. Your little successes spur you to big successes. As you face fears in one area, it becomes easier to face them in another. Your courage will grow. So will you—socially, professionally, emotionally. Your sense of self-worth will become a big part of you. Just keep saying, "Others have done it. I can do it too." Recently, one publishing executive who read this book in manuscript told me, "All my life I thought I had terrible diseases because of my palpitations, dizziness and other such symptoms. Now I know I'm agoraphobic. Now I also know what to do about it. Recently, I was at a meeting and those terrible feelings washed over me and I thought I was going to die right there. But, even though I felt so scared, I made myself sit through the meeting. I didn't die. I felt so happy with myself. I was in charge of my fear."

•Just as you have learned to live with your fear, you can learn to live without it.

You may think there is so much to do, so much to remember. There really isn't. It all lies in one sentence, "Face your fear."

The choice is yours. You can do it if you try.

APPENDIX I

Full Relaxation Exercise

The following is a script of the taped relaxation exercise I give to patients for home practice. You may record it in your own voice or you may choose someone with a soothing voice to record it for you. In the first part of the exercise, the muscle tension should be held for about seven seconds. Allow a five-second interval between each specific muscle group relaxation. In the second part, allow about fifteen seconds for the relaxation of each body area. In the last part, again allow five seconds for each part to relax. If the entire tape takes between twenty and twenty-five minutes to play, your timing is probably right. Except for the muscle-tightening instructions, which should be brisk, the entire tape should be recorded with a soothing, lulling quality. Before you actually do the exercise, be sure you have your "pleasant scene" in mind.

Lie down. Make yourself comfortable. Your arms are at your side, your fingers open. Your eyes are closed throughout these exercises. If stray thoughts come to you, you calmly tell yourself STOP!, push them away and concentrate on whatever you are doing.

The first part of the exercise deals with tightening up large groups of muscles. Your job is to concentrate on the tension, study where you feel the tension and then, on instruction, to relax.

You start with the lower part of your body. Put your toes together pigeon-toed, heels slightly apart. Push your toes down away from you (that tightens your legs). Tighten your thighs. Tighten your buttocks. Tighten the muscles deep inside the buttocks, the muscle around the rectum. Study the tightness. Hold the tightness. Tense . . . tense . . . tense . . . now let go, just relax.

Feel that tension flow out. Now concentrate on the muscles of your toes; relax them . . . relax the muscles of your legs; let them go . . . relax your thighs . . . relax the muscles of your buttocks; let them go . . . now concentrate on the muscles around your rectum; relax them.

Once again, concentrate on each part as I mention it. Toes relaxed . . . legs relaxed . . . thighs relaxed . . . buttocks relaxed . . . muscles around the rectum relaxed. All the tension out . . .

One clue you might get: As the muscles relax and stop fighting gravity, you may start getting that pleasantly heavy feeling. If at any point during this exercise you get that pleasantly heavy feeling anywhere in your body, let it build up. It's another way to get the muscles to relax.

Now the muscles of your abdomen. Tighten up your abdominal muscles as if a little boy was going to push a football into your stomach. Just get them tight. They're long muscles. Study where you feel the tension. Hold it. Tense . . . tense . . . tense . . . and now relax. Feel the tension flow out. Concentrate on the feeling of the tension flowing out and relax the muscles of your abdomen. Let them go. Now try to relax the muscles deep in the abdomen, the muscles of the stomach and gut. There is some little voluntary control over them. Try to think them relaxed.

Now the muscles of your back. Arch the small of your back and get tension in there. There are two long columns of muscles, one on each side of the spine. That might be where you feel it. Wherever you feel it, get to know it. Hold it. Tense . . . tense . . . tense . . . and now let go. Just relax the muscles of your back, let them go. Try to let your back just melt into the mattress, more and more relaxed.

Now the muscles of your chest. Take a deep breath through your mouth and hold it. As you hold it you may notice spots of tension building up in your chest. If you do, take note of them. Remember where they are. Keep holding. Now as slowly as you can, let it out. At the end breathe easily and comfortably, the way you do in a deep sleep. If you have noticed spots of tension in your chest, take them—a spot at a time—and let them go. Relax the muscles of your chest. Just keep relaxing them.

Once again, concentrate on each part as I mention it: abdomen relaxed . . . muscles of the stomach and gut, some tiny control of the tension there . . . back relaxed; let it melt into the mattress . . . chest relaxed, breathing easily and comfortably the way you do in a deep sleep.

Now the muscles of your fingers and your arms and your shoulders. Make a tight fist with each hand. Get your elbows stiff and straight and raise them from the shoulder to about a forty-five-degree angle. Now feel the tension. You feel it in your fingers, your forearms, upper arms, shoulders. Hold it. Tense . . . tense . . . tense . . . and now relax. Just let your arms come back to the sides, fingers open. Feel the tension flow out. Now concentrate on relaxing the muscles of your fingers, just let them go . . . relax your forearms . . . the muscles of your upper arms and shoulders, let them go.

Once again, concentrate on each part; fingers relaxed . . . forearms relaxed . . . upper arms and shoulders relaxed . . . Try to let your fingers and arms feel pleasantly limp and heavy, as the muscles stop fighting gravity . . . more and more relaxed.

Now the muscles between your shoulder blades and

the muscles of your neck. These are muscles very sensitive to nervous tension. Pull your shoulders back, so your shoulder blades almost touch, and at the same time arch your neck and point your chin to the ceiling. Feel the tension. Get it in the back of the neck muscles. Hold it . . . don't strain, but let it build up. Tense . . . tense . . . tense . . . now let go. Feel the tension flow out. Relax the muscles between your shoulder blades. Let them go. The muscles in your neck, relax those. The eventual aim is to get those neck muscles so relaxed that they're not supporting your head . . . your head falls limply back to the pillow . . . more and more relaxed.

Now the delicate muscles of the face. We'll start with the upper part. Squeeze tight the upper part of your face. Squeeze your eyes tightly shut. Wrinkle the bridge of your nose. You feel the tension in your forehead and scalp, between your eyebrows where you frown and in the cheeks under your eyes. Hold it . . . don't strain. Tense . . . tense . . . tense . . . now relax and feel that tension flowing out. Just concentrate and relax the muscles of your forehead and scalp, let them go. The muscles between your eyebrows where you frown, relax those. Relax your eyelids. As they relax they may begin to feel heavy. You may start getting a pleasantly sleepy feeling, but don't go to sleep. The aim is to get the body relaxed and keep the mind awake, alert and in control. Relax the muscles on the bridge of your nose, let them go. The cheeks under your eyes where they feel tight, relax those.

Now the muscles of your jaws and tongue. Squeeze your back teeth together so you get your jaws good and tight. You feel it by your temples, by your ears, wherever you feel it. Now, keeping your jaws tight, push with your tongue against the back of your bottom front teeth so your jaw is tight and your tongue is tight. Tense . . . tense . . . tense . . . then relax, let it go. Relax the muscles of your jaws, let them go. Relax your tongue. Your teeth should be slightly parted. Your jaw hanging slack. More and more relaxed.

Now the lower part of your face. Make a grin showing your upper and lower teeth and pulling the corners of your mouth back. You feel the tension by your nostrils, around your mouth and chin, wherever you feel it. Hold it. Tense . . . tense . . . tense . . . now relax. Feel that tension flowing out. Now relax the muscles around your nostrils; let them go. The muscles around your mouth and chin, relax those. Now try to relax the muscles of your throat. The soft part of your throat, near where you swallow, relax those. The muscles around your voice box, relax those . . . more and more relaxed.

For the second part of the exercise. In this part we check over different parts of your body. Even if it feels relaxed, try to get it still more relaxed. Remember, if stray thoughts come to you, you calmly tell yourself STOP!, push them away and concentrate on whatever we're doing.

Now ask yourself: Is there any tension in my legs or my thighs or my buttocks? If there is, take it a spot at a time and let it go. Even if it feels relaxed, you can get it still more relaxed.

Now ask yourself: Is there any tension in my abdomen, my back or my chest? If there is, take it a spot at a time and let it go . . . breathing easily and comfortably, the way you do in a deep sleep.

Now ask yourself: Is there any tension in my fingers, in my arms, in my shoulders? If there is, take it a spot at a time and let it go. Try to let them feel pleasantly limp and heavy as the muscles relax and stop fighting gravity.

Now ask yourself: Is there any tension between my shoulder blades or in my neck? If there is, just let it go . . . your head falling limply back to the pillow . . .

Now ask yourself: Is there any tension in my face, in my jaws, or in my throat? If there is, let it go . . . let all the tension out.

Now for the third part of the exercise.* Imagine some kind of neutral pleasant scene, like being on a beach, walking in the country. If there is any difficulty with that, then just imagine or think of the word calm, C-A-L-M, calm. If your mind wanders, always bring it back to your pleasant scene or the word calm. And while you keep that in mind, just relax the muscles of your toes, let them go . . . relax the muscles of your legs, let them go . . . relax the muscles of your thighs . . . and the muscles of your buttocks, let them go . . . the muscles around your rectum, relax those . . . your pleasant scene, the word calm, and relax the muscles of your abdomen, let them go . . . the muscles of your stomach and gut, some little control, relax those . . . relax your back, let it melt into the mattress . . . and the muscles of your chest, breathing easily and comfortably . . . imagine the pleasant scene, the word calm, and relax the muscles of your fingers, let them go . . . relax your forearms . . . the muscles of your upper arms and shoulders . . . let them go . . . the muscles between your shoulder blades, relax those . . . the muscles of your neck, your head falling limply back to the pillow . . . your pleasant scene, the word calm . . . relax the muscles of your forehead and scalp, let them go . . . the muscles between your eyebrows, where you frown, relax those . . . relax your eyelids, let them feel heavy . . . and the muscles on the bridge of your nose, let them go . . . the muscles around your nostrils, relax those . . . relax your jaw muscles, teeth slightly parted, jaw hanging slack . . . and the muscles around your mouth and chin, relax those . . . the muscles of your throat, the soft part of your throat, where you swallow, relax those . . . you keep imagining the pleasant scene or the word calm . . . check out your body, if there are any spots of tension, take them a spot at a time and let them go.

Just keep letting go . . . your whole body getting calm and relaxed . . . calm and relaxed . . . calm and relaxed . . . calm and relaxed.

Now I'm going to count from three to one and at the count of one, you'll open your eyes and sit up, wide awake and alert and feel very refreshed. Three . . . two . . . one.

Intermediate Relaxation Exercise

This is an abbreviated version of the Full Relaxation Exercise. It takes only seven minutes to do. Instead of tightening each muscle group separately, you tighten your whole body at once. Tighten the muscles enough so that you feel the tension build up. Do not strain the muscles. You hold the tension for seven seconds and, when told to relax, you let it explode out.

Usually people use this exercise after they have mastered the longer one. However, some people get better results by using this one first. Try each one and do what is best for you.

Lie down. Make yourself comfortable. Arms at sides. Fingers open. Eyes closed. Throughout this exercise if stray thoughts come to you, calmly tell yourself STOP!, push them away and concentrate on whatever you're doing.

First part of exercise: Tighten your whole body all at once. Not so tight that it is strained, but tight enough so that you can feel the tension build up. Your job is to study the tension, to get to know where you feel tight.

Put your toes together pigeon-toed, heels slightly apart, and push your toes down away from you. That tightens your leg muscles. Tighten your thighs . . . tighten your buttocks . . . tighten your abdomen. Raise your arms from your shoulders, fists clenched, elbows stiff. Squeeze your eyes tight shut . . . clench your teeth . . . keeping your face all tight, arch your neck, point your chin to ceiling. Just hold it. Hold it (*about seven seconds*). Let it explode out. Arms back to your sides, chin down. Concentrate on feeling of tension flowing out (*about ten seconds*).

Now check out the muscles of legs and thighs. Any tension? Take it a spot at a time and let it go (*about five-second pause*). Relax the muscles of your abdomen and back (*five-second pause*). The muscles of your fingers and arms, let them feel pleasantly heavy (*five-second pause*), the muscles of your face and jaws, relax those (*five seconds*).

Now take a deep breath through mouth and hold it. Just keep holding it (*fifteen- to twenty-second pause*). Now slowly let it out (*pause*), and at the end breathe easily and comfortably the way you do in a deep sleep.

And now picture your pleasant scene* (*continue from paragraph one, page 374 to end of that exercise*)

APPENDIX II

Model Hierarchies for Use in
Systematic Desensitization in Fantasy

Fear of Spiders

This is the hierarchy I might have used for Miss Muffet. It follows a principle that may be used for many animal fears: You bring the animal closer and closer.

1. You look at a picture of a spider in a nature magazine.

2. You see a spider crawling up the far wall of a large room.

3. You see a spider climbing up a tree trunk about four feet from you.

4. You see a spider dropping from the ceiling on a thread about four feet from you.

5. You're sitting at a picnic table and see a spider crawling on the far end of the table.

6. You see a spider crawling along the ground about a yard away.

7. You look closely (inches away) and see the spider climbing up the tree trunk.

8. You see a spider dropping from the ceiling about a foot away from you.

9. You see the spider crawling on the picnic table about twelve inches from you.

Fear of Spiders (continued)

10. You look down and see a spider crawling over the toe of your shoe.

11. You see a spider on the leg of your slacks.

12. A spider drops from the ceiling right by you.

13. A spider drops from the ceiling onto your shirt front.

14. A spider drops from the ceiling onto your bare arm.

15. You feel something crawling on your leg, look down, and see a large spider.

16. You feel a spider crawling along your neck and onto your face.

17. You feel a swarm of spiders crawling all over you.

Fear of Death

Some people have excessive fears of their own death; others of the death of someone close to them. However, there are also people whose fear is not that specific—they just have a general fear of anything connected with death. One woman came in because of her chronic state of high-level tension. Behavioral analysis revealed this to be her anxiety responses to the many things in our surroundings that reminded her of death. When that fear was removed, her tension came down to normal levels. Here is the hierarchy used.

1. Glimpse of newspaper headlines telling about the death of a famous person.

2. Ambulance racing down the street with siren going and lights blinking.

3. Seeing a crate that reminds her of a coffin.

4. Walking across the street from a funeral parlor.

5. Hearing funeral music on radio.

6. On television seeing a film of President Kennedy's funeral.

7. Seeing an empty hearse drive by.

Fear of Death (continued)

8. Watching a crime movie and seeing victim sprawled on floor.

9. Walking past a funeral home. No one in front.

10. Hearing that a neighbor she didn't know has died.

11. Watching a funeral procession on TV news.

12. Walking past funeral parlor with group of mourners standing outside.

13. Seeing a funeral procession pass by a block away.

14. Hearing that a friend died.

15. Seeing a dead bird in the street.

16. A funeral procession passes right by her as she's starting to cross the street.

17. Riding in a funeral procession.

18. Seeing coffin carried out of funeral parlor and put in hearse.

19. Watching coffin being lowered into ground. Everyone crying.

Fear of Tough-looking People

With the great increases in the number of crimes being committed, we do have to take precautions. However, one woman was so frightened of anyone who looked tough that she could go places only by arranging for door-to-door taxi service. Her concept of "tough" depended on the way they were dressed and on age (teen-agers, especially in groups, were the most terrifying).

1. Tough-looking gray-haired man walking on opposite side of the street.

2. Tough-looking gray-haired man walking about ten yards in front of you.

3. Tough-looking gray-haired man walking toward you.

4. Tough-looking man in his thirties walking toward you.

Fear of Tough-looking People (continued)

5. Tough-looking man in his early twenties walking toward you.

6. Tough-looking teen-ager walking toward you.

7. Two tough-looking teen-agers walking toward you.

8. Three teen-agers walking toward you. They're acting "wild."

9. Big group of teen-agers walking toward you. They're acting "wild."

10. Across the street you see a teen-ager grab a woman's purse and run off.

11. Across the street you see a group of teen-agers punch a woman and kick her down.

12. Across the street you see a group of teen-agers knock a woman down and kick and beat her. She is screaming.

13. A teen-ager grabs your purse and runs off.

14. You're surrounded by a group of teen-agers. They punch you and knock you down.

15. You're lying on the street surrounded by wild teen-agers. They're kicking you and beating you. It hurts and you're screaming.

Fear of Anger

This patient came in with a problem in assertiveness. He had great difficulties in standing up for himself, in saying "No" and in being spontaneous in social situations. However, my examination showed that these were not primarily due to lack of assertiveness but rather a severe fear of people's being angry with him.

Desensitization in fantasy was part of the treatment. The hierarchy we used is a good example of a personalized hierarchy that can be used for many social fears. First he ranked a number of people according to how much fear each would set off if he did become angry. Mary (his sister) was least. Jim (his immediate supervisor) was most. We had him imagine each person expressing different degrees of anger.

Fear of Anger (continued)

1. Person saying with mild annoyance in voice, "I'm pretty annoyed at what you did."

   a. Mary (sister)

   b. Bob (old friend)

   c. Joan (wife)

   d. George (co-worker)

   e. Murray (neighbor)

   f. Tom (aggressive friend)

   g. Jim (immediate supervisor)

2. Person saying in angry tone, "That was a pretty rotten thing to do."

   Repeat a–g listing.

3. Person in rage, face red, eyes glaring, shouting or yelling, "You're a no-good, goddamn bastard!"

   Repeat a–g listing.

Fear of Authority

This woman was brought up to be obedient and was also trained to be frightened of anyone in a position of authority. Now, as an adult, she turns everyone into an authority figure and so is always frightened. So much tension and fear exist in her life that any little thing can cause her to burst into tears. Her husband describes her as "fragile." The hierarchy used was made up of things that had actually happened to her in impersonal situations. Later we made up one for more personal situations.

1. Movie usher telling people to keep in line.

2. Butcher firmly telling her to take a cut of meat she didn't want.

3. Salesperson pressing her to buy a scarf she did not like.

4. Subway conductor telling her to stand back.

5. She's on a crowded sidewalk. Policeman tells her to move on.

6. Salesperson looks at her impatiently.

Fear of Authority (continued)

7. Dentist tells her she should take better care of her gums.

8. Minister's wife mentioning she had missed her the past Sunday.

9. Driving. She stops for a red light and sees a police car alongside her.

10. Headwaiter shows her and her girlfriend to a bad table.

11. Doctor (woman) asking her how she caught cold.

12. Bank teller carefully examining the check she had just given him.

13. Meter maid giving her a parking summons.

14. Minister scolding her for her recent absences from services.

15. Bank official on phone telling her she had overdrawn her account.

Fear of Being Watched at Work

This person was a draftsman who worked for a large architectural firm. He worked in a large room with a number of other draftsmen. Other people constantly came in and out of the room. Any time anyone looked in his direction while he was working, he would become upset to the point where he couldn't work. His work was starting to get very bad and he was worried. The fear had no content. For example, he was not afraid of being criticized. It did not matter who did the looking. What did matter was: how long the look was, how many people were looking and how close to him they were. In the hierarchy we used, all the scenes took place in his office.

1. Person at far end of room glances briefly in his direction and then moves on.

2. Person at far end of room looks at him for about ten seconds.

Fear of Being Watched at Work (continued)

3. Person at far end of room watches him work for about half a minute.

4. Person at far end of room stares at him for several minutes.

5. Two people at far end of room watch him work for about half a minute.

6. Two people at far end of room stare at him for several minutes.

7. Group of about five people at far end of room all staring at him for several minutes.

8. Two draftsmen about halfway across the room glance in his direction.

9. Two draftsmen about halfway across the room watch him work for about half a minute.

10. Two draftsmen about halfway across the room stare at him for several minutes.

11. Draftsman at next table watches him work for about half a minute.

12. Draftsman at next table stares at him for several minutes.

13. Everyone in the room looks at him working.

14. Same. They keep staring at him.

15. Same. One person standing over him.

16. Same. Two people standing over him.

17. Everyone crowding around him, watching what he is doing.

Fear of Fire

This divorced man in his mid-forties was constantly frightened of fire. Not of fire in general but very specifically that his brownstone apartment would burn. He was not afraid of physical injury or even the loss of his possessions. He was just afraid that there would be a fire in his apartment. Every evening when he returned from work, he had a distinct feeling of relief when he saw the house was intact. Whenever he heard a fire engine, he felt a surge of fear that his apartment was on

Fear of Fire (continued)

fire. He had had this fear since adolescence but it was minimal as long as he resided in an apartment house. Since moving to the brownstone apartment some ten months previously, the fear kept increasing. An actual fire would, of course, be terribly disturbing. The aim here was to remove the irrational part of the fear and so to remove his constant, inappropriate fear responses and worries.

1. He is in a different city and hears a fire engine siren.

2. Reading a newspaper headline about the increasing number of fires in New York City.

3. He's in Battery Park (far from where he lived) and hears a fire engine siren.

4. Watching a burning brownstone on a TV news show.

5. Neighbor telling him of a fire in a brownstone on the next block.

6. Walking in his neighborhood and hearing the sirens of approaching fire engines.

7. Walking toward his street after work and smelling smoke.

8. In the apartment and smelling smoke.

9. Watching firemen fight a fire in a house on the next block.

10. Watching firemen fight a fire two houses from his house.

11. Seeing fire engines turn into his street (he is a block away on a cross street).

12. Seeing fire engines in front of his house. Fireman assures him it was a false alarm.

13. Same. Fireman telling him it was a small fire and it is all out now.

14. Coming home from work and seeing his apartment windows broken and gaping black from a fire.

15. Looking around his apartment at minor fire damage. Some smell of smoke.

Fear of Fire (continued)

16. Looking at his apartment completely destroyed by fire. Everything black and charred. Heavy smell of smoke.

Fear of Sexual Inadequacy

This patient was a thirty-year-old man, married for six years. Because of his inability to have an erection during sex play, the couple had not even attempted to have intercourse for almost two years. He would often wake up in the morning with an erection, but it would disappear if he even turned toward his wife. Also there were times he would get an erection when fantasizing about sex or when he was just being affectionate. He had little trouble getting an erection when he masturbated. It was during sex play with his wife, when he felt he must have an erection, that there was difficulty. A number of treatment methods were used, but the crucial part of treatment turned out to be fantasy desensitization to the following hierarchy.

1. Your wife is manually playing with your penis:
   a. You get a 100 percent hard erection—as hard and stiff as you can imagine it being.
   b. She keeps playing with you and you stay hard.
   c. You get a 90 percent hard erection—just a slight bit of softness.
   d. She keeps playing with you, but you don't get any harder.
   e. You get a 75 percent hard erection. It's somewhat soft but you would be able to enter her for intercourse.
   f. She keeps playing with you but you don't get any harder.
   g. You get a 50 percent hard erection—about half hard, half soft. Only some chance that you would be able to enter her for intercourse.
   h. She keeps playing with you but you don't get any harder.

Fear of Sexual Inadequacy (continued)

   i.   You get a 25 percent hard erection. Your penis is mostly soft.

   j.   She keeps playing with you, but you don't get any harder.

   k.   You get a 10 percent hard erection. There's only the slightest sign of being hard.

   l.   She keeps playing with you but you don't get any harder.

   m.   You get a zero percent erection. There is no sign whatever of any response by your penis.

   n.   She keeps playing with your penis but there is not the slightest sign of any response.

   o.   She has been playing with your penis for over ten minutes and still not the slightest sign of response.

2. Your wife is orally playing with your penis.
    Repeat a–o listing.

APPENDIX III

Script for Desensitization Tape

This tape is to help you to do Systematic Desensitization in fantasy. Before actually using the tape, you must have certain things prepared.

1. You must have prepared a suitable hierarchy. Each scene should be on a different index card. The cards should be in the order you are going to use them with the first card on top. Place the cards near your hand or within easy reach.

2. You must have practiced the relaxation exercise. Be certain you know what "pleasant scene" you are going to use so that you don't have to hunt for one when instructed to imagine it.

3. You must know that the tensions you will experience will not be the same, either in quality or in intensity, as if you were really in the situation. Look for the small signs of muscle tightening anywhere in your body or for subjective changes in feeling, however slight.

4. You must set up your tape recorder so that the on-off switch is easily reached. The best way is to use the switch on the microphone and to keep the microphone right by your hand.

SCRIPT

1. First read into the tape the Intermediate Relaxation Exercise. You should make two minor modifications in this.

a. At the very beginning of the exercise where you tell yourself to "Lie down. Make yourself comfortable," add the sentence, "Be sure the Start-Stop switch of your tape recorder is right by your hand."

b. Eliminate the very end of that exercise where you say that you are going to count from three to one, etc. Instead add the following instructions: "Now check out your tensions. If you are fairly relaxed, go on with this tape. Otherwise either start the tape from the beginning again or else discontinue at this point."

2. Pause for about five seconds and go on with the following instructions: "When I tell you to do so, turn off the tape machine, read the disturbing scene on the top card from the hierarchy you are to work on, then close your eyes and imagine that scene. At the very first sign of an increase in tension, start your tape recorder going again. Now do the scene." At this point in your dictating the script, pause five seconds with the machine running.

After the five-second pause: "Stop. Push that scene away. Take a deep breath through your mouth and hold it. Hold it. Hold it. Hold it. Now comfortably let it out (*about a ten-second pause*). Breathe easily and comfortably the way you do in a deep sleep. Now imagine your pleasant scene from the relaxation exercises or think *calm* and relax the muscles of your toes . . . Let them go . . . Relax your legs . . . Let them go . . . Relax your thighs . . . Let them go . . . Keep imagining your pleasant scene or thinking *calm* and let your whole body get calm and relaxed . . . calm and relaxed . . . if you are not completely relaxed now, turn off the machine and just keep relaxing.

Now again you are going to read and imagine the

scene on your card. Remember to turn the machine back on at the first sign of uptightness. Go ahead (*five-second pause on the tape*). Stop. Switch off that scene. Take a deep breath through your mouth and hold it. Hold it. Hold it. Now, like a big sigh, explosively let it out . . . breathe easily and comfortably . . . now focus in on your relaxing pleasant scene or the word *calm* and once again relax the muscles of your thighs. Let them go. Relax your buttocks . . . Let them go . . . Relax the muscles around your rectum . . . All the tension out . . . calm and relaxed . . . calm and relaxed . . . calm and relaxed.

If you are relaxed now, turn off the machine and read and imagine your disturbing scene. Go ahead (*five-second pause*). Stop that scene. Switch it off. Take a deep breath through your mouth and hold it. Hold it. Hold it. Now comfortably let it out. Breathe easily and comfortably the way you do in a deep sleep . . . and zero in on your relaxing pleasant scene or *calm*. That's important. Now relax the muscles of your abdomen. Let them go . . . the muscles of your stomach and gut . . . Some little control . . . Think them relaxed . . . the muscles of your back . . . let them melt into the mattress . . . pleasant scene or *calm* . . . calm and relaxed . . . calm and relaxed . . .

If you are relaxed now, be sure you know what disturbing scene you are going to do now. Turn off the machine and do it. Go ahead (*five-second pause*). Stop that scene. Take a deep breath in . . . and . . . out . . . Breathe easily and comfortably. Imagine your pleasant scene or *calm*. And relax the muscles of your fingers . . . Let them go . . . Relax your forearms . . . Let them feel heavy . . . The muscles of your upper arms and shoulders . . . Let them go . . . Pleasant scene or *calm* . . . calm and relaxed . . . calm and relaxed . . .

Remember to turn on the machine at the first sign of uptightness. Your disturbing scene, go ahead (*five-second pause*). Stop. Switch it off. Take a deep breath and hold it. Now slowly let it out. Breathe easily and comfortably . . . Imagine your pleasant scene or *calm*. Zero in on it . . . Now relax the muscles of your shoulder blades. Let them go . . . the muscles of your neck . . . your head falling limply back to the pillow . . . pleasant scene or *calm* . . . calm and relaxed . . . calm and relaxed.

Check out that you're relaxed. Now the scene that you're working on. Go ahead (*five-second pause*). Stop that scene. Take a deep breath in . . . and . . . out . . . Breathe easily and comfortably . . . Imagine your pleasant scene or *calm* . . . and relax the muscles of your eyebrows where you frown . . . relax those . . . relax your eyelids . . . let them feel heavy . . . Pleasant scene or *calm* . . . calm and relaxed . . . calm and relaxed.

Be sure you are relaxed and alert. Your scene again. Go ahead (*five-second pause*). Stop. Switch it off. A deep breath in and hold it. Hold it. Hold it. Now, like a big sigh, let it out . . . Breathe easily and comfortingly. Imagine your pleasant scene or *calm* and relax the muscles of your jaws. Let them go. Teeth slightly parted, jaw hanging slack . . . the muscles around your mouth and chin . . . relax those. Pleasant scene or *calm* . . . calm and relaxed . . . calm and relaxed . . . calm and relaxed.

One last time: your scene. Go ahead (*five-second pause*). Stop. A deep breath in and hold it. Now slowly let it out . . . Breathe easily and comfortably the way you do in a deep sleep . . . Now imagine your pleasant scene or *calm* . . . Check out your body. If you feel tension anywhere, take it a spot at a time and let it go . . . keep letting go . . . let your whole body feel calm and relaxed . . . calm and relaxed . . . calm and relaxed.

Now I'm going to count from three to one. At the count of one, you'll open your eyes and sit up. You'll be wide awake and alert. Three . . . two . . . one . . .

BIBLIOGRAPHY

Arieti, Silvano, and Brody, Eugene B., eds. *American Handbook of Psychiatry*, vol. 3. New York: Basic Books, 1974.

Aronson, Marvin L. *How to Overcome Your Fear of Flying*. New York: Warner Paperback Library, 1973.

Baer, Jean. *How to Be an Assertive (Not Aggressive) Woman in Life, in Love, and on the Job*. New York: New American Library, 1976.

Baker, Bruce L.; Cohen, David C.; and Saunders, Jon Terry. "Self-directed Desensitization for Acrophobia." *Behavior Research and Therapy* 2 (1973):79–89.

Baum, Morrie. "Extinction of Avoidance Responding Through Response Prevention (Flooding)." *Psychological Bulletin* 74 (1970):276–284.

Beech, H.R. *Obsessional States*. London: Methuen & Co., 1974.

Bergin, Allen E. "A Note on Dream Changes Following Desensitization." *Behavior Therapy* 1 (1970):546–549.

Bernstein, Douglas A., and Borkovec, Thomas D. *Progressive Relaxation Training*. Champaign, Illinois: Research Press, 1972.

Blanchard, Edward B., and Draper, Douglas O. "Treatment of a Rodent Phobia by Covert Reinforcement." *Behavior Therapy* 4 (1973):559–564.

Cammer, Leonard. *Freedom from Compulsion*. New York: Simon and Schuster, 1976.

Cott, Nate, and Kampel, Stewart. *Fly Without Fear*. Chicago: Henry Regnery Company, 1973.

Ellis, Albert. "Rational-Emotive Therapy." In *Direct Psychotherapy,* edited by Ratibor-Ray M. Jurjevich. Coral Gables, Florida: University of Miami Press, 1973.

—————. "The No Cop-Out Therapy." *Psychology Today,* July 1973.

Ellis, Albert, and Harper, Robert A. *A Guide to Rational Living.* North Hollywood, Calif.: Wilshire Book Company, 1973.

Errara, Paul. "Some Historical Aspects of the Concept, Phobia." *Psychiatric Quarterly* 36 (1972):325–336.

Eysenck, H. J., and Rachman, S. *The Causes and Cures of Neurosis.* San Diego, Calif.: Robert R. Knapp, 1965.

Feather, Ben W., and Rhoads, John M. "Psychodynamic Behavior Therapy." *Archives of General Psychiatry* 26 (1972):496–511.

Fensterheim, Herbert. *Help Without Psychoanalysis.* New York: Stein & Day, 1971.

—————. "Behavior Therapy of the Sexual Variations." *The Journal of Sex and Marital Therapy,* November 1974.

—————. "Behavior Therapy Approach: The Case of Marion." In *Three Psychotherapies,* edited by Clemens A. Loew, Henry Grayson, and Gloria Heiman Loew. New York: Brunner/Mazel, 1975.

Fensterheim, Herbert, and Baer, Jean. *Don't Say Yes When You Want to Say No.* New York: David McKay Company, 1975.

Fink, David Harold. *Release from Nervous Tension.* New York: Pocket Books, 1973.

Frankl, Viktor E. "Paradoxical Intention." *American Journal of Psychotherapy* 14 (1960).

Franks, Cyril M., and Wilson, G. Terence, eds. *Annual Review of Behavior Therapy.* New York: Brunner/Mazel, 1973.

Freedman, Alfred M.; Kaplan, Harold I.; and Sadock, *prehensive Textbook of Psychiatry.* Baltimore: The Williams & Wilkins Company, 1967.

Freedman, Alfred M.; Kaplan, Harold I; and Sadock, Benjamin J., eds. *Comprehensive Textbook of Psychiatry/II.* Baltimore: The Williams & Wilkins Company, 1975.

Frazier, Shervert H., and Carr, Arthur C. "Phobic Reaction." In *Comprehensive Textbook of Psychiatry,* edited by Alfred M. Freedman and Harold I. Kaplan. Baltimore: The Williams & Wilkins Company, 1967.

Freud, Sigmund. "Analysis of a Phobia in a Five-Year-Old Boy." *Collected Papers,* vol. 3, pp. 149–289. New York: Basic Books, 1959.

Friedman, Paul, and Goldstein, Jacob. "Phobic Reactions." In *American Handbook of Psychiatry,* vol. 3, edited by Sylvano Arieti and Eugene B. Brody. New York: Basic Books, 1974.

Gelder, M. G.; Bancroft, J. H. J.; Gath, D. H.; Johnston, D. W.; Mathews, A. M.; and Shaw, P. M. "Specific and Non-specific Factors in Behavior Therapy." *British Journal of Psychiatry* 123 (1973):445–462.

Gertz, H.O. "Experience with the Logotherapeutic Technique of Paradoxical Intention in the Treatment of Phobic and Obsessive-Compulsive Patients." *American Journal of Psychiatry* 123 (1966):548–553.

Goldfried, Marvin R., and Davison, Gerald C. *Clinical Behavior Therapy.* New York: Holt, Rinehart and Winston, 1976.

Goorney, A. B. "Treatment of Aviation Phobias by Behavior Therapy." *British Journal of Psychiatry* 117 (1970): 533–544.

Gray, Jeffrey. *The Psychology of Fear and Stress.* New York: McGraw-Hill Book Company, 1971.

Hand, I.; Lamontagne, Y.; and Marks, I. M. "Group Exposure (Flooding) *in vivo* for Agoraphobics." *British Journal of Psychiatry* 124 (1974): 588–602.

Hennig, Margaret, and Jardim, Anne. *The Managerial Woman.* Garden City, New York: Anchor Press/ Doubleday, 1977.

Hersen, Michel. "The Behavioral Treatment of School Phobia." *Journal of Nervous and Mental Disease* 153 (1973):99–107.

Hersen, Michel; Eisler, Richard M.; and Miller, Peter M., eds. *Progress in Behavior Modification,* vol. 1. New York: Academic Press, 1975.

Homme, Lloyd E. "Control of Coverants: The Operants of the Mind." In *Behavior Change Through Self-control,* edited by Marvin R. Goldfried and Michael Merbaum. New York: Holt, Rinehart and Winston, 1973.

Jacobson, Edmund. *Self-operations Control.* Philadelphia: J. P. Lippincott Company, 1964.

Jones, Mary Cover. "The Elimination of Children's Fears." *Journal of Experimental Psychology* 7 (1924):382–390.

———. "Albert, Peter and John B. Watson." *American Psychologist,* August 1974.

Kanfer, Frederick H., and Seidner, Meryl L. "Self-control: Factors Enhancing Tolerance of Noxious Stimulation." *Journal of Personality and Social Psychology* 25 (1973):381–389.

Karst, Thomas O., and Trexler, Larry E. "Initial Study Using Fixed Role and Rational-Emotive Therapy in Treating Public-speaking Anxiety." *Journal of Consulting and Clinical Psychology* 34 (1970):360–366.

Kazdin, Alan E. "Covert Modeling and the Reduction of Avoidance Behavior." *Journal of Abnormal Psychology* 81 (1973):87–95.

Krumboltz, John D., and Thoresen, Carl E. *Behavioral Counseling: Cases and Techniques.* New York: Holt, Rinehart and Winston, 1969.

Lazarus, Arnold A. *Multi-modal Behavior Therapy.* New York: Springer Publishing Company, 1976.

Marks, Isaac M. *Fears and Phobias.* New York: Academic Press, 1969.

Marks, Isaac M. "Behavioral Treatments of Phobic and Obsessive-Compulsive Disorders: A Critical Appraisal." In *Progress in Behavior Modification,* edited by Michel Hersen, Richard M. Eisler, and Peter M. Miller. New York: Academic Press, 1975.

Melville, Joy. *Phobias and Obsessions.* New York: Coward, McCann & Geoghegan, 1977.

Meichenbaum, Donald B. "Examination of Model Characteristics of Reducing Avoidance Behavior." *Journal of Personality and Social Psychology* 17 (1971):298–307.

Meyer, V., and Levy, R. "Behavioral Treatment of a Homosexual with Compulsive Rituals." *British Journal of Medical Psychology* 43 (1970): 63–68.

Mower, O.H. "A Stimulus-Response Analysis of Anxiety and Its Role as a Reinforcing Agent." *Psychology Review* 46 (1939):553–565.

Nemiah, John C. "Phobic Neurosis." In *Complete Textbook of Psychiatry/II,* edited by Alfred M. Freedman,

Harold I. Kaplan, and Benjamin J. Sadock. Baltimore: The Williams & Wilkins Company, 1975.

Rachman, S. *Phobias: Their Nature and Control.* Springfield, Illinois: Charles C. Thomas, 1968.

Richardson, Frank C., and Suinn, Richard M. "A Comparison of Traditional Systematic Desensitization, Accelerated Massed Desensitization and Anxiety Management Training in the Treatment of Mathematics Anxiety." *Behavior Therapy* 4 (1973):212–218.

Richardson, Frank C., and Tasto, Donald L. "Development and Factor Analysis of a Social Anxiety Inventory." *Behavior Therapy* 7 (July 1976).

Rohrbaugh, Michael, and Riccio, David C. "Paradoxical Enhancement of Learned Fear." *Journal of Abnormal Psychology* 75 (1970):210–216.

Salter, Andrew. *Conditional Reflex Therapy.* New York: Farrar, Straus and Giroux, 1949; Capricorn Book edition, 1961.

Schott, Joseph L. *No Left Turns: The FBI in Peace and War.* New York: Praeger Publishers, 1975.

Seligman, Martin E.P. *Helplessness.* San Francisco: W.H. Freeman and Company, 1975.

Sharpe, Robert, and Lewis, David. *The Success Factor.* New York: Crown Publishers, 1976.

Solyom, L.; Garza-Perez, J.; Ledwidge, B.L.; and Solyom, C. "Paradoxical Intention in the Treatment of Obsessive Thoughts: A Pilot Study." *Comprehensive Psychiatry* 13 (May 1972).

Solyom, L.; Heseltine, G.F.D.; McClure, D.J.; Ledwidge, B.; and Kenny, F. "A Comparative Study of Aversion Relief and Systematic Desensitization in the Treatment of Phobias." *British Journal of Psychiatry* 119 (1971):299–303.

Solyom, L.; Shugar, R.; Bryntwick, S.; Solyom, C. "Treatment of Fear of Flying." *American Journal of Psychiatry* 130 (April 1973).

Stern, Richard, and Marks, Isaac. "Brief and Prolonged Flooding." *Archives of General Psychiatry* 28 (February 1973).

Tasto, Donald L.; Hickson, Robert; and Rubin, Stanford E. "Scaled Profile Analysis of Fear Survey Schedule Factors." In *Annual Review of Behavior Therapy,* edited by Cyril M. Franks and G. Terence Wilson. New York: Brunner/Mazel, 1973.

Watson, J. B., and Rayner, R. "Conditioned Emotional Responses." *Journal of Experimental Psychology* 3 (1920).

Wax, Judith. "Mission Employable." *The New York Times Magazine*, June 20, 1976.

Weekes, Claire. *Agoraphobia.* New York: Hawthorn Books, 1976.

————. *Peace from Nervous Suffering.* New York: Hawthorn Books, 1972.

————. *Hope and Help for Your Nerves.* New York: Hawthorn Books, 1969.

Wenrich, Wes W.; Dawley, Harold H.; and General, Dale A. *Self-directed Systematic Desensitization.* Kalamazoo, Mich.: Behaviordelia, 1976.

Wolpe, Joseph. *The Practice of Behavioral Therapy* (2nd edition). New York: Pergamon Press, 1973.

Yates, Aubrey J. *Behavior Therapy.* New York: John Wiley & Sons, 1970.

INDEX

LAUREL

Classic Fiction

Quality paperbacks for serious readers

☐ 30028-2-99 **THE ADVENTURES OF HUCKLEBERRY FINN**, Twain, $3.50

☐ 30845-3-17 **BULFINCH'S MYTHOLOGY (Abridged)**, Fuller, ed., $4.50

☐ 31675-8-69 **DAVID COPPERFIELD (Abridged)**, Dickens, $2.50

☐ 33308-3-94 **GULLIVER'S TRAVELS**, Swift, $3.50

☐ 36914-2-28 **THE PICTURE OF DORIAN GRAY**, Wilde, $2.95

☐ 37640-8-84 **THE SCARLET LETTER**, Hawthorne, $2.50

☐ 39154-7-96 **TURN OF THE SCREW** and **DAISY MILLER**, James, $2.50

☐ 39728-6-93 **WUTHERING HEIGHTS**, Bronte, $2.75